Ordinary People Dancing

# Ordinary People Dancing

ESSAYS ON KATE O'BRIEN

Edited by

Eibhear Walshe

CORK UNIVERSITY PRESS

*First Published in 1993 by*
*Cork University Press*
*University College*
*Cork*
*Ireland*

© *The Editor and Contributors 1993*

**British Library Cataloguing in Publication Data**

A CIP catalogue record for this book is available from
the British Library.

ISBN 0 902561 65 0 Hardback
ISBN 0 902561 66 9 Paperback

Typeset by Tower Books of Ballincollig, Co. Cork
Printed in Ireland by ColourBooks of Baldoyle, Dublin

# Contents

# Notes on Contributors

*Eibhear Walshe* lectures in the Department of English in University College, Cork. He is a section editor in the forthcoming *Field Day Anthology of Irish Writing, Vol. 4* and is also advisor on new Irish writing at the Abbey Theatre, Dublin. His doctoral reseach is in contemporary Irish drama and his published work includes examinations of the Irish novel, gender and writing, and dissidence in Irish literature.

*Eavan Boland* is a successful poet with her first collection being published in 1967. Her more recent books include *The Journey* (1987), *Selected Poems* (1989) and *Outside History* (1990). She has also been a reviewer and critic for numerous publications.

*Ailbhe Smyth* is Director of the Women's Education, Research and Resource Centre (WERRC) at University College, Dublin, where she teaches Women's Studies. She writes on feminist politics and culture and is editor of a number of collections, including *Wildish Things: An Anthology of New Irish Women's Writing* (Attic Press, 1989) and *The Abortion Papers: Ireland* (Attic Press, 1992).

*Emma Donoghue* studied English and French at University College, Dublin before moving to Cambridge to work for a PhD on the literary friendships of early English novelists. Her study of eighteenth-century British lesbian culture, *More Than Holding Hands,* is due out from Scarlet Press in Autumn 1993. Her first novel, *Stir-Fry,* will be published by Penguin in 1994.

*Patricia Coughlan* is a lecturer in the Department of English, University College, Cork. She has written several essays and articles on Anglo-Irish literature, especially on seventeenth-century writings and on gender in twentieth-century texts. She has edited a collection of essays *Spenser and Ireland* (Cork University Press, 1989), and is preparing a book on English writings about Ireland, 1630–1680.

*Anthony Roche* is a lecturer in Anglo-Irish literature at University College, Dublin and Chairman of the Irish Writers Union. He has published extensively on Irish writing and his book on contemporary Irish drama is forthcoming from Gill & Macmillan.

*Anne Fogarty* lectures in the Department of English, University College, Dublin. She has published articles on Renaissance literature and women's writing. She is currently working on a study of sixteenth-century colonial writing in Ireland, entitled *Colonial Plots: Reading History in Edmund Spenser's The Faerie Queene.*

*Fanny Feehan* was music critic with the *Sunday Tribune* and has written extensively on Irish music and literature.

*Michael O'Toole,* journalist with the *Evening Press,* is the author of the memoir *More Kicks than Pence* (1992).

*Michael Cronin* has taught in Tours and Paris and is currently lecturer in the Faculty of Communications and Human Studies at Dublin City University. He is a founder member and current chairperson of the Irish Translators' Association. He is co-editor of *Tourism in Ireland: A Critical Analysis* (Cork University Press, 1993).

*Mary Breen* teaches in the English Department at University College, Cork. Her research interests include gender and Irish writing and the work of James Stephens and George Moore.

# Acknowledgements

In preparing this volume for publication, I received a great deal of help and encouragement as well as practical assistance, and I wish to acknowledge this. Firstly I want to thank the O'Brien family, Mrs Rosemary O'Brien and Donough and John O'Brien for permission to quote from the writings of Kate O'Brien and help with biographical and photographical material.

This research was carried out with the help of a UCC Arts Faculty Research fund and with a travel grant from the Department of English and I want to thank Professor Colbert Kearney and Professor Eamon Ó Carragain for all their help and encouragement. I'd like to thank, in particular, my colleagues, Dr Pat Coughlan and Mary Breen in UCC and Dr Anne Fogarty in UCD, for insightful comments and for their great interest in O'Brien.

Trinity College, Dublin, The National Library of Ireland and The British Library were all sources of information and I wish also to thank Charles Seaton of *The Spectator* for invaluable help with O'Brien's journalism. RTE radio and television archives gave me hitherto unconsidered material on O'Brien and I am indeed grateful.

A special mention of thanks goes to Barra Ó Seaghdha for all his care and attention in working on these essays with me. Friends of Kate O'Brien in Ireland, such as Professor Lorna Reynolds, Paul Smith, Mrs FSL Lyons, Mervyn Wall, Michael O'Toole and Fanny Feehan, were most co-operative in helping me, as was Mary Stewart in London and Professor Jim and Kate Hughes, Mrs Sylvia

Hitchcock and Mr and Mrs Dempsey in Canterbury. Thanks also to Sir John Gielgud and Sir Stephen Spender for their recollection of Kate O'Brien.

Finally, I would like to thank Sara Wilbourne of Cork University Press for making this project possible, through her commitment, her enthusiasm and her support throughout. In addition, I am very grateful to Eileen O'Carroll and Anne Lee for all their care and professionalism in working on this project.

# Introduction

This collection of essays takes its starting-point from the inescapable fact that Kate O'Brien is a deeply problematic figure. The problems arise directly from the nature of her writing, her literary reputation, her cultural placing, her sexuality, and her intellect. Together these conspire to create a sense of unease. There is, undoubtedly, a distance and an uncertainty in public perception of O'Brien as an Irish writer. She falls into no ready category, judged as appearing to vacillate between popular fiction and 'literature', Catholic conscience and Wildean dissidence, English letters and Irish writing, bourgeois history and feminist fable. Marginalised, along with Joyce, Beckett and other mainstream Irish writers, and then, like them, rehabilitated and reprinted after years of critical (not popular) neglect, her work failed to find any comfortable place within this mainstream.

More damaging has been the limited popular and critical interest that O'Brien *has* managed to attract, perpetuating uncertainty as how exactly to categorise her writing. Critical perspectives vary from the casually anecdotal (evading direct confrontation with the implications of her fiction, instead concentrating on the ambiguities of biography), through uncritical championing, to the overtly dismissive. In many ways, this unqualified championing and reclaiming of O'Brien as successful proto-feminist and victorious, uncomplicated radical is as counterproductive as outright neglect.

All of this has contributed to a distinct problematising of O'Brien and her fiction, a problematising that fails to engage with her fiction and its inherent complexities. There is no doubt that O'Brien's writing is, in part, flawed, uneven and complex, yet I would argue that it is these very complexities and flaws that make her fiction so revealing. It is revealing because it is informed by O'Brien's struggle to articulate cultural and aesthetic debates subversive to the Ireland in which she wrote. O'Brien's is a voice rarely heard in Independent Ireland, the voice of an intellectually informed, sexually dissident, (col)lapsed Catholic. The disturbances and conflicts within her novels are consequent on this isolation and therefore worth examining.

This book takes on and engages with this dissidence, this disturbance in a number of ways. In this introduction I examine the way in which Kate O'Brien is discussed and constructed as a cultural figure, especially after her death, becoming the focus for speculation in terms of her writing and her sexuality. Then I want to consider critical views on O'Brien, questioning how these add to partial and limiting notions of her fiction and arguing that they serve to perpetuate her difference, her outsiderness. Finally, within the essays themselves, a critical context for all of O'Brien's writings, novels, essays, travelogues, journalism, is realised, allowing for a complete overview of her importance as cultural commentator. For the first time, a coherent scholarly perspective emerges from which to consider this remarkable and unique woman.

I take the title of this collection from a 1962 RTE television programme on Kate O'Brien, *Self-Portrait*. In it, O'Brien reflects on her life and her writing and attempts to define the impulse that informed her imagination.

> Essentially, my novels arise from reflections on people. I am always rather influenced by music - dance music and the human singing voice, help me, move, give me ideas. I don't know why. I suppose it's something to do with the sight of ordinary people dancing, something so poignant about it.

*Ordinary People Dancing* seems, on the face of it, to be an inappropriate title for a book on Kate O'Brien. This celebration of ordinariness, of the poignancy of the human singing voice, of dance music, seems surprising from a writer who has been perceived as being essentially remote, intellectual, outmoded and different. Yet I choose the title deliberately, as a strategy for radical reappraisal and rethinking. There is, as I have argued, an unease with O'Brien, a sense of distance and of difference, and this needs to be confronted. We need to reconsider her as a novelist who drew her inspiration from popular culture, writing fiction from within the mainstream of this popular culture rather than above it. Thus much of the critical and cultural attention paid to O'Brien must be challenged. In this section I want to examine the ways in which O'Brien has been perceived, both in scholarly studies and also in terms of public debate.

In 1984, ten years after O'Brien's death, a commemorative seminar was held in Limerick to celebrate her life and her writing, and from this occasion the Kate O'Brien Weekend was born. An annual literary event, this weekend focuses on different aspects of her fiction and attracts much academic and popular interest and, also, controversy. (It is significant that this, the only literary school in Ireland about a woman writer, takes place over a weekend, unlike the Yeats, Joyce and Synge schools, which stretch to a fortnight.) The keynote lecture, often given by a friend and contemporary of O'Brien, has been a notorious occasion for antagonism and controversy and it is revealing to consider the aspects of O'Brien's identity, both as writer and as woman, that continue to trouble such occasions.

It is worth noting the qualified terms deployed to describe O'Brien. Her *Irish Times* obituary (14 August 1974) refers to her as a 'writer . . . who could exert and sustain an *unusual* power [my emphasis] with nothing to shout about but much to admire'. The playwright J. B. Keane saw her as 'This majestic figure who towers over her contemporaries' and her friend Benedict Kiely recollects: 'A handsome, well-built woman with mannish hairstyle who had a direct way of speaking. She put you on your toes and kept you there.' Apart from these slightly forbidding and intimidating views of O'Brien, two distinct and contentious arguments have, in the words of the press reports, 'flared up' in relation to her. Both are highly charged, as one concerns her sexuality and/or fertility and the other concerns, of all things, her beauty.

During the 1988 Kate O'Brien Weekend, the keynote speaker, John Jordan, drew attack from O'Brien's family on the subject of her sexuality. In an article entitled 'Family defends writer's reputation' *The Irish Times* reported Jordan as saying

> that the novelist had certain problems of her own in that she was mannish in her ways and had difficulties in personal relationships. It was possible that she even had a child, and after her divorce from her Dutch husband she made more friends among women. At this stage, Ms Mary O'Mara, whose mother-in-law, she said, was Kate O'Brien's sister, denied the implications of what Mr Jordan had said. She was in possession of all the relevant legal documents which dismissed such a possibility. Other speakers defended the Limerick novelist and the chairman of the session said that Kate O'Brien's high status as an author will continue.

(One wonders exactly what legal documents existed to dismiss the possibility that Kate O'Brien was 'mannish'!)

The implications behind this comic interlude are most significant, the notion that O'Brien's 'problems' included her mannishness, that she needed to be defended from this taint of unnaturalness and that, in 'protecting' her against the charge of lesbianism, her family are also defending her status as a writer. Many of these subterranean issues also surface in a sharp interchange between Kevin Myers of *The Irish Times* and writer Louise Hermana on the related question of Kate O'Brien's beauty.

Commenting on a photograph of the young Kate O'Brien (*Irish Times*, 21 February 1989) Myers says:

> Certainly the image she left behind in this world is of a frail, but stern old lady with cropped hair and a fierce, glinting intelligence in her eyes. . . . But nobody could guess from looking at the old lady just how very beautiful the young woman was. Look at that photograph and look at that beauty – a proud beauty, fine but determined. That is one side of O'Brien that one hears nothing about. Another side is her lesbianism, about which, I am told, Limerick, her native city, – which only now is learning to claim her, gets distinctly edgy. But if she were lesbian and had women lovers and looking at her, who could blame them?

It would appear, on first reading, that Myers is attacking the prurience and unease with which O'Brien's sexuality and her writing is viewed and is indeed celebrating what he terms 'the sheer courage that emanates from the magnificent face.' But consider the hidden implications of this rediscovery of O'Brien's beauty. Myers correctly identifies that the popular image of O'Brien in Ireland was of the older, more severe woman. However when photographs of the young, beautiful woman superseded this received image, then her aberrant sexuality suddenly becomes permissible, understandable, allowed. Myers, in calling attention to her appearance, was seeking to normalise and make acceptable the perception that O'Brien was different, difficult and intimidating. Beauty as a supreme value, according to this argument, breaks down normative sexual taboos and removes the stigma of abnormality from same-sex desire.

Louise Hermana, in a subsequent article (*Irish Times*, 1 March 1989), attacks a bewildered Myers for his dubious championing of O'Brien and points out, quite perceptively:

> The neglect which Kevin Myers accurately identifies as being O'Brien's lot is further compounded by the offensive reference he makes to her appearance "look at her face" he says. Why must women be subjected to this kind of sexist and public scrutiny? You don't have to argue that Kate O'Brien was beautiful to prove she was a good writer. Did people not read her because once she looked forbidding and start reading her now that Kevin Myers has given her the sanction of his approving eye.

Myers, to be fair to him, didn't seem to understand the nature of Hermana's objection, but for him to find the young, beautiful O'Brien a more suitable object for female desire than the older, formidable woman is unsound. In a sense the valuation of her appearance becomes entangled with the issue of the accessibility of her fiction. What Myers is searching for, in actuality, is the acceptable face of Kate O'Brien.

Much of this unease and difficulty is also reflected in scholarly attention to O'Brien and her work. I want to consider two accounts in particular, Lorna Reynolds's full-length 1987 study, called, significantly enough, *Kate O'Brien: A Literary Portrait* and Adèle Dalsimer's *Kate O'Brien: A Critical Study* (1990). Both give unsatisfactory accounts of O'Brien, Reynolds's because of evasions and consequent digressions into the anecdotal, Dalsimer because of a sense of incompleteness, of a reluctance to explore fully the implications of her initial project.

*Kate O'Brien: A Literary Portrait* is a lively, exasperating and exceptionally well-informed biographical study, given the advantage of Reynolds's lifelong friendship with O'Brien (as she puts it herself, 'a memorable and stormy friendship' (p. 83)), but a study whose partial and sometimes elusive narrative renders O'Brien's fiction even more inaccessible. ('The world of Kate O'Brien's novels is a sombre place.' (p. 129)). In terms of biography there is as much information about Reynolds's own antecedents as there is about O'Brien's, and the aristocratic pretensions of the O'Brien family are highlighted ('Certainly Kate O'Brien commanded all the aptitude for hauteur any aristocrat could desire' (p. 28)), as well as O'Brien's own disdain for the mundane and the domestic ('The uses of Vim were unknown to her'(p. 38)). Throughout, Reynolds provides a portrait of a formidable and impatient intellect, but dismisses key areas of imaginative concern and development in O'Brien's fiction, furthering the sense of distance and of difficulty.

Where Reynolds is at her most perceptive is in her analysis of the intellectual and moral context of O'Brien's novels. Accurately, she identifies the centrality of education in these parables of female empowerment, and rightly sees the tyranny of familial power-structures as the target for O'Brien's dissent. An understanding of Irish Catholicism is a necessary point of departure, in Reynolds's view, for any reading of her fiction. Thus, her chapters dealing with *Without My Cloak* and *The Land of Spices* tend to be the most insightful, arguing coherently that O'Brien's 'exile' was in fact voluntary and freely made and not part of some Joycean aesthetic.

However, it is with the deployment of sexuality as a destabilising force that Reynolds finds fault with O'Brien and parts company with her. She considers *Mary Lavelle* (O'Brien's first novel to be banned and powerfully subversive), 'not well-made', calls the protagonist 'rather dull', and sees the pivotal moment of adultery and death as 'unnecessary'. Reynolds chooses to foreground the adulterous affair between Mary and Juanito as the causal factor for the novel's banning, ignoring the depiction of lesbian sexuality in the figuring of Agatha Conlon. (There is a fascinating subtext within Reynolds's study, a series of encoded references operating below the surface of her literary portrait. For example, she gives an account of the visit to O'Brien's house in Roundstone, Co. Galway, of the writer Enid Starkie and of Starkie's penchant for cross-dressing, a source of much amusement to the locals!)

Furthermore, Reynolds contends, '*That Lady* was, in a way, a step sideways', because it seemed to deflect her from her obligations to the liberation of the Irish bourgeois female and also because it was a compromise forced on her by the trauma of censorship. (As I argue in my essay, *That Lady*, rather than evading censorship, directly confronts it.)

The most damaging aspect of Reynolds's study is the implication that Kate O'Brien's fiction disimproved. In her analysis of *As Music and Splendour*, O'Brien's most open portrayal of lesbian desire, Reynolds makes a most revealing assertion:

> In the character of Vittoria, who presents us with a figure of declining ambitions, combined with "art neglected, but when as now picked up for a lazy moment, still gold, pure gold", we are perhaps justified in seeing a picture of the author herself in her declining years. Vittoria is not the only artist who dissolved the problem in the anodyne of alcohol (p. 94).

There are two points to be made here. Firstly, Fanny Feehan in her essay on *As Music and Splendour* has argued convincingly that the character of Vittoria can be read as a portrait of the celebrated Irish diva Margaret Burke-Sheridan, a contemporary and acquaintance of O'Brien. Secondly, to portray O'Brien as dissolving her talent in alcohol is to undermine and demean the achievement of *As Music and Splendour*, her last novel and her most radical, in terms of representation of sexual and artistic independence.

Adele Dalsimer's *Kate O'Brien: A Critical Study* provides a committed and enthusiastic account of O'Brien's creative journey and, unlike the Reynolds portrait, has a directness and a refreshing lack of evasion. There is a commitment to placing O'Brien's work within a more radical literary and cultural context. Furthermore, Dalsimer structures her study in a more methodical and linear fashion, supporting her assertions with scholarly cross-referencing and supplying a full bibliographical framework for the novels.

This critical study takes as its basis the notion that 'all of Kate O'Brien's novels assert loudly the need of women and writers for aesthetic, emotional and sexual freedom', and this is indeed a given in her fiction. However, there is a tendency in this study to elide cultural complexity. Dubbing O'Brien's Mellick burghers 'Big House Catholics' is a cultural misnomer symptomatic of a broader lack of precision in her analysis.

Elsewhere in this collection, contributors like Emma Donoghue and Mary Breen will challenge Dalsimer's readings of particular novels, like *The Land of Spices* and *Mary Lavelle*. What I want to do here is to point out the extent to which she unwittingly reaffirms the misconception that O'Brien was essentially conservative. Dalsimer seems to see no contradiction between her claiming of O'Brien as 'a pioneer' and the assertion that 'An almost childlike sense of connectedness encases Kate O'Brien's Ireland, so that any sorts of love her heroines choose fail to replace the love of family.' Again and again, Dalsimer, whether consciously or not, interprets the novels in terms that perpetuate the misconception that O'Brien is, ultimately, conformist and tied to the religion of her culture as, for example, when she states that 'the passion that Mary Lavelle experiences is too ephemeral to resist her Irish Catholic values.'

Dalsimer is astute in identifying O'Brien's disinterest in the lasting significance of the erotic but incorrect, I would argue, in ascribing this disinterest to O'Brien's residual beliefs. This is a common complaint against her fiction, the notion that she is too much of her time, foregrounding Catholicism in her fiction to an excessive degree. The novelist Francis Stuart complains that she 'was far too concerned with the Catholic dimension . . . and was a social commentator rather than a creator of literature in its true sense'. At the centre of my argument and indeed the central purpose guiding this collection, is the idea that Kate O'Brien refused to participate in simple, reductive exercises in subversion, in the mode say, of Stuart's own *Black List-Section H*. Instead, her strategies of attack were much more sophisticated, locating her novels within the culture that sought to marginalise her, intellectualising her religious and moral dissent, respecting and at the same time opposing the true nature of the Catholic paternalism that attempted to outlaw her.

Her tactics against the Franco Regime in her 1937 travelogue *Farewell Spain* perfectly illustrate this stratagy of informed attack from within. Instead of simply condemning the Nationalist cause, O'Brien converts her lament for the threatened Republican cause into a celebration of Castilian history and culture, a reclaiming of the figures of Teresa of Avila and Philip II and of those medieval centres of learning, Toledo, Salamanca and Madrid. In other words, she manages to occupy the cultural territory formerly appropriated by Franco, capturing key symbols of Catholic Nationalism and making them her own, thus complicating the over-simplified dichotomy between rebel and conservative. This subversion from within is the real radicalism underlying O'Brien's fiction and it is her respect and interest in Catholicism, not as a dogma but as an intellectual pursuit, that engenders the real difficulty in treating with her work. She confuses comfortable oppositions, theologically too well-informed both for conservative critics, already uncomfortable with her sexual politics and also for self-styled 'outsiders' like Stuart, dismayed by her interest in mainstream Catholic belief.

O'Brien's imaginative development is, thus, the focus of interest and of examination in this collection, the movement away from Mellick and from the constrictions of family towards Europe and the discovery of individual conscience. Teleologically, her writing moves away from collective belief and towards the enabling of this concept of individual conscience. The difficulties and contradictions inherent in this development will be discussed by the contributors, the problematic nature of O'Brien's representation of sexual role, for example, yet, all in all, this study will establish O'Brien's importance and achievements as an artist.

Joseph Conrad called Henry James 'An historian of fine conscience' and I borrow this term for the process by which O'Brien appropriated Catholic intellectual rigour and secularised it. Two factors influence and shape O'Brien's fiction in this locating and empowerment of secular conscience; firstly, her fictive representation of sexual difference and secondly, her banning and consequent resistance to this silencing. This collection of essays will trace this process of empowerment, suggesting areas of unease within her texts and, ultimately, allowing for a clearer, more defined sense of O'Brien's distinctive and remarkable imaginative powers.

In this collection, the essays are ordered thematically, structured around a series of linked concerns and debates within O'Brien's writing. The contributors deal with five central areas of interest; firstly, O'Brien's place within the tradition of Irish women's writing (Eavan Boland, Ailbhe Smyth), then constructions of sexual and lesbian identity within her fiction (Patricia Coughlan, Emma Donoghue), intertextuality, music, and popular fiction (Anthony Roche, Anne Fogarty, Fanny Feehan) the context of O'Brien's critical writings and journalism (Michael Cronin, Michael O'Toole) and, finally, subversion and resistance in O'Brien's novels (Mary Breen, Eibhear Walshe). Taken as a whole, this study thus offers a series of readings or re-readings of O'Brien that call into question the partial or limited versions of Kate O'Brien hitherto presented.

Eibhear Walshe

# Biographical Note

Kate O'Brien was born in Limerick in 1897, the youngest daughter of Thomas and Catherine O'Brien, into a well-to-do middle-class milieu. One of nine brothers and sisters, she lost her mother at the age of five when Catherine O'Brien died of cancer and consequently she became a boarder at Laurel Hill, a convent school in Limerick. She spent in all fourteen years at this school, later fictionalised in *The Land Of Spices* and it was from this French-run institution that O'Brien first encountered a European-centred system of education and of thought. Indeed, Laurel Hill was sneeringly dismissed by more nationalist educationalists as producing only 'wives of colonial governors'. (Later in her career, when her novels were earning her some notoriety, a subsequent principal of Laurel Hill wrote to O'Brien, remonstrating with her and asking why she wrote such scandalous novels. Her telegraphed reply was 'Pounds, Shillings and Pence'.)

In 1916 her father died and, as the family fortunes were in decline, efforts were made to get her a position in a bank. However, with the help of a county council scholarship, she went instead to UCD, reading English and French for her B.A. Her teachers included the poet Austin Clarke, who commented on her essays as being 'an outward sign of inward grace' and the French Professor, Roger Chauviré. Listening to him lecturing on French poetry, she remarked that this was when she grew up. She graduated from UCD in 1919 and then moved to England in search of work, joining two of her sisters there. She did some freelance journalism and then became foreign language translator for *The Manchester Guardian,* earning the rich sum of £5 per week. At this time, Irish politics and the War of Independence were dominating English newspapers and O'Brien tells of a colleague who used to taunt her during the prolonged hunger strike of the republican Lord Mayor of Cork, Terence McSweeney. Each morning this colleague would greet her with the jibe, 'thirty-two days now, Miss O'Brien, and you still tell me he's on hunger strike'. *The Manchester Guardian,* however, soon after decided to discontinue its foreign news page and O'Brien turned to teaching. From January 1921 she taught a term at St Mary's Convent in Hampstead, London, one of her pupils being her lifelong friend and literary executor, the painter Mary O'Neill, illustrator of several of her books.

In the autumn of 1921, O'Brien went as secretary to America with her brother-in-law, Stephen O'Mara, who was co-ordinator of de Valera's Bonds Drive, and there became friends with Harry Boland, an intimate both of de Valera and also of Michael Collins, and later killed during the Civil War. (Legend has it that O'Brien wore the Russian crown jewels as a fund-raising stunt during a public reception!) She returned to London in 1922 and, as she was considering marriage with a Dutch journalist, Gustaaf Renier, she decided to go to Spain for a year as a governess, before marrying. Bilbao was her home for 1922/23, where she taught English to the children of the Areilza family. (Subsequently the son of the house, Don José María De Areilza, became Spain's foreign minister and he and O'Brien corresponded on the subject of *Mary Lavelle,* her novel inspired by her time in his family home. However, as a banned author, she was on opposite sides to him politically and their correspondence ended.)

On her return to London in 1923 she married Gustaaf Renier, but ended the marriage after eleven months, returning to journalism and the editing of a newspaper for the Sunlight League. (In later life, she would refer to 'poor Gustaaf, now in his grave', but in actual fact, this was inaccurate. He survived O'Brien, having achieved some fame with his book *The English, Are They Human?*)

Her literary career began with the overnight success of her first play *Distinguished Villa,* written in six weeks for a bet and produced in May 1926. It provoked the salute from Sean O'Casey: 'Dublin ventures to congratulate Limerick'. On the strength of an advance from Heinemann, she wrote her first novel, *Without My Cloak,* which became a best-seller and won her the Hawthornden and James Tait Black memorial prizes. A sequel, *The Ante-Room,* was published in 1934, and then her first novel to be banned for obscenity, *Mary Lavelle,* was published in 1936. At the same time, she began reviewing fiction for *The Spectator,* being among the first few critics to recognise Beckett as an important new voice in fiction.

*Farewell Spain,* her 1937 travelogue, was banned in Spain for its outspoken criticism of Franco and she was barred from entering Spain until 1957. She recalled the efforts of the Irish ambassador to persuade the Spanish government to lift the barring order: 'He had to tell a lot of lies, I was a reformed Character, a High Class Convent Girl.' *Pray For The Wanderer,* a more directly autobiographical novel, was published in 1938.

During the war O'Brien lived in Oxford, and while working for the Ministry for Information she wrote *The Land Of Spices,* her second novel to be banned, published in 1941. She moved as a paying guest to the house of the novelist E. M. Delafield in 1942 and wrote *The Last Of Summer,* later produced as a play in 1944, directed by John Gielgud. At the same time, O'Brien edited a collection of essays called *The Romance Of English Literature,* contributing an essay on English letters and diaries, published in 1943.

In 1946, she published her only historical novel *That Lady,* later filmed in 1955 as *For One Sweet Grape,* and the royalties O'Brien earned from the stage adaptations of the novel, including a Broadway production with Katherine Cornell, enabled her to buy a house in Roundstone, Co. Galway, where she lived between 1950 and 1960. (She wrote a piece for *Vogue* on Greta Garbo and her mystique, hoping to entice Garbo out of retirement to play Ana de Mendoza in *That Lady,* but she was unsuccessful, and Olivia De Havilland eventually played the role.)

Her time in Roundstone brought a decrease in creativity, one novel, *The Flower Of May* (1953) and a study, *Teresa Of Avila* (1951), and her notoriety as a banned author made her something of a local character. (There is one story of her attending a local wedding of some young friends and of the sermon being directed at her, in censorious terms that apparently amused her.) She published her final novel *As Music And Splendour* in 1958 and in 1960, bankrupt and neglected critically, she was forced to sell her house in Roundstone and moved to Boughton, in Kent, where she spent her last fourteen years. She did publish another travelogue, *My Ireland*, in 1962, and a memoir, *Presentation Parlour*, in 1963, but her efforts to write a final novel, *Constancy*, were in vain and she died in Canterbury in 1974, having allowed herself to be given final rites. Her grave, in the grounds of a Carmelite convent in Faversham, Kent, has her name, and the inscription *Pray For The Wanderer*.

*Chapter 1*

# Continuing the Encounter

*Eavan Boland*

There is an irony, at least in retrospect, about my one meeting with Kate O'Brien. She came to our house on an October evening at the start of the 1970s. The weather was cold for the time of year. Rain splashed from eaves and gutters; our road glistened under streetlamps. We had been in the neighbourhood only a few months and I thought all the building would never be finished. Houses were under construction: roofs were half-done and windows were left leaning against unfinished walls. The trees were a study in contrasts. The big firs and spruces of a former woodland looked ill-sorted beside the rowan trees, their trunks enclosed in chicken-wire. Kate O'Brien was then in her early seventies, but frail and not far from her death. My husband, Kevin Casey, collected her and brought her to the house. He was editing a book of Irish short stories and he had sought her out, writing to her, hoping for a contribution. She had written back, sending all four chapters of a new novel called *Constancy*. He had a clear, unshakeable admiration for her work. Now he pulled into the drive with her beside him.

The irony of that evening lies in its lack of communication.

Now that I look back at the huge distinction and sweetness of her achievement, it seems I should have been ready with a hundred questions about writing, about women, about Ireland: about her relation to all three. The truth is I would not even have known how to frame them. I was in my mid-twenties; I had published one book of poems. I was still, to all intents and purposes, writing someone else's poem. I had a sense of disquiet, the first stirrings of a malaise about being a woman and a poet in a country which kept those words magnetically apart. But I had no words for it.

It is also difficult to dissociate that encounter from the more downright meeting between woman and woman. There was, for instance, the simple matter of what to do for dinner; and I had complicated it horribly. Earlier in the week, I had taken down her book *My Ireland* and had read, with fascination and unease, her account of how not to entertain her: 'I may be afraid of bossy waitresses,' she had written, 'but I am not at their mercy . . . I have asked, for instance, if I could have a minute steak, a plain green salad and a glass of wine. Always no . . . I have been so driven to experiment that I have asked for a linen napkin, instead of a paper one. (But that last may have been a bit unreasonable.)'

I was puzzled and deferential. I provided the steak, the green salad, the linen. I hardly knew how to take this woman with her cropped head and deep voice and a way of slicing right through a conversation. Afterwards, we sat at right angles to one another in the carefully heated room, the curtains drawn, the drama of the suburb shut out. She was a graceful guest but with a keen ear for evasion and rhetoric. When I reflexively defended one or two people on the grounds that they had a good sense of humour, she made a half-turn and fixed her eye on me. I was too young to appreciate the deft combination of mirth and menace in her tone: 'I am entirely against', she said, 'the promotion of a sense of humour as a philosophy of life.'

We had recently moved house. We had packed up the books, the curtains, the still-obvious wedding gifts − all the icons of a first year of marriage − and moved to the new place. We had left a flat in the centre of Dublin, near the Canal and the coffee-bars, to come to this landscape we hardly recognised. Our first days in the house had been flurried and lucky. A friend had moved into it and got married from it, all within the space of three days. It was a good start.

But there were still raw floors and empty spaces. Through all the comfortless days of transit, one set of books remained unpacked and available: Kate O'Brien's novels. I had been reading them, off and on, for months. There was a cadence and delight which led me from one to the other – from the Galsworthy-like expansiveness of *Without my Cloak* to the charm and estrangement of *Presentation Parlour.* I sat in the white kitchen, the window facing out on newly-planted poplars, and took the book up and set it down. The breviary of another womanhood, another Ireland.

The Ireland from which Kate O'Brien emerged was not the Catholic Ireland of nineteenth-century lore; of hand-to-mouth hardship and bleak survival. Her people must have known these things once; then it changed. By the end of the century they had advanced from handcarts and evictions to a settled prosperity. The characters in her novels have a certain worldly pride. They can tell the difference between Carrickmacross and Guipure lace. They send their children to school in Dublin. They furnish their long tables with silver and ivory-handled cutlery and their minds with all kind of strivings which were unknown to their less fortunate compatriots.

The apparent difference was horses: trading in and telling between: Kate O'Brien's father, Tom O'Brien, ran a successful carriage-horse business. With his brother Michael he bred and sold such horses, sometimes bringing over businessmen and even minor European royals to stay at Shannonview and Boru House to view the animals before purchase.

Other differences ran deeper. Kate O'Brien's world was perishing almost as soon as she had discovered it. It was an ethos and a mythos that would vanish completely with the First World War, absorbed into the shriek of steam-trains and the bright chrome of touring cars; whose pretensions to grace and separateness fell at Ypres and the Somme. It was a world whose outward gestures masked an inward yearning for certainty and structure: qualities which the modern world would dispense with; and not always politely.

I sat reading Kate O'Brien in another Ireland. Our window looked out on a small garden and the start of my neighbour's hedge. At the front of the house the Dublin hills at night were dark, strung with a few lights. These things would creep into my language, my poetry; they would become mysteries of imagery and memory. But they had been fatal to the world she knew. Every year the lights on those hills would increase, the suburbs would march out to the foothills, eating the distance, replacing the cow parsley and marigolds with bicycle wheels and garages. The Ireland she had known, of discreet gesture and separation, would disappear in that advance. The ironies of conscience set against privilege, which she had explored in *The Ante-Room,* could not happen in the same way again. Even more, the important structures of faith and rule-making she relied on were also disappearing. 'I think a crucial aspect of Kate O'Brien's exploration of women in her work', Lorna Reyolds had said, 'comes from an awareness of the Catholic girl, trained in the abstract dogma of the Catholic church, suddenly confronted with the ambiguities of human living and with dilemmas of conscience.' The ambiguities were still there, but the contexts were vanishing.

That rapid spread outside our window, that vista of exigency, was something she could not like. Kate O'Brien was a romantic elitist. She held to the nineteenth-century view that the extraordinary define themselves against and not with the many. She had a clear perception of the small, doomed group — again *The Ante-Room* is the text — in which the elegy for order produces a conflict of identity. The intuition I had even then of the life of ordinariness — of the bicycle wheel and the bang of the garage door — as itself a source of vision was not one I could have commended to her. I had no understanding of that world and I felt she would have little sympathy for mine. For me womanhood and the body gave access to the visionary adventure; for her they were the source of those conflicts which define the spirit. There was not much common ground between us, even had I been able to articulate the ground at all, which I was not. But I had some understanding then — and I think more since then — of what it must have been like to have emerged from an Irish world to be a woman writer.

We live in a time when women writers of the past — they have no choice in the matter — are politicised by the present discourse about literature and gender. This is not the same as saying they are political writers. Therefore it seems especially important to me that they are not obliquely silenced by that politicisation: that the complex refusals and ethical withdrawals which made up their world are not swept away by our own. Even with one meeting — though even a superficial reading of her novels would have shown it — I recognised that Kate O'Brien was neither an Irish writer nor a woman writer in the accepted sense of those terms; that new terms were therefore needed. The internal exile was evident in small pieces of body language. That night at dinner, for instance, her way of talking had seemed to me eloquent but alien, as if a shy woman had masked herself with a theatrical voice. It was not so much a social manner as a literary one, suggesting a hinterland somewhere between Bloomsbury and Roundstone. And indeed she had left Ireland for England in 1918. She graduated from UCD, did some newspaper journalism. She became a teacher in Hampstead and then visited the United States with her brother-in-law. By 1923 she was in Spain, in Bilbao, working as a governess and taking in the sights and sounds of a country which would influence her deeply. By the late 1920s she was back in London and writing and publishing there.

These are the places where she was; where she was not is just as important. Whether by accident or design, she had left Ireland at a moment of national introspection and self-definition. During the 1920s Irish fiction writers for whom the national question was both idiom and instruction would come to the fore. The heady theme of new power applied to old wounds was hard to escape; and yet she left it behind. If Kate O'Brien was not particularly drawn to leave — there is no evidence of quarrelsome estrangement — she was also not particularly drawn to stay.

For a poet like myself who began to write in a culture inflected at every turn by male assumptions, the absence of a writer like Kate O'Brien was an important mystery. As I developed as a poet, as I found my voice, I recognised the way in which the Literary Revival had mediated national idioms into literary forms. To judge from short stories clotted with small towns and predictable actions, or poems wounded by a self-conscious rhetoric, it was almost as if an invisible script had been passed from hand to hand, from writer to writer. It contained specious arguments and a false pastoral; it proposed supporting roles in a corrupt scenario. A poet like Patrick Kavanagh, some years later, recognised this for what it was and was scathing about the Dublin literary establishment which had enabled the climate: 'When I came to Dublin', he wrote, 'the Irish Literary Affair was still booming. It was the notion that Dublin was a literary metropolis and Ireland as invented and patented by Yeats, Lady Gregory and Synge, a spiritual entity. It was full of writers and poets and I am afraid I thought their work had the Irish quality.' And again: 'In those days in Dublin,' he wrote — about a period slightly later but ethically similar — 'in those days the big thing besides being Irish was peasant quality. They were all trying to be peasants. They had been at it for years but I hadn't heard.'

In that dangerous corridor between a national ethos and its literature women writers were at particular risk. The script provided for women in general to be images, emblems, icons — the ornamental parts of the poem, the passive objects of the narrative. For a woman poet or novelist, wishing through her particular statement to avail of a psycho-sexual as well as an historic identity, this was a crucial barrier; the more oppressive for being unseen and unadmitted.

Certainly I knew, without needing a theory for it — although not yet clearly enough on the night I met her — that there were acts of power and elements of exclusion in the Irish literary world. The Irish poem was attended by permissions and prescriptions. There were things you could put in and things which were left out. You could have a murder in that poem, but not a baby; you could have the Dublin hills but not the suburbs under them. You were deemed to write the Irish poem if you were deemed to be an Irish poet and it was not easy, nor always acceptable, to be Irish and a woman and a poet all at the same time. There might even have been an undertow of argument that the categories were — if not mutually exclusive — then mutually compromising.

All of this engages hindsight and it would be wrong to read Kate O'Brien's work as in any way a gloss on this analysis. She came from a different world; her absences inform her themes and her themes are integral to her achievement. Neither the intellectual climate of the Ireland of the 1920s, nor the conflicts it engendered, suited her. If she was disillusioned by de Valera's

Ireland — and she was — she lacked the profile and intent of the overtly political writer. Her subversions, her politic would be deeply private. In that half-lit and imprecise world where writers suffer the evaluations and devaluations of their time she could call on rare but not immediately obvious resources. The national idea would remain invested for decades in the feminine as a passive literary trope. It would be hard — right up to my generation — to break out of it. Kate O'Brien did not seek to disassemble that trope in any immediate or obvious way. But because her destiny as an imagination would be to explore a delicate compound of conscience and sexuality — and how one can illuminate and torture the other — she would be a powerful part of its unravelling. She is today, and in the light of retrospect, that very agent of a changing perspective in Irish literature which she did not seek to be in her time. And she is this partly because her private and steadfast vision was inclusive of several dispossessions of identity — sexual, ethical and historical. But above all, because it is almost impossible to maintain the intricate oppressions necessary for a woman to be a passive object of a literature once she becomes a powerful voice within it. Kate O'Brien is such a voice.

I look back at that meeting now with different eyes. More than twenty years have passed and in the interim the raw suburb has settled down. The new trees slowly became indistinguishable from the old ones. The roads filled with flowers and cars and the faces of neighbours' children; and then my own. Somewhere in that time I found the poem I wanted to write; and wrote it. The years have not convinced me that there are fewer distances between my view of things and Kate O'Brien's. But they have persuaded me of something which I suspect is true of many meetings between readers and the writers they admire: that the face-to-face meeting is the least revealing one. That the encounter continues — beyond time and occasion — through memory and re-readings. And if the distances are not less, they are themselves an index of something I treasure in a literary tradition largely deprived of it: the richness of dialogue and difference with an Irish woman writer of another generation.

But the differences must be respected. Kate O'Brien lived in another ethos as well as another era. I am not sure, for instance, that she would have been drawn to the argument that a literature is strengthened expressively in proportion to its breaking of old and historic silences. She loved French writing and English fiction; she wrote eloquently about Greville and Pepys. Similarly, the struggle of a generation of women writers to secure an invisible truth by drawing the visible life of a woman nearer to elite literary forms might – or might not – have commended itself. It was the individual woman who interested her rather than the community of womanhood. And in the individual woman it was the interaction between sexuality and selfhood that caught her particular attention.

And even here – at this powerful centre of her achievement – there are flaws. Her heroines are heroines indeed: they are allowed stature by an elite and fastidious imagination which at times glamorised womanhood to the point of sentimentality. But Kate O'Brien was an honest artist; her heroines are also wounded women. In each one the wounds is the outcome of unresolved choice. Anna Mendoza in *That Lady* is a hurt captive: between carnal choice and spiritual loyalty to her friend. The nun in *The Land of Spices* is a hostage to the memory of her father, caught in 'the embrace of love' with another man; and therefore a hostage to her own doubts about the purity of her vocation. Perhaps a clue to the whole achievement – its complex sexuality and reticent pain – is in her portrait of Teresa of Avila, wounded from fantasy to sanctity: 'She was an easy, fluent, careless writer of prose', wrote Kate O'Brien, 'who, compelled again and again by high necessity, could say in plain words because she had to, what greater writers could never say.' Is there a hint there of Kate O'Brien's own lost purpose? And if there is, is it part of a privacy which is itself an unresolved choice? I regret that inferences in her argument – the love between women, the political and spiritual identity of the sexual outsider – were not made more plain and therefore more persuasive.

But in the end a writer must be valued for what he or she is: every choice, every refusal is part of that. There are few Irish writers who have meant more to me than she does. When I think of her achievement I like to remember her own words about Teresa of Avila. The line-drawing is not quite accurate – she is not incomprehensible and she looked coolly on rapture – but it suggests something of the complex celebration which is there in her best work: 'Dangerous as her territory may be we do not find it barren as the flowers we know. The trouble is, that incomprehensible as she may be, we cannot help liking her. The charm lives with the sanctity, the wit with the vision, the human simplicity with the ineffable raptures.'

# Chapter 2

# Counterpoints:*
# A Note (or Two) on Feminism and Kate O'Brien

*Ailbhe Smyth*

*Counterpoint*: 'Song pointed against'; a contrary point; the opposite point. (*OED*)

'The subject of feminism', Lorna Reynolds reminds us, 'is never openly raised in Kate O'Brien's work.' No, although *sotto voce*, in a kind of counterpoint, once or twice.

> She thought with pleasure now of the green, white and purple ribbon around the dusty panama hat. She hoped that perhaps Miss Robertson would give her a piece of ribbon. Not that she would wear it, but she'd like to show it to Norrie O'Dowd.
> Anna Murphy in *The Land of Spices*.

'The song pointed against' is difficult not to hear when you are reading for it, which is as pointed a way of reading a text, I agree, as deciding not to hear it. But why not read for the 'other' melody, the opposite view, the counterpoint?

*Can a woman read otherwise? Can she write otherwise?*

The question is not whether Kate O'Brien was or was not a feminist writer, nor even whether or not she was a feminist (a shifting term if ever there was one), which is not altogether the same thing. I am not in the least interested in the geometry of Kate O'Brien's feminism and have no intention of proving that she was or disproving that she wasn't (which is, I think, the same thing). What interests me is the question of how the historical and material fact of Kate O'Brien's sex (she was a woman then, in her terms, whatever it may mean now) was reflected in her writing: what did she see, how did she see it?

Also, the corollary question of how the end-of-century and material fact of my sex is reflected in my reading of her writing? What do I see and why do I see it?

*What happens when neither woman denies her sex, although each in her own way, and in her own time, recognises the taboos, the 'necessary silences', so long and so tightly stitched into women's sexuality? What conversation is possible between us? If there is one, it has its tensions and its reticences. I'm nervous of imposing, even more of transposing into an inappropriately direct idiom. By what right (in both senses) would I question, far less judge, the writer before me? I have the strongest sense Kate O'Brien would, in any case, have been extremely irritated by attempts to define (confine) her in any terms but her own.*

> And be the judge of your own soul; but never for a second, I implore you, set up as the judge of another. Commentator, annotator, if you like, but never judge.
> Reverend Mother to Anna Murphy in *The Land of Spices.*

Throughout Kate O'Brien's novels, women ceaselessly talk to one another, across and through imposed silences. Why not also across time?

> Darling, good night now, I must fold up this letter, dull as it is, and say good-bye for a little time. Surely you are safe by now in Buenos Aires? When can I expect to hear from you? When do you open? What is the list?
> Clare, writing to Luisa, in *As Music and Splendour.*

Is what differentiates us more or less important than the accords? Can we ever see the same?

> I see a sense of women's quest for freedom. Freedom from the owner-
> ship of patriarchs: fathers, husbands, priests and nation-states. Freedom
> for a woman to live on her own terms, wherever and however. Whether
> in pain and perplexity, almost always with great difficulty.
>                    Ana, *'That Lady',* refusing to be owned.

I read the titles: *Without my Cloak, The Land of Spices, As Music and Splendour . . . .* Faintly exotic, enigmatic, secretive, not releasing meaning easily, signalling that we need to seek it out beneath a surface smoothed over by conventions. Coded titles, 'hiding [their] bravery', inviting us, contrarily, to look through a different lens. And see a different world. How different?

Enough for her work to be, not exactly shunned, but certainly not canonised. For Kate O'Brien suffered a long banishment to the outlying regions of (Irish) canonical acceptability. Not totally dismissed but not considered central either. As if, somehow, she had not quite proved herself one of the boys and must therefore wait, on the off-chance of being called to glory, in a kind of ante-room. Doing time in the literary Styx. Awaiting a judgement which might never come (she who hated such things) and when it did, might wound even more fiercely with its nonchalant incomprehension.

Kate O'Brien has been admired (not passionately acclaimed – there is a world of difference) for her certainties, her deftness with the conventions of realist fiction, her perceptive representation of the Irish Catholic bourgeoisie. Around the dilemmas and enigmas deeply embedded, even encoded, in her work there is a resonant silence. I think that, in a very important sense, Kate O'Brien's work has been *neutralised* by the literary law-makers. They either ignore it altogether (Seamus Deane's *A Short History of Irish Literature* is a useful reference-point here) or render it innocuous, unthreatening, 'respectable' – and very much less interesting than it really is – by refusing to acknowledge, far less to decipher, its coded disruptions of conventional narrative structures.

James Cahalan cheerfully hails her as 'the best Irish writer of the 1930s and 1940s and one of the most important novelists of any period'. But her work is briskly dealt with in less than three pages, in a medley selection entitled 'Women Novelists' (a strategy used twice for women in the same book, by the way). Elizabeth Bowen, Molly Keane, Kate O'Brien, Maura Laverty and Mary

Lavin (less than eight pages for the lot of them) are inelegantly lumped together, and on the most tenuous grounds: (a) because they are of the same generation (so what? so were Patrick Kavanagh and Samuel Beckett), and (b) because of their 'devotion to realism', whatever that may mean, the 'devotion' having the effect of osmosing them all into unthinking (female) emotionalists. Cahalan certainly does not explain *why* Kate O'Brien should be considered one of the most important novelists of the period. Fine words do not soften the blow of substantive critical negligence.

Mind you, it's unfair to single out James Cahalan, because he is one of the very rare male critics to have written about Kate O'Brien at all. But why are the (male) critics, if not totally mute, then at best tight-lipped? Is it faintheartedness, downright dislike or just plain incomprehension? Of course, it may well be that muteness is the only plausible (i.e. least disgraceful) position for canon-makers to adopt, when they are unwilling or unable to read the song against itself.

Is it possible (I ask the question quite disingenuously), that a man critically reading Kate O'Brien's novels may, from time to time, feel ill at ease with such a strongly woman-centred world? Is there not a marked case in male-generated Kate O'Brien criticism of marginalising what does not quite fit the image of the 'lady novelist' (preferably a creature from the conveniently distant 'early days' of Irish fiction anyway), and is therefore doomed to placelessness in the Irish literary cartography?

 *But how, I ask myself, could a woman survive at all, never mind live creatively, passionately, fully in an environment which would stifle her so utterly? As Clare says to Rose, in* As Music and Splendour, *talking about female*  *roles in opera: 'They seem all to go either mad or bad – there's no other way out!' All of Kate O'Brien's work is about an 'other way out'.*

Cahalan himself remarks of Kate O'Brien's 'fictional focus on women', that it 'included an understanding of the stresses of their sexuality and the psychology of their relationships with other women'. I would put it a great deal more strongly: these novels do not simply 'include' an understanding of female eroticism, whether heterosexual and/or lesbian: eroticism is a *vital* axis of her narratives, with the possible exception of *Without My Cloak*. Although already in that first novel the dangerous consequences of denying the erotic are presented quite unambiguously:

> Love, that Caroline had so long forgone, then found and flung aside and wept for, had now become a thing she hated to consider.

Caroline, poor Caroline, failed by her nerve, and her lover, at the eleventh hour so that she lost her chance for love and for freedom. And went on resenting it, and herself, for the rest of her life. Caroline sees herself as having to choose between two starkly opposed possibilities, and that is her tragedy:

> There is no way to get rid of a whole life. I thought there was. Oh, love, I thought there was.

Later, the choices are not so simple. Not even for Agnes Mulqueen. Especially not for Agnes, whose erotic desire is fixed on a fantasy-creation. She constructs an object out of the material to hand — Vincent — precisely, of course, because he is mostly not to hand and her desire is therefore free to develop unfettered by the codes of her class. But as Deirdre Madden suggests, one feels this love is doomed partly because it is not 'born out of freedom' and partly (most significantly):

> because it is a love between a woman and a man. In the world of O'Brien's novels, such a love seldom, if ever, develops into a lasting joy.
> Deirdre Madden.

But how was Kate O'Brien to represent as 'lasting joy' what could barely be represented at all? How to write what could scarcely be spoken?

> 'Lesbian' is a word written in invisible ink, readable when held up to a flame and self-consuming, a disappearing trick before my eyes where the letters appear and fade into the paper on which they are written, like a field which inscribes them.
> Elizabeth A. Meese.

The challenge was immense — to make the ink readable: the ink of female eroticism. For what Kate O'Brien explores primarily are the intricate complexities of women's desire: the 'stresses'

indeed, but also, and more, the dilemmas, perplexities and con-
fusions of a desire which can hardly recognise itself and which
— even if it dares to do so — has no language readily available
in which to mark that desire. And yet this is precisely what Kate
O'Brien succeeded in doing:

> Still Orpheus and Eurydice, their brilliantly made-up eyes swept for
> each the other's face, as if to insist that this disguise of myth in which
> they stood was their mutual reality, their one true dress wherein they
> recognised each other, and were free of that full recognition and could
> sing it as if their very singing was a kind of Greek, immortal light,
> not singing at all.
>
> Clare and Luisa in *As Music and Splendour.*

Meeting that challenge, finding a language, was a transgression
punishable by the severest sentence of all: silence or denial before
such a profound breaking of the 'laws'. But what else did Kate
O'Brien, surely the least naive of writers, expect? In that very
first novel, Eddie, whose excessive love for his sister Caroline
breaks a deeply rooted taboo, gently, wisely and sadly predicts
the future:

> And these loves of ours are out of order and can come to no good.
>
> Eddie in *Without My Cloak.*

It is so much less troublesome to erase the naming of women's
sexuality in all its diversity than to try and understand it. So much
less threatening to the given order to pretend that women do not,
cannot, have an independent sexuality: that is, a sexuality which
is neither male-defined nor male-dependent for its very existence.
So much easier to behave as if it doesn't exist at all. For what
does not exist cannot be written about.

*The reverse is also true. Is it not?*

When I first read Kate O'Brien, as a very young woman, I did
so with something of a *frisson:* I thought it was very daring to
read a banned author. I cannot now read Kate O'Brien's work
without being acutely aware of the significance and consequences
of the silencing of women through acts of censorship. And side-
lining, or faint praise for less than the whole story, are altogether

as dangerous a form of censorship as the banning of her novels under the Censorship (Obscene Publications) Act.

Now, when I read it is with admiration (among other things) for the honesty of her exploration of what it means to live as a woman, in a woman's body, with a woman's desires, in a culture which allows women meagre credit and credence on condition that they remain voiceless, mindless, pleasureless, powerless and unswervingly male-focused. What I admire is Kate O'Brien's persistence in searching for ways of naming experiences which women had not (yet) dared to name, even to themselves, and which swerve close to, if not right into, the 'wild zone' of a space beyond the rigid boundaries of convention.

We say, of course, that much has changed since the repressive decades of the Censorship Acts, of the 1937 Constitution, the Dancehalls Act, and so on. But I wonder who has most benefited from those changes? Women are still not free, as I write in the autumn of 1992, to determine our sexuality. And the witch-hunts continue, although in different forms. And we are still afraid to name them.

Lorna Reynolds remarks: 'Today it is difficult to understand all the furore' (over the banning of *Mary Lavelle* and *The Land of Spices*) — the commotion over that single sentence, so delicately phrased, 'the embrace of love', in *The Land of Spices*. But then, the censors and the hunters will always ferret out the merest flick of a tone of voice which, to them, betrays the true subversive. The single sentence was the hook on which to peg their loathing (and fear).

*As Philip sought a noose for Ana's neck.*

Why? Certainly, because Kate O'Brien wrote about male homosexuality. Even more certainly, because she strove to represent the coming to selfhood, socially, emotionally, creatively and sexually, of women. The women in her fiction encounter classic — almost emblematic — and seemingly immovable obstacles in their struggle to realise themselves. Mary Lavelle rejecting both father and fiancé, Helen Archer confronting the bishop, Ana challenging the might of the state: each one in her way refuses to have her life, her passion, her desire — whatever it may be —

defined by the institutions of patriarchal heteroreality. Kate O'Brien was censored because her heroines expose and, to differing degrees, resist the bondage of patriarchy and all its paraphernalia — family, marriage, property, religion, class, and all the rest of it. They come to knowledge, if not to sweet and lasting joy, through experiences which are not defined or controlled by men.

Without such independent knowledge, women cannot survive. Some women never make it. Mollie Considine dies, literally, of dependency and silence: the price she pays for experiencing sexual pleasure (which she cannot even name), is death through childbirth. Caroline is embittered, emotionally cut off. Señora Arriavaga, perfect wife and mother, lives (her husband recognises) a kind of death in life: pleasure cannot so much as enter her vocabulary, so well has conditioning done its work of repressing within her even desire itself. But Mary Lavelle and Milagros, even 'the misses', certainly Helen Archer, possibly Anna Murphy, Ana and Bernardina, Clare and Rose, all inhabit worlds in which men are incidental to women's survival. Not that independence is necessarily synonymous with happy endings. On the contrary. Kate O'Brien's heroines do *not* end up doing what women are supposed to end up happily doing. They do not indeed 'end up' at all, for how do you end a story which has only just begun, tentatively, to be told? Kate O'Brien, having effectively disabled the conventional heterosexual ending of marriage (i.e., male—female mating), then reaches the realisation that what might (diversely) replace it had yet to be invented or, perhaps, was quite simply unrepresentable.

For Kate O'Brien, women are the 'primary presence' (in Adrienne Rich's phrase) and women's relationships to and with one another are what significantly shape her fiction. And those relationships are loving, passionate and persuasive in ways that her heroines' heterosexual relationships are not. Helen Archer's education (in its full Latin sense) of Anna Murphy is at the very centre of her life. Agnes Mulqueen sacrifices herself, in effect, for love of her sister. Clare's existence is defined primarily — even exclusively — in terms of Rose and Luisa. *That Lady* is a magnificent novel of female friendship — and so rarely read as such. Ana and Bernardina are bound together in the most powerful, tender and intimate ways, each enabling the other to be more fully herself than she could otherwise have been. Together, these two women constitute a formidable threat to the ruling caste. For which, to be sure, they are punished.

The 'communities of women' which Kate O'Brien first implies and then develops more boldly in her later novels, are not perfect – this is no romanticised paradise – but they do function to enable women to speak and to act, to live and to love (however fleetingly). They are separate spaces, sometimes chosen and carefully constructed (the convents and schools), sometimes externally imposed, as punishment, and lived with difficulty (Ana's incarceration), sometimes seemingly unconscious, almost accidental (the café in *Mary Lavelle*), but each one providing a measure of freedom from a narrowly-bounded, misogynistic world, and greater self-determination for women.

The same-sex relationships in her work are, I believe, profoundly erotic in that they are rooted in love – the love of women for women, variously understood and expressed, sometimes sexual, more often not. Does this mean that Kate O'Brien is a lesbian writer? But what does the question mean? And who is asking it, and why? I am most wary of the question, firstly because I suspect, in some cases at least, it is motivated by a homophobic (and prurient) desire to 'out' a writer by imposing on her an anachronistic identity she would not have recognised. I am wary too because the question suggests that it is possible to reconstruct the life-experience on the basis of the fiction. Let us remind ourselves, as Reina Lewis put it, that good gossip is not useful literary criticism. We do indeed need close readings of Kate O'Brien's work which explore her representations of women's sexual desire and of how it is constantly thwarted or stifled by patriarchal institution. We also need a biographical account which does not evade the issue of sexuality, but which does not either construe 'sexual identity' as the only signifier of self.

'Feminist' is often used as a kind of polite euphemism for 'lesbian' (as if that were a rude word), which slip-sliding conflation solves nothing at all. In this case, and given that definitions of 'lesbian' are even more problematic – and historically and culturally located – than definitions of feminism, perhaps it might be useful to take Audre Lord's discussion of 'lesbian' as a point of departure (if not of arrival):

Strongly women-identified women where love between women is
open and possible, beyond the physical in every way.

One way and another, harmonious and erotic accords between
women are represented in Kate O'Brien's writing as serious
possibilities, although always liable to be sanctioned. For the
patriarchy cherishes docile daughters and obedient wives. But Kate
O'Brien's heroines are hardly docile, however politely their dis-
obedience may be phrased, and may (even) evade if they do not
reject the pleasures of wifehood. Their freedom is not easily attained, often it is heavily burdened by pressures to conform which
bite deeply into social and moral conscience. If some appear to
be ultimately defeated, it is not without an intense struggle between desire and the internalised forces of oppression. But even
defeat may not be conclusive, for Kate O'Brien's endings, often
melodramatic or romantic, are the least (or the most) 'satisfying'
aspect of her narratives.

To write this, of this, like this – to refuse the solutions of the
system – is a radically subversive act which undermines the bases
of the Establishment, its values and practices. Kate O'Brien could
not be allowed to continue unchecked. Nor was she. For how
many might follow?

But what of the inner censors? So much more stifling than the
overt bully-boys and their laws. For all Kate O'Brien had the
courage to write, what did she feel, know, imagine, desire but
have to leave unsaid? The inner censors must surely have hedged
her words, taught her codes and circumlocutions?

What Kate O'Brien certainly explored, and why she is therefore
of inestimable value as a foresister (and why she had to be silenced),
is women's coming to a sense of power that is strongly marked
by eroticism, in a particular culture, granted, and at a particular
moment in time (as I too am located as 'her' reader). To read her
work chronologically is to follow a path to adult womanhood,
to knowledge and self-knowledge, to passion and desire. She provides a perspective, a vocabulary for exploring what it can mean
to be a woman and what one can become if we embrace freedom,
with all the risks and uncertainties it brings. If we can refuse to
take existence at face-value but insist on exploring it on our own
terms, in the wholeness of ourselves as thinking, acting, feeling,

pleasuring beings. Not the only perspective, indeed, but significant in a landscape where the markers are few.

Take a patriarchally (pre)determined destiny, infuse it with 'this tangle of our longings', and give it leave to 'sing my own, to my own heart'. This is not an answer, rather a possibility: 'the words swam before her in a new, wild mist of tears', leading us – perhaps, who knows – to a land of spices. In any event, out and away from the ante-room where women have been condemned to do time, always the objects, never the subjects, of their own stories.

Whether Kate O'Brien would have called herself a feminist or not may not matter so very much. What her writing gives us is a perspective which is firmly woman-centred, which will accept nothing less for women than the unquestioned (but always questing) right for women to live their lives as they will, without constraint and without opprobrium. Kate O'Brien does not, I think, write about the experience of women's oppression; she does not, on the whole, linger with the victim. Rather, she strikes out, ventures forth and charts a way towards freedom. And what else is feminism about, however we phrase it?

*Censored, silenced, sentenced, punished: sent (back) to the ante-room. The women's room. Were it not for women's presses (Arlen House the first of them) and women scholars (Lorna Reynolds, a lone voice for so long), there is no knowing for how long we would have been deprived of Kate O'Brien's harmonies. Women, pointing her song against the prevailing chant.*

## Works cited

James M. Cahalan, *The Irish Novel: A Critical History,* Dublin, Gill andMacmillan, 1988.

Seamus Deane, *A Short History of Irish Literature,* London, Hutchinson, 1986.

Reina Lewis, 'The Death of the Author and the Resurrection of the Dyke', Sally Munt (ed.) *New Lesbian Criticism: Literary and Cultural Readings,* Hemel Hempstead, Harvester Wheatsheaf, 1992.

Audre Lord, *Sister Outsider,* Trumansburg, New York, Crossing Press, 1984.

Deirdre Madden, 'Afterword' to *The Ante-Room,* London, Heinemann, 1934 (London, Virago Press, 1989).

Kate O'Brien, *Without My Cloak,* London, Heinemann, 1934 (Virago Press, 1986).

Kate O'Brien, *The Ante-Room,* London, Heinemann, 1934 (London, Virago Press, 1989).

Kate O'Brien, *Mary Lavelle,* London, Heinemann 1936 (Virago Press, 1984).

Kate O'Brien, *Land of Spices,* London, Heinemann, 1941 (Dublin, Arlen House, 1981).

Kate O'Brien, *That Lady,* London, Heinemann, 1946.

Kate O'Brien, *As Music and Splendour,* London, Heinemann, 1958.

Lorna Reynolds, *Kate O'Brien: A Literary Portrait,* Gerrards Cross, Bucks., Colin Smythe, 1987.

*Shorter Oxford English Dictionary.*

*Chapter 3*

# 'Out of Order'
# Kate O'Brien's Lesbian Fictions

*Emma Donoghue*

To understand the feeling of unreality that dogs me as I begin this essay, you may need to play a little game. Imagine that a certain writer, let us say Elizabeth Bowen, had never been written about as Irish. Imagine not only that most essays assumed her Britishness (as many do), but that Irish scholars had failed to claim her as part of their literary tradition, because they had never heard of her. Imagine that anyone who pointed out the Irish settings of several of Bowen's fictions was told that she wrote them from a sympathetic outsider's perspective. If anyone presumed to mention the influential years of childhood and adult life she spent in Ireland, they would be told that there was no way of conclusively proving that she thought of herself as 'Irish' or even 'Anglo-Irish' (terms notoriously difficult to define), and that therefore they had no right to speculate.

Reading Kate O'Brien as a lesbian novelist is as fruitful and as necessary, I suggest, as reading Elizabeth Bowen as Irish, Jane Austen as middle–class, or Alice Walker as black. But because 'lesbian' is more easily denied and avoided than these other labels, even in the 1990s, such overdue work on Kate O'Brien has not been done. The Irish literary establishment has generally lauded her as a realist, leaving out the most innovative subject she was realistic about, and failing to reprint her last novel. Lesbian historians and critics seem never to have heard of her, or know of no context of 'Irish lesbian fiction' in which to place her.[1] She falls down the gaps between traditions.

I think it would be fair to say that during her life and after it, Kate O'Brien, her family, biographers, critics, and friends all colluded to keep her in the closet. Not so much by covering up her bonds with women, as by denying that those partnerships were of any relevance to her work. Rather than the traditional strategies for heterosexualising a reputation – summarised by Lillian Faderman as 'bowdlerization, avoidance of the obvious, and *cherchez l'homme*'[2] – most of those who have written on Kate O'Brien have simply avoided the lesbian issues in her work. The spotlight gets shifted, the subject is changed, other things are talked of. The bibliography of criticism on O'Brien provided by Adèle Dalsimer[3] shows that most discussions of her novels manage to leave out *Mary Lavelle* and *As Music and Splendour*, and the only essay which concentrates on the latter is about opera – which is rather like writing about horse-riding in *The Well of Loneliness*.

Leaving aside the difficult task of wresting biographical information from censored or reluctant sources, let us consider how we might go about reading Kate O'Brien as a lesbian novelist.

We could look at her attacks on the heterosexual family, as Susan Crecy has done in a recent lesbian reading of Ivy Compton-Burnett.[4] From her very first novel, O'Brien is sardonic about the effects of marital commitments on women's lives. Some good work here has been done by Adèle Dalsimer, who points out, for example, that *The Land of Spices* manages to validate every kind of love *except* that between adult heterosexuals, and provides a sort of map of 'alternatives to familial bonding'.[5] Many of O'Brien's characters resist marriage, seeing, with Matt Costello in *Pray for the Wanderer*, that 'life might fruitfully be a lonely track or a jealously personal adventure'.[6] It would be interesting to read O'Brien's novels as a series of interrogations of the institution of matrimony, and to analyse the figure of the independent, nunlike spinster who crops up in so many of her novels, from

Fanny in *The Flower of May*, to Nell Mahoney who looks like a cross between — a crucial pairing — St Catherine and Sappho.[7]

A feminist understanding of the 'lesbian spectrum' would allow a critic to work line by line through O'Brien's novels, plucking out every moment of warmth or *frisson* between women. But this is simply too vast a scope; it includes mother–daughter, sisterly, friendly, and rivalrous relationships, which may have an erotic element but profit not at all from being lumped in together. If we read a woman's longing for a mother figure as essentially lesbian, as Adèle Dalsimer does with Clare's nostalgia for her grandmother in *As Music and Splendour,*[8] we risk reducing lesbianism to a problem for psychoanalytic theory to solve; also, this reading cuts heterosexual women off from the female quest for the mother. Sisterly love won't fit either. Kate O'Brien sometimes gives bonds between sisters a romantic and self-sacrificial tone (for example, Agnes and Marie-Rose in *The Ante-Room,* or Eleanor and Julia in *The Flower of May*), but the structure of sororal devotion contains the emotion and harnesses it to respectable ends. A character like Agnes may feel troubled by excessive love for her sister, but that love is not presented as in any way taboo.

And taboo, I suggest, is the key word for Kate O'Brien's lesbian fictions. Not one taboo, but many; a whole world of forbidden attractions, and the moral conflicts they provoke. I want to approach O'Brien's work by probing the network of illicit relationships, the loves she presents as 'out of order'.

O'Brien's lesbian perspective governs not just the content but the structure of her novels, the careful mixing and contrasting of loves. A common strategy of the closet is to write about homosexuality of the opposite gender; many gay men and lesbians have found it safer to write about each other than themselves. Kate O'Brien not only uses this device, presenting clearly homosexual male characters in *Without my Cloak* and *The Land of Spices*, but brings in other unlawful passions such as incestuous devotion in *Without my Cloak* and *The Last of Summer*, and (in most of her novels) heterosexual passion which could lead to adultery. These loves are all forbidden, and the distinction between those the Church merely forbids, and those it castigates as unnatural, is far from clear. They are presented not to crudely symbolise O'Brien's lesbianism, but to broaden her appeal to a wide audience.

This strategy of diverse presentations of the same basic theme allows O'Brien to make, not a special plea for lesbians, but a grand argument for moral accountability and tolerance. So without writing a string of clearly lesbian novels — without in fact having noticeable lesbian content in more than two of them — O'Brien managed to argue, over and over again, for sexual self-determination. *As Music and Splendour*, I will argue, is not a late effort, but the climax of all her novels, the making explicit in a lesbian context of so much she has been arguing for in other novels.

'I see no story unless there is a moral conflict',[9] Kate O'Brien said of her work. It is possible to read her entire corpus in terms of stages on a moral journey — not from natural to unnatural, but from easy or lazy loves to brave commitments (whatever the sex of the love-object).

To begin with, O'Brien pays little narrative attention to those whose love can be contained in a respectable bond — whether marriage, sisterly devotion, or a generous mother–daughter relationship such as that between Ana and Anichu in *That Lady*. Then there is a category of selfish loves, such as the parental greed of Anthony in *Without my Cloak* and Hannah in *The Last of Summer*. Refusing to admit that they are guilty of anything, these greedy lovers win their love-objects, but earn the narrator's disapproval. O'Brien reminds us not to judge a relationship by the nominal, virtuous roles of the participants. For example, fathers are allowed to love sons, but we are told that Anthony's hysterical love for Denis, 'if it was paternal, would bear no resemblance to the orthodox family feeling'. The problem is not what he feels but what he does — he greedily establishes a connection between them which will allow Denis no freedom, and at the end has won at the cost of a kind of demonic possession, his eyes watching the returned prodigal with 'blazing love'.[10]

This essay will concentrate on the next two categories: those who take moral responsibility, and step back from sin, and (generally in the later novels) those who are equally responsible, and choose to walk into sin, from motives of love. There is no great difference between them. The point is not whether they commit the sexual sin or not (which often depends, for example in Agatha Conlon's case, on whether a love is reciprocated), but the responsibility and integrity they show in the choice. As Dalsimer repeatedly points out, Kate O'Brien is far from idealistic about the prospects for romantic love, but I want to show that she is hopeful about the moral growth that can be prompted by romantic and other loves.

By the time contemporary readers of Kate O'Brien met Agatha Conlon in *Mary Lavelle* (1936), they had a moral framework to read her in. She is the grand example of the early O'Brien character who comes to know herself through an unlawful love, and withdraws from danger. Agnes in *The Ante-Room* discovers this strength in herself when she withholds love from her brother-in-law out of loyalty to her sister. In *Without my Cloak,* a similar generosity is shown by two men. Denis's friend the priest Martin Devoy is furious with Anthony for chaining Denis in his love; when Martin realises that he is jealous, because he loves Denis himself, he immediately removes himself from temptation – but probably more to save his soul than to save Denis. His is a limited moral code: 'He had done no harm and would do none.'[11] Early in her career, Kate O'Brien tended to link homosexuality and self-sacrifice – a common way for lesbian novelists to win readers' sympathy for their characters.[12]

A subtler generosity than Martin's is found in Eddy, who combines several taboos. A dandified London bachelor with hands like a woman's, vague about his lifestyle and friends, Eddy sets his Mellick family on edge. They know his lifestyle must hide some sin or mystery, but they are not sure what. In a deliciously comic passage, his sister Teresa speculates: 'And still there remained something about this brother that dimly frightened the shrewd Teresa in her heart of hearts. Something vague and unfamiliar about his ways. There had even once been a rumour, vehemently hushed up by charitable Tom, that Eddy did not always go to Mass on Sunday.' After the details of his secret, effeminate characteristics, the heavy hints that he is gay, comes the bathos of his small crime.[13]

Eddy's loves are unveiled gradually, beginning with the information that he would rather have a sister than a wife, and would only take a wife if she were his sister Caroline's twin. This strong hint of incestuous devotion is clarified when Caroline runs away from her marriage to stay with Eddy in London. She quickly falls for Richard, the friend (lover?) Eddy has been travelling in Italy with. Wounded but generous, renouncing his own stake in both of them without fuss, Eddy stays out all evening to allow them to draw closer. When he hears they have missed their chance, he is disappointed by the waste: 'I thought by staying out to make you happy', he tells Richard sadly. Since there is nothing to lose now, he can tell Richard the story of his romantic love for Caroline:

> She turned me against women, except when adventure with them could be cheap as cheap. . . . I've never loved a woman except Caroline; and you love her, and I love her more perhaps than I love you, more even than I love myself. And these loves of ours are out of order and can come to no good.[14]

Notice how the hint of homosexuality, his love for Richard, is cleverly slipped in between heterosexual attraction to his sister and self-love. But this is not just a way of disguising it; O'Brien is pointing out the similarities between all three. They are all loves which may be 'out of order', and can find no fruition in Mellick, but they compare well in tenderness and generosity with the passionless 'order' represented by Caroline's marriage. Loves which, if admitted, bring their sufferers together in solidarity across the lines of sexual choice; which join Caroline, Eddy and Richard together in a bodiless intimacy that her husband Jim will never know.

The banning for 'immorality' of *Mary Lavelle* (1936) by the Irish Censorship Board, it has usually been assumed, was for the explicitness of Mary's affair with Juanito, but O'Brien's pioneering treatment of the Agatha Conlon subplot must have scandalised the Board too. The two women have parallel experiences. Both are virginal, with a pronounced disinterest in heterosexual contact, until the year they meet in Spain. Mary dislikes her fiancé's kisses: 'all she experienced was a mild physical discomfort and, at the roots of her virgin spirit, an inadmissible distaste'; unable to admit it to anyone, she keeps this 'unnaturalness' in the back of her mind. Similarly, Agatha has never known 'anything about attraction to other people or about the sensation of pleasure human beauty can give'. They have both come to Spain to reject female roles. Mary, though outwardly conventional, longs for her childhood dream: 'To be alone for a little space, a tiny hiatus between her life's two accepted phases. To cease being a daughter without immediately being a wife.' Agatha has escaped both these roles, by allowing her 'hiatus' to last for twenty years. Finally, Agatha and Mary are alike in that each blossoms into her true self through a love which is taboo — Mary falling for the married son of her employer, Agatha falling for Mary. Both of them find the strength, after an initial self-indulgence, to withdraw from their beloveds' lives, and (as Martin Devoy would put it) do 'no harm'.[15]

Agatha Conlon is an intriguing and well-developed character who has received practically no attention from O'Brien critics, perhaps because they have no idea of the lesbian literary tradition from which she comes. Despite the commitment of Adèle Dalsimer's study to 'deal more directly than any of its predecessors with the issue of sexual preference', she has a curious blind spot about Agatha; in a chapter which analyses the political symbolism of every member of the Areavagas family, Dalsimer refers to her only as 'the homosexual Agatha Conlon, tormented in her impossible love for Mary'.[16] This makes it sound like the love is impossible because it is homosexual, but in fact it is an unrequited love much like any other.

When *Mary Lavelle* opens, Agatha Conlon is thirty-eight, having escaped from Ireland at twenty-one. Unlike the other ever-Irish 'Misses', she has not clung to her roots, but has learned Spanish and blended into the culture which offers her more freedom than Co. Wexford did. Agatha is introduced as 'queer', acidic and blunt, with the fanatical, noble, boyish face of your average sexual deviant. The mark of the martyred androgyne 'Stephen Gordon' in Radclyffe Hall's influential *The Well of Loneliness* (1928) is apparent; and perhaps there is also an echo of the fanatically religious lesbian Cecilia in George Moore's *A Drama in Muslin* (1886). But Agatha is no stereotype, and compared to the tortured lesbians of Djuna Barnes's lurid *Nightwood* (1936), for example, she is full of life and energy. Agatha is still a pious Catholic — something both her home and adopted cultures are centred on — and is described as nunnish, which often operates as a code word for lesbian. What keeps her from being a nun, she explains wryly, is her 'evil nature'.[17]

But this is not a re-run of *A Drama in Muslin*, with the frustrated lesbian being absorbed into the Church. What Agatha is fanatical about is not Catholicism, but the bullring. Addicted to its drama, she goes to bullfights whenever she can. The first sign of change in her solitary life is when she invites Mary along: 'I never in my life before asked anyone to go with me to a fight.' They are both deeply stirred by it, and in the exhilaration Mary begins to see past Agatha's spinsterish manner: 'The hungry, unbalanced face looked smooth and young. "You might take her for a boy just now," Mary thought.' The imagery of the bullfight is explicitly sexual, and the effect on Mary is described almost as a rape: 'The wound of the bullfight was in fact — though she tried to forget and ignore it — the gateway through which Spain had entered in and taken her.'[18] (Dalsimer reads this as a foreshadowing of sex with Juanito, ignoring the fact that it is Agatha who brings Mary to the fight, Agatha whose passion for heroic, bloody Spain Mary finds so disturbing and attractive.[19])

But as Mary falls in love with Juanito, she begins to avoid Agatha Conlon, fearing the self-exposure such meetings bring. 'Her eyes, so blind and fanatical, could sometimes search with savagery. If only she were kinder, or anyhow not so mad.' Conlon is not so much mad as touchy. Rather than the predictable behaviour of a caricature, she acts according to mood. The emphasis is not on her static qualities but on metamorphosis; for example, when Mary asks permission to call her by her first name, we are told that 'A very faint flush rejuvenated most tragically the starved, thin face.' Mary comes to realise that Agatha can be 'as sensitive as she was crude', and sometimes she forgets to be afraid of her friend. "How beautiful the creature can seem!" Mary thought, and the irrelevant reflection calmed her.' Kept on the borders of *Mary Lavelle's* official love story, kept in the margin of meaning, the two women's 'irrelevant' bond can avoid the spotlight of a reviewer's gaze. For most of the book, Agatha only hints at her feelings, for example in irritated asides about Mary's procrastinating fiancé, or once, when Mary asks would she like a husband herself, in looking at Mary 'as if she might strike her'.[20]

But eventually the clues, the hints begin to grate. It is all too obvious that we are moving towards a dramatic confession. It may help to remember what an early attempt this is at the

characterisation of a likeable lesbian. The tradition available to
Kate O'Brien, in a flood of novels published in the early decades
of the century, was one of evil vampires and barking head-
mistresses. Mary Renault, another lesbian novelist trying to write
'literary' novels in the 1930s, deftly mocked the clichés available
to her: 'Colonna, by all the laws of literature, ought to have been
plain, heavy, humourlessly passionate and misunderstood, pursuing in recurrent torments of jealousy the reluctant, the in-
experienced and the young. She ought to have behaved like
someone with a guilty secret.' O'Brien's Agatha certainly fits most
of these adjectives — but what she also has is an essential
seriousness, a central place in the novel, a story of her own.
Whereas in order to avoid the 'laws' of such gloomy literature,
Mary Renault turned instead to the tradition of lesbian decadence,
and gave her Colonna much charm but little substance. 'Colonna,
it appeared, accepted her own eccentricities much as she did the
colour of her hair, though as a source of more amusement.'[21]
This kind of characterisation avoids the risk of embarrassment,
but tends to marginalise the lesbian as a jester; it is just as limiting
a role, whereas Kate's serious secretive Agatha has a key place in
the moral web of *Mary Lavelle*.

The two women's love-stories build to a simultaneous climax.
Allowing herself to dream of a life with Juanito, Mary feels jarred
when Agatha suggests that the two women might holiday together
in Avila. She tells Agatha she is returning to Ireland in a few days
— which brings on a flood of revelations. For the first time in
her life, Agatha explains, she has fallen into, not a 'romance' (she
only uses that high-status word for heterosexuality), but a 'crush',
an 'absurd infatuation'.[22]

It is interesting at this point to recall that when Mary commented that it was probably a sin to watch a bullfight, Agatha
laughed and said 'Not for me, until the Church says so.' This may
be a hint that on some level she was always aware of her desire
for women, but unwilling to feel guilty about it until the Church
specifically told her to. This respite lasts only a few weeks; Kate
O'Brien does not allow her heroines any loopholes. In the
confession-box, a priest tears away Agatha's illusions. She had
not intended to say anything to Mary, but as a sort of revenge
for Mary's plan to go home, she now blurts out her new-found

knowledge. The terms of the discussion, for an Irish novelist in
the 1930s, are bravely explicit, emphasising the physicality of the
passion and its equivalence to heterosexual desire. 'I like you the
way a man would, you see. I never can see you without – without
wanting to touch you. I could look at your face forever. . . . I knew
it was wrong; but lately I've been told explictly about it in confession. It's a very ancient and terrible vice.' Notice that Agatha's
torment is specifically Catholic; she does not loathe herself for
being a lesbian as such. Mary reacts neither with horror nor much
surprise; she says how sorry she is, and tries to comfort Agatha's
conscience by telling her 'Oh, everything's a sin!' When Agatha
apologises for 'talking rot', Mary insists 'It wasn't rot.' Thinking
about this afterwards, Agatha is rather amazed that Mary didn't
seem 'frightened or repulsed', and decides that in the best moral
sense the Catholic girl from Mellick is a 'pagan'.[23]

Mary's may seem a mildly liberal reaction, reading it today, but
to put it in context we can compare this scene with a similar
declaration of love in a contemporary play, Lillian Hellman's *The
Children's Hour* (1934). When Martha tells her friend Karen 'I have
loved you the way they said', Karen tries every kind of denial,
from 'You're crazy' to 'We never thought of each other that way.'
Having won no response, no acceptance from her beloved, Martha
does the decent (lesbian) thing and shoots herself.[24]

By contrast, Kate O'Brien's treatment of a similar situation in
*Mary Lavelle* is calm, positive, almost cheerful. Rather than
elaborate defences of the lesbian as a type, she concentrates on
the similarities between all relationships. What she stresses above
all is the equivalence between Agatha and Mary, whose sexual
sins have the best of motives.

> Mary watched the baize door swing and swing again in the porch of
> San Geronimo and caught each time the gleam of candles. People go-
> ing in incessantly to pray, as Agatha did so often, as she did, as Juanito
> too, perhaps, seeking strength against the perversions of their hearts
> and escape from fantastic longings.

So far, the vocabulary is orthodox enough; illicit love is 'fantastic'
and a 'perversion'. But watch out for the next sentence: 'Seeking
mercy, explanation and forgiveness because they are so vicious
as to love each other. . . . Oh, Lord have pity! Help us to have

pity on each other, to make some sense sometime out of this tangle of our longings!'[25] O'Brien allows 'vicious' and 'love' to collide; the effect is almost sarcastic. Nor is the cry for pity a conventional sinner's plea; what the speaker is asking for is not divine mercy, but divine help with the human project of mutual mercy. The longings do not form a sewer, a pit, a cage – merely a tangle, because people rarely long for each other in neat couples. This conversation takes place as Mary and Agatha sit opposite the cathedral steps – a significant setting, hinting at proximity to a church yet exile from it.

Considering her background, Agatha Conlon comes across as a brave and sturdy woman; she may not have the sophisticated self-acceptance of, say, Mary Renault's lesbian characters, but nor is she as guilt-ridden or masochistic as most of the lesbians in pre-1970s fictions. It is interesting that she is quite demanding of Mary, and mixes her self-reproach with loud protest, as in the following sentence: 'I shouldn't have said this at all. To-morrow, I'll go half-mad when I remember. But the cool way you said you're going in a week! Must you do that?' Another key element in her characterisation is her maturity. Far from sobbing at Mary's feet, Agatha is the one who consoles Mary in their 'tangle of longings'. After the confession of love, it is Mary who weeps, and Agatha who pats her awkwardly and tells her 'You're young. It'll be all right. Don't cry.'[26]

An exceptional feature of the book is its delicate analysis of how their relationship develops *after* the revelation. Not having chosen any of the spurned lesbian's traditional options (travel, drug addiction, madness, death, heterosexuality), Agatha stays around, and finds to her surprise that she and Mary grow closer than ever. Mary feels 'discomfort and guilt' about Agatha, because she still intends to leave her and Spain, but 'a certain relaxation' has been won for their friendship. Mary has realised how similar their situations are: as she tells Agatha, 'You take one kind of impossible fancy, I take another.' For neither is it easy; both must take responsibility for their 'sin', and decide how much to risk. Ironically, it is romantic love that brings Agatha and Mary together, in 'sisterly' similarity if not in mutual happiness. Mary allows Agatha close to her 'not so much because Agatha fantastically and perversely loved her but because, like her, she was fantastically and perversely in love'.[27]

This has a double effect. The sense of solidarity and sympathy makes Agatha recover from her confession more easily, feel less guilt. The increase in closeness, however, makes her love Mary more, and suffer more at the parting. But O'Brien leaves us in no doubt that the second pain — simple human loss — is more bearable and more quickly healed than the first, self-hatred. Agatha can face her life alone with considerable gusto; she intends to 'settle into old age', she tells Mary, and become 'the sort of muttering hag children throw stones at!' The Gospel allusion is underlined when Mary responds 'could I throw stones?'[28] If the object of the unnatural love cannot condemn, O'Brien implies, how can the reader?

Part of the hag/witch persona is a lingering love for Mary which Agatha has no intention of giving up. Mary regrets having made her unhappy; 'it'll pass soon — won't it?' she asks wistfully. 'I hope not,' Agatha tells her, and adds defiantly: 'It can't be such a ghastly crime to — to think about you.' Her confessor, she tells Mary with a hint of amusement, calls it 'the the sin of Sodom': 'They have queer names for things,' said Mary. 'They know their business.'[29] But Agatha, an early à-la-carte Catholic, knows her own business: to redefine her sin, and make up her own queer names. The only 'ghastly crime', she decides, is sex (which, not being on offer at the moment, is easy to forgo). 'Thinking about' Mary, on the other hand, and all the love, desire, and self-awareness as a lesbian it entails, is allowable. As a token of her new self-acceptance, she demands a photo from Mary; though she is resigning herself to a life of celibacy, she will not deny herself her feelings.

Though you would not realise it from most critical accounts of the novel, the Agatha Conlon story is not just an incident, but what Bonnie Zimmerman has called 'a coming out novel', within Mary's own more conventional novel of development. Zimmerman finds a similar pattern in a range of such novels from 1928 to 1978: 'the recognition of emotional and/or sexual feelings for another woman, the realization that that love is condemned by society, the acceptance of a lesbian identity either physically (through sexual initiation) or psychologically.' The endings, as Zimmerman sees it, depend on whether the book is written before or during the Women's Liberation Movement of the 1960s and 1970s. Most of the early endings are 'tragic and violent'; the 'feminist lesbian novel', however, ends in 'freedom'.[30] But Kate O'Brien's works are difficult to fit into such a generalisation. Agatha Conlon does not escape into an idyllic lesbian community nor find true romance, but neither does she choose the death or madness offered to most early heroines. Unlike the teenager Zimmerman identifies as the usual adolescent lesbian heroine in the coming-out novel, Agatha is thirty-eight; already living in exile from her homeland; she has no need to run away. Spain allows her the space (and privacy, and employment) to come to terms with herself. So when we add Kate O'Brien to Zimmerman's survey, it becomes more complex, less polarised into gloomy 'pre-feminist' and celebratory 'feminist' novels. This is a good example of the lesbian literary tradition being improverished by O'Brien's absence.

What I find so satisfying about working on Kate O'Brien rather than on other lesbian novelists, quite apart from the quality of her writing, is her honesty. She is explicit — not about sex (concerning which she has little to say) but about moral issues, decisions, hard words. Reading the works of her contemporaries, even those as apparently 'out' as Gertrude Stein, we have to struggle through euphemisms and code-words, layers of innuendo and ambiguity, all designed to protect the writers from embarrassing accusations. Romantic friendships, especially in the girls'-school literary subgenre (a powerful example is Dorothy Stratchey Bussy's *Olivia* (1949)), are often given a degree of intense eroticism that can only be called lesbian — yet nothing can be proved. Whereas Kate O 'Brien, on the two occasions when she writes about passion between adult women, calls it exactly that; no coyness veils her analysis of lesbian relationships.[31] She knows, and she makes her heroines acknowledge, that this is not romantic friendship but a quite different thing: something equivalent to marital love, though outside its social 'order'; something punishable and costly, but often worth the price.

Which is why I cannot agree with Adèle Dalsimer's reading of *The Flower of May* (1953) as a naive lesbian fairytale.[32] After the crisp honesty of *Mary Lavelle*, why would O'Brien hide her lesbian meaning within the outmoded convention of romantic friendship? Dalsimer seems irritated with O'Brien for allowing Fanny to reach the end of the story 'still unaware that her feelings for Lucille are sexual' – but those feelings have never been shown to be sexual. The friendship is peaceful, supportive, occasionally a little possessive and romantic – rather like the relationship of sisters in *The Ante-Room,* and acceptable within the same moral 'order'. Neither Lucille nor Fanny shows any sign of feeling a serious, taboo passion like Agatha Conlon's. Lucille does have something on her mind which is never articulated, but she shows no constraint or self-consciousness in her embraces and conversations with Fanny, so I cannot agree with Dalsimer that Lucille's 'secret' is that she knows she is a lesbian. The girls' friendship is described in terms of 'relief', 'strength', 'warmth' and 'help'.[33] It is a strong partnership, but never sounds like the passionate, exclusive bonds of eighteenth- and nineteenth-century romantic friendship to which Dalsimer compares it. Much as I might like to find another O'Brien novel about lesbians, this is not one.

Another Kate O'Brien novel which is not about lesbians, by the way, is *The Land of Spices*; the bond between Anna and her Superior is a calm, distant mutual support, and nothing more. According to Bonnie Zimmerman, most lesbian novels of development are set in women-only environments such as schools.[34] The main problem with that, as far as I can see, is that the lesbian love can be easily read as an adolescent phase or an environmental stress. By the 1940s, the lesbian school or college novel was already a cliché, and one O'Brien was clearly determined to avoid; in *The Land of Spices* she makes clear that the shallow *Schwärmerei* of convent life are unimportant, and have nothing to do with adult love between women.[35] Her lesbians discover their true selves in the outside world, making the point that it is not for lack of men that they love women.

In her later novels, Kate often focuses sympathetically on characters who enter into sexual relationships in full knowledge of their actions. For example, Helen's father in *The Land of Spices,* whose passion for seventeenth-century religious verse is not incompatible with the 'embrace of love' he gives to a male student. Helen comes to regret having run away from him at eighteen, and to realise that her own sin of 'arrogant judgement' was far worse than any sexual crime he may have committed. When she meets him again, she finds him 'to be visibly happy, guiltless and

good – who was guilty and evil, theology said'.[36] The case for
the virtue of the sinner is developed in *That Lady* (1947). Marked
out from adolescence by her missing eye, Ana is a strongly spiritual
woman – another of O'Brien's heroines who has come close to
being a nun – who decides that it is worth risking her soul for
a love-affair with a married man.

> "I've found something that has been missing always," she tells her con-
> science, and that may indeed be just as important as what your voice
> tells me of. And I don't feel this sense of sin you warned about. No
> doubt I shall, but meantime – this is a battle, with rules, exactions
> and trials you concealed from me; this love, this sin has a morality
> of its own that I find I understand. I see my plight, and I acknowledge
> still your old imperatives. But I can't obey them now – I must take
> a chance.[37]

As I read Kate O'Brien's career, these investigations into the
'morality' of sinful love reach their climax, their most daring version, in her final novel. As Irish censorship eased up in the 1950s,
O'Brien allowed herself to return to an explicitly lesbian plot.
*As Music and Splendour* (1958) is like *Mary Lavelle* in that the story
unfolds far away from Ireland, but is much franker and more
celebratory in its account of a relationship between two women.
Instead of playing a supporting role, the lesbian is one of the two
heroines, whose stories are presented equally and in parallel. Set
at a safe distance in place (Paris and Rome) and time (the 1880s),
*As Music and Splendour* nonetheless manages to create a modern
Irish lesbian and give her a startling voice.

We meet Clare and Rose at sixteen, in a Parisian convent, lonely
for the families and homes they have had to leave behind in Ireland.
Geographical exile is soon overlayed with moral exile, when the
bohemian society of Rome draws them into sexual relationships.
Here O'Brien structures the book very cleverly: we follow the
parallel growth and adventures of Rose and Clare – nice wholesome girls, referred to by others as the Irish songbirds, the Irish
angels, known for their 'sisterliness'. Clare is described as cool,
reserved, almost nunnish. Discussing her choice of career, she explains that she could have been a nun but could not have borne
to be a wife; again, O'Brien makes nunnishness hint at sexual ambiguity.[38] Only more than half-way through the story, when the

readers should be fully involved with both heroines, does O'Brien reveal that Clare is a lesbian; she has been in love with her Spanish friend Luisa as far back as the convent in Paris. Lorna Reynolds explains tactfully: 'What Kate O'Brien wants to emphasise is rather the nature of love than its direction. Clare is the least promiscuous, the most austere and disciplined of all the young people in the novel. Love is love, the deduction seems to be, whether it is homosexual or heterosexual.'[39] This is a complex strategy; not only is the lesbian heroine given advantages of likeability and morality over most of the other characters, to counteract her deviance, but her life is paralleled with Rose's heterosexual adventures, to show how little difference there is between their 'sins'.

When Luisa and Clare are singing in an opera together, with Luisa playing the hero, their roles hint at their passion for each other:

> Still Orpheus and Eurydice, their brilliantly made-up eyes swept for each the other's face, as if to insist that this disguise of myth in which they stood was their mutual reality, their one true dress, wherein they recognized each other . . . so lightly they kissed, and turned away to wash and cold-cream themselves back into the ordinary Roman night.[40]

O'Brien's use of theatrical roles here can be read two different ways. On the one hand, a nervous reader could assume that these basically normal girls got carried away by the travesty; as Lorna Reynolds suggests, 'we are free to think' that the myth 'beglamoured' Luisa and Clare into thinking they could be happy together.[41] But on the other hand, I suggest, the roles may be seen as temporarily liberating them into the truth, unconventional behaviour becoming 'their mutual reality'. A very different text by Lorna Reynolds adds weight to this interpretation. In 1954 she was on sabbatical in Rome, where her friend Kate O'Brien was researching *As Music and Splendour*. Seven years later she wrote a sensuous lyric called 'Euridyce' which used the very same roles to suggest an endlessly deferred escape from secrecy into freedom, 'the long tunnel from night to day'. In her repetition of the phrase 'You Orpheus, me Euridyce' at the ends of verses, Reynolds emphasises that these are not the 'real' king and queen, but names for roles which are available to anyone for playing out a hazardous journey.

Cowslip-sweet the breath
Blown down the dazzling southern-facing shaft,
As we climbed and wound from dusty underground,
Up far on the way, you leading me,
You Orpheus, me Euridyce.[42]

The almost imperceptible drawing-together of nunnish Clare and
gay Luisa is delicately charted in this slow-moving novel. For example, when Clare discovers that Luisa is having an affair with
her 44-year-old male music teacher, though it troubles her, the
revelation also pulls her closer in intimacy. Their scenes are subtle without being coy, full of unfinished sentences and kisses on
eyelids. Not until the tenth chapter, in a letter from Luisa who
is away on tour, do we learn for sure that they are lovers.

Clare's gloomy suitor, Thomas, flushes out the truth in a scene
that oscillates very convincingly between furious argument and
inconsequential chat. Clare's simple explanation avoids self-hatred
and relies on no essentialist theories: 'Easily I might have loved
you. But − she caught my heart before I knew what was hap-
pening, Thomas. And I think she's lovely, and I love her. I can't
help it. It's true.' It is clear that Clare has skipped the Agatha stage
of suddenly realising her pure love is adult and sinful; she has
known about society's homophobia, and loved in spite of it, from
the start. But Thomas sees it as a schoolgirlish crush, a *schwarm*,
and explains (in the language not of his pre-sexologist 1880s but
of Kate O'Brien's Freudian 1950s): 'Your development has been
delayed.' Clare is affectionately scornful: 'you must not bring your
clever talk against something you know nothing about'. O'Brien
makes Thomas a figure of fun by giving him ludicrously lurid
exclamations like 'You pale, self-loving ass! You − you stinking
lily, you!' Clare answers his insults informatively, never losing
her temper, and so comes across as very powerful and sure of
herself. She resists his labelling of her as 'amoral', and turns his
weapons against him:

Certainly I am a sinner in the argument of my Church. But so would
be if I were your lover. So is Rose a sinner − and she knows it − in
reference to our education and faith . . . We are so well instructed that
we can decide for ourselves. There's no vagueness in Catholic instruction.[43]

The irony here is that sin is used as the great leveller, the common denominator for all sexual orientations. By carefully paralleling the lesbian and straight relationships, O'Brien makes the point that they are equally criminal in the eyes of the Church, and equally likely to produce happiness or sorrow. As Clare tells the reproachful Thomas, 'You can argue as you like against my loving Luisa. But I can argue back all your unbridled sins. We all know the Christian rule – and every indulgence of the flesh which does not conform to it is wrong. All right. We are all sinners.'[44] All being 'wrong' makes Clare's situation 'all right'; sin feels relative, so it is a comfort to Clare that she is no worse than all her sexually-active friends. Her relationship with Luisa breaks up after a year and a half, but loss is not presented as a direct consequence of the sin of lesbianism.

Bonnie Zimmerman finds that in most lesbian novels of development, 'the protagonist's first lover is inadequate or inhibiting. She either betrays the young lesbian, usually leaving her for a man, or fails to protect her from the vindictive outside world.'[45] O'Brien resists both these hackneyed endings. Luisa has a male lover but feels far more strongly about Clare – if she leaves Clare 'for' anything it is the world tour which will help her career. Nor does she need to protect Clare, who is confident and has enough friends to keep a mildly vindictive world at bay. The lovers break up because of the pressures of absence, Luisa's other lovers, and being closeted, but not because lesbian love is essentially frail or ephemeral.

During her relationship with Luisa, it is clear that Clare would prefer to be monogamous; for example, she cries when Rose mentions Luisa's affair with her male teacher. But in arguing with Thomas about Luisa's infidelity, Clare turns the victim status he taunts her with into a powerful generosity. 'If you were a man you couldn't endure that. No. Men, as you call them, don't seem to be able to endure things. I don't know what sex you suppose me to belong to, but I can endure Luisa's life.' And Thomas is finally brought to admit that Clare knows more than he does about love. Later, when Luisa's lover Duante insists that Luisa is a wanderer, 'incapable of fidelity', Clare retorts even more hotly: 'And are we in charge of her?'[46] She refuses to let men set the terms of her relationship with Luisa, or despise it for not being a complete possession.

Much as I like this element of Clare's characterisation, I am made
uneasy by it. Such generosity is quite a common theme in early
lesbian novels, but its overall effect can be to render women's love
harmless to society. Whereas Radclyffe Hall and Gale Wilhelm
showed their lesbians voluntarily giving up their beloveds, slightly
later novels tend to replace self-sacrifice with a vague generosity
or tolerance of non-monogamy — but the effect is the same. The
more truly loving lover tends to lose the girl. In Mary Renault's
*The Friendly Young Ladies* (1944), for example, Leo's devoted partner Helen feels only 'the breath of loneliness that passes for
jealousy in generous souls' — as a result, however, she loses Leo
to a man.[47] Elizabeth Craigin's *Either is Love* (1937) contrasts the
purity and freedom of the heroine's love for Rachel with her husband's masterful, possessive love for her. As Jane Rule points out,
the greedier marital love wins: 'Either may be love, but the first
exists in a freedom that becomes limbo if for the other the rights
and privileges of ownership have been reserved.' Another writer
who does this, Rule points out, is Colette, who tends to 'idealize
love between women in a way to make it too rare and too pure
against the greater realism of heterosexuality'.[48] So while in *As
Music and Splendour* it might make sense that Clare would behave
in this way, we have to remember that 'generosity' is a common
strategy of lesbian novelists for taking the threat or sting out of
women's love.

At the end of *As Music and Splendour*, the reader is left with a
vivid impression of Clare and Luisa's time together — radiant Sunday mornings peeling peaches, snatches of opera, internal
monologues of troubled tenderness — and the jealous heterosexual triangles in which Rose is involved sound rather miserable
by comparison. A 'Catholic agnostic' herself,[49] Kate O'Brien
took seriously the Catholic consciences of her heroines, but Clare
comes across as no more *angst*-ridden than any heterosexual
heroine: 'We are all sinners', she concludes almost cheerfully. Her
liking for precision leads her to accept pejorative labels calmly:
'If to be a bohemian is to have forsaken the moral standards of
properly instructed people,' she asks Luisa, 'then surely I am one?'
And a last visit to Ireland makes her realise that she will never
return to live 'the simple, clean, courageous and uncomforted life'
of her dying grandmother.[50]

The one thing Clare does not do is worry about being a lesbian. She uses neither that word, nor any synonym, to describe her 'type'. Holding to the hard facts — her love for Luisa, her committal of and commitment to a sin — Clare wastes no time on speculations about her sexuality in general. She is a refreshing change from other early lesbian heroines, who tend to think of themselves as society's extras or leftovers — for example, Mary Renault's Leo who sees lesbianism as a way for 'surplus' women in wartime population imbalance to 'arrange themselves'. Nor does Clare feel any need to change her friends or run from her social circle in case they will not accept her as the knowledge of her affair with Luisa begins to percolate through their conversations. Again, it is interesting to contrast her with Mary Renault's Leo, who advises lesbians that 'the thing to do is to like and be liked by as many ordinary people as possible'.[51] The difference in Clare's case is that she has not had to think of herself as different from ordinary people — because those who surround her are all bohemians, eccentric exiles, and free spirits. And indeed in Kate O'Brien's novels, those whose loves are 'out of order' are so thick on the ground that it is hard to find anybody who is 'ordinary' in Leo's sense. In O'Brien's world of 'ordinary people dancing', it becomes impossible to see the artificial differences between them.

Books on lesbian literature almost never mention Kate O'Brien's name; it is always as an Irish novelist, closeted in nationality, that she is known. But *As Music and Splendour* is the most exuberant and thought-provoking 1950s lesbian novel I have read, outshining such classics as Claire Morgan's calm romance *The Price of Salt* (1952). These quiet, genteel, early lesbian novels can profitably be read side by side; they cut through the centuries of sensationalist clichés about androgynes and vampires, making a simple case for individual freedom.[52]

One reason why *Mary Lavelle* and *As Music and Splendour* have not received recognition from lesbian critics is that in each case only half the plot is about a lesbian — whereas classics like *The Price of Salt* are about nothing else. Putting it negatively, we could say that O'Brien hid her lesbians in subplots within heterosexual romantic novels, for fear of having the spotlight turned on them. But I want to suggest that, whatever her motives may have been, the effect is rather utopian.

After a few decades of lesbian–feminist novels about coming out of heteropatriarchy into women's community, many of us are beginning to look for more complex stories about a range of sexualities, a variety of loves outside the 'order' we were reared in. *As Music and Splendour* could be a prototype for the kind of novels that will be written in the 1990s — novels primarily about ideas, relationships, eras, opera or horse-riding if you like — but profiting from a lesbian perspective. Lesbianism and bisexuality are not topics in Kate O'Brien's fictions; they are realities. She writes about women who love each other and the realisations and complications that brings; what she does not write about is lesbian identity as such, divorced from context. And this, I suggest, is what gives her such importance as a teacher to my generation. In *The Flower of May*, the spinster Aunt Eleanor who stayed home for love of her sister gives her house to her niece Fanny, to enable her to study abroad with her beloved friend. As she explains in a tone of exasperated reproach, 'You young ones don't see how much some of us desire to promote freedom of action among the intelligent.'[53] Kate O'Brien's lesbian fictions do not promote lesbianism so much as freedom of action.

## Notes and references

1   See my essay, 'Noises from Woodsheds: The Muffled Voices of Irish Lesbian Fiction', Suzanne Raitt (ed.), *Volcanoes and Pearl Divers*, London, Onlywomen, forthcoming.

2   Lillian Faderman, 'Who Hid Lesbian History?' Margaret Cruikshank (ed.), *Lesbian Studies: Present and Future*, New York, The Feminist Press, pp. 115–16.

3   Adèle M. Dalsimer, *Kate O'Brien: a critical study*, Dublin, Gill & Macmillan, 1990, pp. 132–5.

4   Susan Crecy, 'Ivy Compton-Burnett: Family as Nightmare', Mark Lilly (ed.), *Lesbian and gay writing: an anthology of critical essays*, London, Macmillan, 1990, pp. 13–22.

5   Dalsimer, *Kate O'Brien*, p. 63.

6   Kate O'Brien, *Pray for the Wanderer*, Harmondsworth, Penguin, 1951, p.6.

7   *ibid.*, p. 12.

8   Dalsimer, *Kate O' Brien*, p. 120.

9   Kate O'Brien, quoted in Vivian Mercier, 'Kate O'Brien', *Irish Writing*, vol. 1, 1946, pp. 86–100, p. 98.

10   Kate O'Brien, *Without my Cloak*, (1931), Harmondsworth, Penguin, 1949, pp. 34–5, 509.

11  ibid., pp. 230, 234, 242–5.
12  In Radclyffe Hall's *The Well of Loneliness* (1928), her heroine Stephen gives up her lover Mary to a man; in Gale Wilhelm's *We Too Are Drifting* (1935), Jan nobly refrains from seducing her beloved, and so loses her.
13  O'Brien, *Without my Cloak,* pp. 64, 48.
14  ibid., pp. 62, 212.
15  Kate O'Brien, *Mary Lavelle*, London, Heinemann, 1936, pp. 32, 298, 34.
16  Dalsimer, *Kate O'Brien* pp. 1, 39.
17  O'Brien, *Mary Lavelle,* pp. 84, 97, 100, 207.
18  ibid., pp. 119, 117, 128
19  Dalsimer, *Kate O'Brien*, p. 36.
20  O'Brien, *Mary Lavelle,* pp.187, 210, 197, 201, 207.
21  Mary Renault, *Purposes of Love* (1939), Harmondsworth, Penguin, 1986, p. 41. Also see Mary Renault, *The Friendly Young Ladies* (1944), London, Virago, 1984, p. 197.
22  O'Brien, *Mary Lavelle,* pp. 283, 285.
23  ibid., pp. 119, 284–6, 295.
24  Lillian Hellman, *The Children's Hour* (1934), in *The Collected Plays,* London, Macmillan, 1972.
25  O'Brien, *Mary Lavelle,* pp. 119, 284–6.
26  ibid., pp. 285, 286.
27  ibid., pp. 296–7 .
28  ibid., pp. 296, 298.
29  ibid., pp. 297–8.
30  Bonnie Zimmerman, 'Exiting from Patriarchy: The Lesbian Novel of Development', Elizabeth Abel *et al* (eds.), *The Voyage In: Fictions of Female Development,* Hanover and London, University Press of New England, 1983, pp. 244–57, pp. 245–7.
31  This distinction was not obvious to all O'Brien's contemporaries. Some useful advice on how to read sensitively the differences between women who loved women 'innocently' and women who knew they were 'different' is offered in Leila J. Rupp,' "Imagine My Surprise": women's relationships in mid-twentieth century America', Martin Duberman, Martha Vicinus and George Chauncey, Jr. (eds.), *Hidden from history: reclaiming the gay and lesbian past,* London, Penguin, 1991, pp. 395–410.
32  Dalsimer, *Kate O'Brien*, pp. 100–2.
33  Kate O'Brien, *The Flower of May*, London, Heinemann, 1953, pp. 295, 336.
34  Zimmerman, 'Exiting from Patriarchy', p. 247.
35  Kate O'Brien, *The Land of Spices,* London, Heinemann, 1941, pp. 3, 5, 78, 171–2.
36  ibid., pp. 157, 160, 22.
37  Kate O'Brien, *That Lady,* London, The Reprint Society, 1947, pp. 180–1.
38  Kate O'Brien, *As Music and Splendour,* New York, Harper & Brothers, 1958, pp. 175, 189.
39  Lorna Reynolds, *Kate O'Brien: A Literary Portrait,* Irish Literary Studies No. 25, Gerrards Cross, Bucks, Colin Smythe, 1987, p. 111.
40  O'Brien, *As Music and Splendour,* pp. 175, 113.

41  Reynolds, *Kate O'Brien*, p. 129.
42  Lorna Reynolds, 'Euridyce' (1963), A. A. Kelly (ed.), *Pillars of the House: an anthology of verse by Irish women from 1690 to the present*, Dublin, Wolfhound Press, 1987, p. 104.
43  O'Brien, *As Music and Splendour*, pp. 211, 207, 209, 207.
44  ibid., p. 208.
45  Zimmerman, 'Exiting from Patriarchy', p. 253.
46  O'Brien, *As Music and Splendour*, pp. 195, 211, 293, 295.
47  Renault, *The Friendly Young Ladies*, p. 182.
48  Jane Rule, *Lesbian Images*, London, Peter Davies, 1976, p. 188.
49  See Reynolds, *Kate O'Brien*, p. 118.
50  O'Brien, *As Music and Splendour*, pp. 208, 253, 343.
51  Renault, *The Friendly Young Ladies*, pp. 164, 178.
52  For the subversive impact of such novels, see Kate Adams, 'Making the World Safe for the Missionary Position: Images of the Lesbian in Post-World War II America', Karla Jay and Joanne Glasgow (eds.), *Lesbian Texts and Contexts: Radical Revisions*, London Onlywomen, 1992, pp. 255–74.
53  O'Brien, *The Flower of May*, p. 330.

*Chapter 4*

# Kate O'Brien:
# Feminine Beauty, Feminist Writing
# and Sexual Role

*Patricia Coughlan*

I

In this essay I propose to investigate some problems raised by
the depiction of feminine beauty in Kate O'Brien's fiction. In her
novels, the physical descriptions of central female characters ex-
travagantly stress their visual attractiveness. These descriptions
typically employ a wealth of allusions to art-objects and icons
enjoying classic status in the tradition of Western art, as well as
to powerful, sometimes destructive, figures in mythology and to
objects of amorous idealisation in European literature. The narrative regularly invokes the rhetoric of beauty as an ideal quality,
transcending time and cultural difference, an aesthetic incontrovert-
ible, in the course of these passages. These constructions of
O'Brien's protagonists form a complex which associates art, here
understood as an instance of the ideal, with the sense of potentially dangerous sexual charisma and with sophisticated sensual
pleasures, the arena for the exercise of that bourgeois imperative,
refined taste. These pleasures are *metaphorically* conjured up in the
guise of flowers, food, and wine, thus presenting the characters

described as delicious erotic consumables; they are simultaneously given a matching *metonymic* context in that insistence by the respective narrators on a lavish upper middle-class *mise-en-scène* which is a hallmark of O'Brien's fictions. There are qualities both of metropolitan glamour and of faintly *risqué* modernity (in a 1920s mode) about many of these portraits of feminine beauty, with their mentions of Renaissance masterpieces on the one hand, and their daring references to paganism in the form of Greek goddesses on the other.

Yet as earlier generations of readers, especially women readers, already recognised, and as Irish and some international feminists are now discerning more and more clearly, Kate O'Brien's work has a strong radical moment, however uneasily it may sit with her sensational—realist mode, near-rococo verbal style and over-stuffed settings. Her writings not only take an unmistakably oppositional stance towards the general cultural narrowness, prudery and ruralist exclusions of Free State Ireland — the common targets of all dissident writers and cultural critics in the decades between 1920 and 1955 or so — but also institute an interrogation of the forms of oppression specifically visited on women.[1] This interrogation is conducted in a whole series of novels which are, it should be admitted at the outset, of uneven quality, largely lacking in stylistic elegance and apparently innocent of the great modernists' developments in narrative technique, if not altogether in vision. Yet under the dismayingly wordy surface, O'Brien conducts a delicate and searching examination, even an anatomy, of the constrictions of women's lives and the pain of feminine consciousness. This critique is focused largely on the culture of the Irish provincial bourgeoisie, though O'Brien's work does also sometimes employ European settings, to particularly good effect in the historical novel *That Lady* (1947), in *Mary Lavelle* (1936) and in her last novel *As Music and Splendour* (1958). Evident in her work taken as a whole is an intense interest in the various forms of social regulation which infantilise women, restrict their development and ensure their domination. This project must surely have been influenced, no doubt at some removes, by the great nineteenth-century novels which so vividly render the tragic consciousness of doomed heroines such as Emma Bovary, Anna Karenina and Effi Briest, and perhaps by the pessimistic determinist naturalism of Zola or Hardy. In O'Brien's early best-seller *Without My Cloak* (1931), the aim is still evidently the faithful representation of the agony of a woman, Caroline Considine – spirited, not without self-awareness – on whom the prison doors of an uncongenial marriage have closed, and who fails utterly to find the means of any self-liberation. Later, however, this vision is altered by the various shapes of new plots, each of them variants on the protagonists' invention, and their wresting free of potentially autonomous but none the less feminine selves from the dominant masculine authority and the given ideological forms.

It is when we put together this quite crisply feminist project, however little it is overtly named as such, with the fictional representation of the physical appearance of these heroines, that a curious contradiction begins to emerge. It is one thing to show women as all surface, glossy, glowing and sumptuous, or as classically perfect of countenance, drawing admiring and envious glances from a chorus of less fortunate female mortals in supporting roles, and from males a mixture of fascination, fear (expressed in Medusa and Gorgon-images), and the desire to possess – a possession imagined, in the time-honoured manner, nakedly and erotically as a form of subjugation. It is usually quite another to concentrate in one's fictional discourse on the interiority of such female characters, on their struggle to recognise themselves as active subjects within the offered social forms, and on the acts and stratagems by which they may aim to seize autonomy and make themselves real in the world. My topic in this essay is to explore that contradiction.

## II

Employing the language of our own contemporary feminist critique of representations, we would say that the scopic representation of women as objects of the male gaze is very prevalent in O'Brien. In her fictions the narrator consistently focalises through, that is to say s/he adopts the viewpoint of, male characters in the story. In the extended account in *Mary Lavelle* of Don Pablo's vision of Mary, and subsequently of his son Juanito's, and in Eddy's description in *Without My Cloak* of his sister Caroline, the

salient fact is the astounding beauty of the two women who are
the objects of description. That beauty is mystified by a rhetoric
which gestures towards the domains both of the (paganised)
sacred, in *Mary Lavelle,* and of the radiance and exalted mode of
being of art, in both of these and in other texts. The beauty of
Caroline and of Mary is seen as constitutive of their respective
feminine selves. This apprehension of their personal beauty as an
essential, self-defining quality is sometimes even attributed to such
characters themselves; it is true, however, that O'Brien does
generally mark this as an unreflective, shallow and basically narcissistic form of feminine subjectivity. This is true of the school
beauty Molly in *Land of Spices,* and of the heroine Agnes's frilly
sister Marie-Rose in the sombre world of *The Ante-Room* (1934):

> Marie-Rose sat at her dressing-table in dim lamplight and brushed
> her silky gold hair, which curled and lolled very prettily against her
> shoulder. In spite of weary lines about her eyes, she was looking –
> she could not but admit – delicious. She ran her hand affectionately
> along her smooth young cheek, and mused with an impartial pleasure
> upon the whiteness of her throat. The white frills of her night-dress,
> the flounces and ruches of her white silk wrap, foamed delicately, and
> made a dramatic darkness of the shadows in which she sat.[2]

I wish to ask what may seem to be a rather simple-minded question, but is nevertheless a necessary one. Why does a woman
novelist, and at that a writer of well-attested lesbian orientation
in her own life – and therefore someone whom one might have
expected to see women as active or desiring subjects on their own
account – perpetuate the representation of women in this object-
ified way? The inevitable surprise and dismay of a feminist reader
at the apparently patriarchal conventionality of her physical
descriptions of female characters is generated not only by the evident feminist intention of her work, but also by the decided difference of O'Brien's own sexual orientation from the prescribed
norm. The most characteristic project of her work would seem
to be to rehearse the attempts at self-liberation of the central female
figures; she is clear-eyed and persistent in pursuing a critique of
the institutions of Irish bourgeois life and the oppressively sexist
ideology underpinning them.

Her near-obsession with what sometimes almost seems an

abstract, essentialised quality of beauty in women sharply conflicts with the process of representing the achievement of freedom
and individual thought by the women in the fictions, because fully interiorised autonomous subjectivity becomes the property of
the male viewer, whose noting and appreciation of feminine beauty
gives him the status of a connoisseur, and sometimes even the kind
of originality of creative perception attributed to an artist. The
quality of beauty itself is nearly always, by this move, presented
as being *unconsciously* possessed by the feminine object viewed; and,
further, in O'Brien's aesthetic discourse beauty is always thrown
back to an earlier ideal – a picture, a statue, the notion of a goddess-
like distance and aura. It is thus firmly situated, and implicated,
in the whole patriarchal system of the scopic and the fetishised
which has been so well described both from the feminist and the
anti-consumerist viewpoint, in the classic instances by Laura
Mulvey and John Berger.[3] O'Brien always presents feminine
beauty as a given, an essential quality, and as surrounded, in accordance with European traditions both visual and literary, by a
mystique. Nowhere does O'Brien show the slightest interest in
relativising the experience of beauty or in exploring – or even
recognising – a moment of its social or cultural *construction*. These
textual instances of beauty attract, rather, a language of the ineffable, of extreme emotion (felt by the male observer); the language
of quasi-mystical experience attaches to them, and they
characteristically produce in their generally male recipients an aporia
indicating the recognition of an experience similar to the sublime
as defined in Romanticism.[4] Dr Curran's admiration of Agnes
Mulqueen in *The Ante-Room* is a good example:

> William Curran fed his eyes with a greed which he thought a life of
> staring would not satisfy. The long, narrow lines of her body, the girlish
> thinness of her arms, the sweet young breast, the soft dark fall of hair,
> her profile, saved from perfection by too much length of bone . . . all
> these beauties raised in him such a conflict of senses as made victory
> and defeat alike unbearable. For if he won her, what skill or right had
> he in such possession, and if he lost – (pp. 66-7)

His experience disorients and obsesses him:

> In regard to her he had left his rules and certainties behind, and lived
> from hand to mouth without direction, so that when she stood before

him, though he steered with credit through automatic talk and gestures,
his only true awareness was of her starry beauty and of the pounding
of his blood. (p. 60)

Her beauty is constantly connected by the narrator, in these
passages focalised on Curran, with the notion of an abstract ideal:

Her face, quite near him, transcended every common thought of beauty.
He smiled at the mortal anxiety that shadowed its immortality. (p. 75)

The role of this discourse of beauty is developed further in subsequent novels: in *Mary Lavelle*, as I shall point out, it is especially
prominent. Here is one of many possible examples from that text:

She sat erect, her hands clasped loosely over her crossed knees, her slender
body outlined as flowingly as if she were a figure in a dream. The curly
edge of her neutral-coloured hair made an angelic nimbus, but there was
nothing Christian in the face it framed. Those featues came unflawed –
oh, impossible marvel – from Greece's most exacting and fastidious time.
A virgin, pagan face. The face of untaken Aphrodite.[5]

How may we understand this state of affairs? Must we simply
conclude that O'Brien could not, or did not wish to resist the
conventional attitudes of her age – and perhaps also of the
Victorian and Edwardian ages preceding it, in which some of her
texts, faithfully realist in mode, are set? Or is there any room at
all for an assumption that while making the scopic gaze of her
male characters constitute female ones as objects, she is also in-
terrogating that gaze? Certainly, in her last novel, the underrated
*As Music and Splendour*, which deals with the training of two young
Irish women as opera singers towards the end of the nineteenth
century, and their successful careers in Europe, one might argue
that she uses the active position, as artists themselves, of Clare
and Rose to show their conscious putting on and off, as opera
heroines, of the stereotyped role of women as objects of consumption. Clare has to learn to 'hop and skip and blow kisses and peep
and scream', to play gypsies and chambermaids amid the 'lunacies
of opera'.[6]

Generally, however, there is little warrant for a comforting
hypothesis of ironic deployment on the author's part of these objectivised female forms; instead some other way of resolving, or

at least understanding, the contradiction between granting and withholding feminine subjectivity in these texts must be found. We should notice that O'Brien gradually comes to invent more and more self-aware central characters: Agnes in *The Ante-Room* improves on Caroline Considine, and Mary Lavelle on Agnes, and Helen Archer in *The Land of Spices* on Mary. Indeed Helen, the Reverend Mother running the convent school, is an embodiment of considerable female authority who, though she is described as a striking physical presence, partakes not at all of the standard objectivised feminine existence of secular women. In Ana de Mendoza, the heroine of *That Lady* (1947), an inner personal force like Helen Archer's and the intense physical magnetism attributed to other protagonists are made to coexist, and that coexistence is to some extent explicitly problematised in the narrative. So the dazzling surface of the early beauties is increasingly complicated by stronger and stronger intimations of interiority, though the narratives never entirely shed their scopic impulse.

## III

Let me examine the problem more closely, and justify my assertions by providing textual instances. Mary Lavelle, in O'Brien's third novel, is a good example of interiorisation and reflexive thought; but there remains a yawning gap between the impression Mary's beauty makes on others, and her own sense of self, for which that beauty is an unthought element. The sensuous narcissism of Marie-Rose in *The Ante-Room* (of which I have already given an instance) or of Molly Considine in *Without My Cloak* causes less of a jar upon the reader's sensibility, but I think this is only because each of them is less fully interiorised, represented as an active, experiencing consciousness, than Mary Lavelle, who is the protagonist of the narrative. Here is a representatively sumptuous description of Molly:

> Their bodies relaxed; Anthony's hand moved over her hair and neck to her warm, silk-covered breast. Familiar, sensual peace crept into them, and they rested a minute together. The man's eyes dreamt over her reflection in the mirror, and she took pleasure in it too.[7]

Male scopic sexuality is not represented as in the slightest degree predatory in this passage, which indeed stresses the couple's mutuality in sensual pleasure. But Molly's own participation in her beauty as spectacle is also evident:

> Cloudily the two saw her reflected . . . her skirts of night-blue silk billowed to the floor; her little bodice, beribboned up and down with velvet and inlet with lace, was faithful to the lovely line of her breasts; pagoda sleeves engulfed her arms, but little jewelled hands gave pretty pledge for them; chatelaine and mighty topaz brooch weighed touchingly upon her slenderness.

Molly's luscious, Winterhalter beauty (the novel is set in the 1860s) is explicitly shown as drawing from her a narcissistic response:

> Blue eyes, misty as Anthony's were bright, smiled faintly *from the pool of glass*; the curve of her mouth had a dream's outline, and over *her indeterminate soft face* shone the appeal of lovely transience. *She was all woman, all fragility,* of the type that flowers enhance, and parasols and jewels; pouring out tea she could look adorable, or dancing a quadrille, or singing at the piano; but beauty unfolded from her voluptuously in hours like this; evening and quietude adorned her like a crown. (p. 31; emphasis mine)

The 'pool of glass' is an explicit signal of narcissistic and mythically destructive self-regard; the other passages I have emphasised help to complete the picture of feminine beauty as quintessentially passive and vulnerable. That this passage is focalised upon the man and that these are primarily his observations (in both senses) is clearly revealed by the next sentence:

> Anthony's thoughts turned back inconsequently to the first time he had stood beside her dressing-table; he remembered the rapturous excitement of that hour. (p. 31)

This whole passage seems a perfect instance of the scopic, and of the proxy nature of women's desire as (and if) it is constructed in patriarchy: Molly admires herself in Anthony's eyes.[8] We may add that this particular character is a doomed figure, who dies in childbirth as a result of the concrete sexual expression of the very desire which is so sensuously described in this passage. (Though it is not here our specific concern, we should nevertheless acknowledge O'Brien's muted but explicit note of protest at the immemorial fate of women in the ages before contraception.)

Mirrors are, of course, themselves deployed in literature and painting as emblematic of the feminine condition; given O'Brien's intense interest in visual impressions, it is not surprising to find her drawing on this traditional item in the vocabulary of Western representation. *Mary Lavelle* contains two significant mirror-moments, but rather different ones from this. Mary's dull pipe-smoking fiancé has given her an antique mirror in which he instructs her to look so as to remind her how she has driven him mad with desire: 'But he liked to bring her random presents – violets or a book of music or silk stocking – or, as one day, an old hand-mirror of thin, exhausted silver. "Look there, my love", he said, "and see why I'm so crazy".'[9] This scene functions as a patriarchal injunction. There could scarcely be a clearer example of the double-bind in which women are placed in patriarchy: Mary is to learn of her reflected beauty, but precisely as that which is a *danger* to John. That is: she is to apprehend her own destructiveness, over which she has no control but which is meant to oblige her to be subordinate to her lover. This is squarely in the tradition of the compliment-as-threat which pervades Western amorous discourse in general, and courtly and Petrarchan love-poetry in particular. It is founded upon a denial of the woman's agency: she is the vessel of the man's passion, a figure falsely exalted, pure object of fascination and fear combined. Historians of the medieval and Renaissance sub-genre of *vanitas* paintings, which show a woman performing her toilette before a mirror, make the useful point that such images give the viewer scopic pleasure in the depiction of a beautiful, sometimes semi-nude female, while simultaneously – and more or less hypocritically – preserving the alibi of a moralising function.[10] O'Brien's invocation of the topos, at least in *Mary Lavelle*, works rather against this than for it; this characteristic duplicity would seem to arise largely in visual art-forms, notoriously, of course, in cinema.

The other instance of mirroring in this novel occurs when, on her arrival in the Spanish household, Mary is made slightly uncomfortable by the enormous mirror in her room:

> She had been brought up in unself-conscious habits and therefore was not so much regretful as relieved that the mirrors' positions made it

> impossible that she should see herself when arranged for sleep – and yet
> she had wondered, lying there, how in fact one did appear in such a cloudy
> resting-place. (p. 12)

It is significant that at this point Mary 'laughed at herself self-consciously' and next takes out and studies her photograph of John: as if she unconsciously invokes him to curb her tendency to independence. I would argue that this, rather different mirror-motif – here as in other narratives concerning personal identity, such as *Jane Eyre* or the writings of Lacan – thematises the individual's obligation to assemble some kind of coherent working selfhood. It thus raises the question of whether, and how, a woman might avoid fitting oneself neatly into the repertoire of roles offered, and more actively, and in the Ireland of the 1930s more transgressively, how one may go about inventing others.

But this particular cautious passage would scarcely justify an argument that the novel adequately addresses the gap between men's appreciation, simultaneously abject and possessive, of Mary's beauty, and the very different nature of her own interest in herself. We would be mistaken if we made too much of it as an indication of a consciousness on O'Brien's part of the gap or disparity I have described above. Elbowing Mary's tentative self-perception out of the way in the text of the novel are the rapturous silent paeans to her beauty by Don Pablo and Juanito, a sample of which I have quoted earlier. This discourse of Mary's absolute beauty – she even pips at the post the Castilian noblewoman Luisa in the unspoken competition which produces some of the novel's sillier passages (pp. 151, 168-9) – is crucially linked with the mystique of the bullfight, described with equal enthusiasm by the narrator, but this time in an extended and eloquent passage which is focalised through Mary herself.[11] The chapter called 'A Corrida' is structurally parallel to the sex-scene between Juanito and Mary which later brings the plot (and the male lead) to a climax.[12] By means of this parallel O'Brien links together intensely erotic images of heterosexual domination-and-submission with a notion of 'art, unconcerned and lawless', as embodied in the violently cathartic spectacle of the bullfight.[13]

There are two further important strands in this complex concoction of desire, death, and aesthetic ecstasy. One is the fact that Mary is brought to the *corrida* by Agatha Conlan, the tormented lesbian character who, along with John, Mary's Irish lover, his Spanish *alter ego* Juanito, and Juanito's father Don Pablo, has fallen overwhelmingly in love with Mary's beauty. I shall leave till later my consideration of the significance of Conlan's sexual orientation. The other strand is that the passage describing Mary and Juanito's lovemaking is not focalised through Mary, which is what a reading of the book as a rehearsal of feminine self-liberation might lead one to expect, but is narrated from Juanito's perspective; and the description dwells in an undeniably sado-masochistic way on images of Mary's specifically feminine vulnerability and pain *as themselves erotic* and constitutive of Juanito's pleasure:

> He took her quickly and bravely. The pain made her cry out and writhe in shock, but he held her hard against him and in great love compelled her to endure it. He felt the sweat of pain break over all the silk of her body. He looked at her face, flung back against the moss, saw her set teeth and quivering nostrils, beating eyelids, flowing, flowing tears. . . . She was no longer Aphrodite, but a broken, tortured Christian, a wounded Saint Sebastian . . . (pp. 308-9)

The images in this dismaying passage vividly recall the violent death of the bull at the *corrida* in their presentation of Mary as animal-like. They also invoke Renaissance paintings of St Sebastian — in which the beautiful, nude young man's body is pierced by arrows, and in which a devotional topic provides a slightly disguised pretext for voyeurism — and reactivate the text's earlier fantasies of Mary as a Greek erotic image of intense and sensual beauty — variously a *kouros* (the genre of statues of young boy-athletes) and Aphrodite, goddess of love:

> Yet, this evening, strolling without premonition . . . he had encountered that against which he believed no man, however old or wise or tired, can be adequately armed. He had met beauty, mythical, innocent and shameless. . . . Her hair . . . was curly and clung to her head like a Greek boy's. Her blue eyes, boyish too, androgynous, were wide and shy, but darkened by dark lashes and by shadows of fatigue. . . . Her carriage . . . most virginal and pagan. (p. 66)

This is from the account of Don Pablo's first vision of Mary; it is supplemented by further mythological allusions, all hinting at the danger to be incurred by viewers of her beauty, which is thus again invested with unconscious destructive potential:

> He would not be afraid of Medusa's face, since it was certainly not
> his business to play Perseus. He had been smitten by a vision in the
> garden . . . (pp. 66-7) [14]

Juanito, Don Pablo's son, sees Mary in a strikingly similar way,
with the recognisable compound of shock, aesthetic appreciation
and sexual desire:

> She sat erect. . . . The curly edge of her neutral-coloured hair made
> an angelic nimbus, but there was nothing Christian in the face it framed.
> Those features came unflawed – oh, impossible marvel! – from Greece's
> most exacting and fastidious time. A virgin, pagan face. The face of
> untaken Aphrodite. (p. 167)

The climactic sex-scene, then, is a kind of apotheosis of the scopic
moments in the book as a whole, and as well as the domination–
submission motif, it restates the idea of a continuum, or even an
identity, between feminine beauty and the objects of specifically
aesthetic experience. So it would seem that in *Mary Lavelle* O'Brien
is driven to objectify Mary both scopically in general and erotically
in particular through the device of her beauty. The result is that
she gives far more imaginative energy to that *relinquishing* of agency
to which Mary is moved by her awakened passion for Juanito,
than to the representation of Mary's making her own of her life
which is the larger concern of the novel.

One must, of course, acknowledge the presence here also of
the notion of sexual initiation as a rite of passage into adulthood.
We might negotiate this minefield by suggesting that two kinds
of liberationist imperative are colliding, and one – the narrative
of specifically feminine self-development – comes off worse than
the other: the recognition, after Freud, Havelock Ellis and D. H.
Lawrence, of the central importance of sexuality in personality,
and the determination to speak it, not let it go unrepresented in
novelistic discourse. In the 1930s this was, of course, a progressive
motive, marking a resistance to Victorian religio-moral repres-
sions. But inevitably *we* read O'Brien's text with a feminist scep-
ticism about doctrines of sexual liberation, hard-won in the
post-1960s disillusion with what largely turned out to be a
masculinist enthusiasm for indiscriminate sex as a panacea for
social and psychological ills, a new form of domination rather

than of freedom.[15] In *Without My Cloak* and elsewhere (in Dr Curran's thoughts in *The Ante-Room*, for instance) there is very clear evidence of the presence in O'Brien's mind of the new discourses of sexology, specifically of the rather positivist inheritance of Krafft-Ebing and Ellis, if not explicitly of the more humanistic Freud. But acquaintance with these discourses is the perogative of the men. Caroline, the sexually unhappy wife in *Without My Cloak*, is shown as scarcely self-aware, at the mercy of feeling, guilt and desperate impulse and incapable of any analysis, such as, for instance, her brother Eddy can engage in. She is represented by the narrator as driven by almost unconscious natural forces, as in the detached reductionism of this passage, where a mechanical and scientistic perspective is employed:

> and here she was, at forty-two, still beautiful and warm, with nerves frayed to tatters from loathing of a man's desire, from disturbance and frustration of her senses. A physiological commonplace – that was all Caroline's trouble, drench it however the silly creature might in tears and modesty and hesitations. (p. 185)

This passage takes care to adopt the worldly, knowing tone of a man commenting on that whereof he knows; it is precisely a knowledge from which Caroline is debarred by the laws of her femininity. In this context to be feminine is not only to be kept in ignorance of the 'facts' newly established by 'science', but to be 'a silly creature', incapable of knowledge of and for herself.

## IV

In the tradition of realist narrative, and specifically of the *Bildungsroman* on which O'Brien draws, the protagonist's struggle for personal autonomy presents her or his internality, the inner reflexiveness at which s/he painfully arrives, as a form of originality. It is that which, within an ideology founded on the idea of the unified subject, guarantees selfhood.[16] But in O'Brien's work this originality — Mary Lavelle's, engaging wilfully in her Spanish adventure, insisting slightly shockingly on a year to herself between daughterhood and wifehood; Ana de Mendoza's, risking the absolutist king's rage in choosing his

minister as her lover — this originality is, for the reader, in tension
with the rhetoric of beauty which is persistently employed in the
representation of these wilful women. Beauty, as I have suggested
above, is recognised in these texts by the observer's sense of being
thrown back upon a preconstituted, ideal sphere. In a manner
recalling the platonic, it is presented as an absolute about which
there could be no dispute; culturally predefined, talked about as
a given. There is never any — so to speak, Kantian — sense that
it might be as much unconsciously constructed by the viewer as
a property of the object beheld. Now, as the feminist critique of
culture has abundantly shown, the mystifying language of art,
literature, and mythology which surrounds the notion of beauty
is itself strongly implicated in the fetishising representations of
women which are ubiquitous in patriarchy. Thus the love-scene
in *Mary Lavelle*, even as it topples vertiginously towards pulp
romance — 'he held her still and murmured wild Spanish words
of love' (p. 309) — is quite in the tradition of Renaissance nudes,
connoisseurship, and high-class voyeurism.

Of course, Kate O'Brien takes the claims of Art at their own
valuation: throughout her work she accepts and celebrates the existence of a sphere of the aesthetic which is set apart from the
actual and transcends it. As well as the ample evidence her own
texts provide for this view, I am also drawing here on remarks
made about O'Brien's thought by her friend the critic Lorna
Reynolds, who stresses O'Brien's belief in, and sense of reverence
for, an ideal sphere of art and beauty.[17] In particular, she insists
that Kate O'Brien would have conceived of such a sphere as utterly
removed from, and as above, gender and sexuality. I have no particular reason to doubt that this view is a reliable indication of
what O'Brien's theoretical position on these matters would have
been if stated discursively, but texts escape the conscious control
of their authors, and that they can do so may be, in my belief,
the chief promise of a continuing life for them in the minds of
future readers.[18] In this essay I may well be reading Kate
O'Brien in part against the grain of her own intentions, or
privileging some of them at the expense of others, but without,
I hope, a lack of sympathy, and unrepentantly. I therefore find
myself diverging from Lorna Reynolds's views, in the following
way.

O'Brien's implicit theory of the aesthetic is a secularly transcendent one. As for metaphysical matters, while she treats the imperatives of Catholicism with a delicate sympathy, particularly in the rendering of Agnes Mulqueen's emotional suffering in *The Ante-Room*, a degree of modern detachment from Irish and institutional Catholicism is evident on her own part.[19] It is the realm of art which instances a kind of sacredness; and her conception of feminine beauty seems quasi-sacramentally connected to that sphere. I would contend that *in her fictions,* at least, sexuality is not distanced or programmatically excluded from the realm of aesthetic exaltation, as it is in some versions of the aesthetic, Schopenhauer's, for example. Rather, she imbricates erotic motives with idealisation, making one work upon the other in a manner reminiscent sometimes of Spanish mysticism (Teresa of Avila, about whom, it will be recalled, she also wrote, and John of the Cross) and sometimes of Plato's celebration of homoeroticism as an elevating force in the *Symposium* (and of the whole tradition of European writings which stem from it and its Renaissance Florentine avatars). This idealising discourse complicates the task of any critic who would wish to take seriously O'Brien's own developed understanding and intentions, without at the same time relinquishing the disturbing sense the reader has of fetishistic and voyeur tendencies in the texts' depiction of women.

## V

At this point it is time to consider the place of Kate O'Brien's own, biographical, sexual orientation in this puzzle, which so far I have done no more than mention. As other contributors show, after a brief and unsuccessful marriage in early adulthood she was predominantly lesbian-identified. In what ways can this be made to relate to the representation of women in her fiction? Later in my discussion, I shall discuss certain more general problems in making that connection. But first I shall stay with the specific issue of the representation of feminine physical beauty. May we deal with the contradiction I have been outlining — between the attempt of her female protagonists to achieve agency, and their generally simultaneous construction as objects of scopic and aesthetic desire — by arguing that she appropriates the normal discourse of masculine narrators precisely to celebrate a real entity, female beauty, and to express desire for the women whose defining property this is? We would then see her as empowering a female viewer to perceive beauty as, previously, only men were allowed to do; except that her discourse differs from that of men-desiring-women in that it is not consuming, dominant, subjugating an Other, but praising, enjoying, sustaining, the Same. According to this perspective, Kate O'Brien would have chosen not to dismantle the conventions of feminine beauty, but to adopt them and refunction them. To put it otherwise and more promisingly, we might see her as resisting the customary Oedipal plot, predicated as it is on sexual difference and feminine lack, and setting up an alternative narrative of homogeneity and sexual affinity.[20] Should we then try to reread the scopic, possessive, sado-masochistic sexualities of *Mary Lavelle* as fantasy games, conventions which O'Brien means to make slip from their moorings in the actual oppression of women, into a free play of pleasure, a set of multiple and shifting subject-positions which would crisscross the traditional binary map of human sexual congress? How far is this a viable interpretative option?

There are only two explicitly lesbian references, to my knowledge, in Kate O'Brien's fiction. One is the representation of Agatha Conlan in *Mary Lavelle*, and the other the love between Clare Halvey, joint heroine of *As Music and Splendour*, and her fellow-musician Luisa Carriaga. The two are separated by twenty-one years, and they differ with intriguing sharpness. I shall deal first with *Mary Lavelle*. Agatha Conlan is an example of what Catharine Stimpson calls the 'dyke' stereotype: the haunted, doomed 'invert', who feels herself accursed and cast out, of whom Radclyffe Hall, not many years before O'Brien composed *Mary Lavelle*, had provided the influential archetype in the person of Stephen Gordon.[21] Agatha is sympathetically portrayed, but carefully held in the novel's margins. Her unsatisfied desire generates one of its moving passages, a puzzled meditation by Mary on the sadness of unsatisfied desire and of unwilled mutual injury:

Mary watched the baize door swing and swing again in the porch of San Geronimo and caught each time the gleam of candles. People going in incessantly to pray, as Agatha did so often, as she did, as Juanito too, perhaps. Seeking strength against the perversions of their hearts and escape from fantastic longings. Seeking mercy, explanation and forgiveness because they are so vicious as to love each other. . . . oh bitter, unforeseen exactions! What an astonishing need there was, as life explained itself, of this incessant in and out to altars. . . . Heart after heart was found to be in pain. . . . Oh, Lord have pity! Help us to have pity on each other, to make some sense sometime out of this tangle of our longings! (pp. 285-6)

But, as we have seen, the plot drives on towards its major resolution in the heterosexual initiation of Mary by Juanito, leaving Agatha as the centre merely, or at least ostensibly, of a subplot, itself the sad pendent to the matching happy outcome of O'Toole's sunny romance with the retired bullfighter Pepe. O'Toole's transgression against class and genteel self-respect, contemptuously rejected by the other 'Misses', is warmly endorsed by the narrator and Mary, and structurally by its place at the close of the novel. The promise of O'Toole's contentment starkly contrasts with Conlan's forsakenness and utter isolation. It is very difficult for readers in these later decades not to go against the grain of the book's overt denouement — Mary's passionate heterosexual fulfilment — and perceive in Conlan's intensity, unhappy and self-condemned, a subtext querying the obligatory discourse of sexual difference. Such readerly tendencies are certainly strengthened by the unusually uncertain and novelettish tone of the Mary–Juanito scene, which I have already noted. But one cannot make bricks out of straw: these readers' responses cannot conjure out of this text any kind of overt rejection of the norms of conventional heterosexuality, with all their implicit subjugation of women, still less a utopian counter-proposal of same-gender affinity to supplant it. *Mary Lavelle*, then, at least, does not seem to offer much support to the argument mentioned above, that O'Brien is appropriating the masculinist construction of women as aesthetic objects with any very confident intention of rehabilitating it as acceptable from within an active feminine subjectivity. Strikingly, she gives Agatha Conlan a love-speech which specifically aligns the nature of her desire for Mary with masculine sexual attraction.

Conlan is left in blank, isolated misery, O'Brien herself remaining true to her vision in giving no hint of a possible moral rehabilitation of Conlan in her own eyes. She does, however, give her a strong interest, amounting to a passion, in the spectacle of the bullfight. After witnessing it, Conlan is described as transfigured, almost beautiful. When, later in the novel, she confesses her attraction to Mary, she explicitly says: 'I like you the way a man would' (p. 285). In this character, then, O'Brien gives an example of an aesthetic viewer, someone with a realised selfhood, however agonised, who is a connoisseur and judge of the aesthetic, as are male figures and narrators elsewhere in the novels. The appreciation of the beauty of the *corrida* shown by Conlan is of a piece with her admiration of Mary, openly denominated as sexual. For the reader, this would seem to entail a division of female sexuality within itself into the binary pattern of dominant and submissive roles, viewer and viewed, familiar from the masculine–feminine stereotype.[22] Juanito and Agatha can be lined up as active agents, desiring *subjects*, each opposite Mary, projected as *object* of desire. This is, of course, to oversimplify: one should immediately recall the crucial fact that O'Brien makes Mary exit the novel in a state of entire openness about her own affective, and indeed vocational, future.

The utopian temptation to read a programmatic, or at least conscious sexual dissidence into *Mary Lavelle* is greatly strengthened by 'reading back' into that earlier novel our impressions of the Clare–Luisa relationship in *As Music and Splendour*. This is an example of relatively carefree lesbian activity, into which the question of guilt does not enter, given to pleasure and joy. Clare and Luisa's capacity for play is emphasised, and their affair is surrounded in the description by a context of pleasurable sensuous consumption, specifically of fruit, wine, and fresh Italian coffee. The relationship is represented as flouting the heterosexual imperative of monogamy, at least on Luisa's side; a situation painful to Clare, but which she is shown as accepting. The narrator makes clear Clare's favourable comparison of Luisa's love with that of two male characters, Iago Duarte and Paddy, the gloomy Irish ex-clerical student. It is Paddy who constructs Clare scopically, in O'Brien's familiar aestheticising manner: he thinks of her as 'an angel or a virgin from some Sienese canvas' (p. 108).

Luisa, by contrast, loves Clare as activity rather than as object. The novel frames their mutual affinity by means of the motif of Gluck's *Orpheus and Eurydice*, in which they are once cast as the spouses. The role of Orpheus is a cross-dressed woman's role, and the story's invocation of undying love, and vulnerability to change and loss frames the whole Luisa–Clare plot as an intense emotional experience. It is poignantly referred to as 'their one true dress' – a striking phrase which acknowledges the endlessly shifting guises and disguises which compose the emotional lives of people in general, whatever their sexual orientation. The aesthetic moment of Clare and Luisa's joint performance holds their love in solution, fixes and glorifies it, in a celebratory moment which transcends the suffering of their real lives. It is one of Kate O'Brien's best fictional ideas; in this motif she triumphantly effects that very particular merging of sexual and aesthetic motives which characterises her strange, characteristic and paradoxical imagination.

This is the place to take up certain general problems, political and theoretical, which are raised by reading Kate O'Brien's writings as lesbian and which I have postponed until near the end of my discussion. Is it appropriate to expect the literary expression of lesbian sexuality to be an instance of utopian freedom from inauthentic and repressive bourgeois sexual norms? Does this not incur risks in two directions? One is the hidden implication of the possibility of free choice of sexual orientation on which this projection is predicated: a view which would be strenuously rejected by many if explicitly stated.[23] The second potential risk arising from the investing of lesbians with the social optimism and utopian longing of 'straight' women and men is the designation of lesbians from outside to occupy a necessarily dissident position in regard to sexuality, a move which ignores the specificity of women's lives. This would merely replicate the tactic of male writers and critics who project their own utopian wishes on to the mode of existence of women in general, treating the condition of femaleness as a blank, a *tabula rasa* waiting to be inscribed with men's yearning to escape the crushing burdens of masculinity. Frances Restuccia has argued this case well in relation to Joyce:

> Joyce shifts the law over to the mother from the fathers/Fathers so that she can assist him in a finely tuned, precisely controlled subversion,

> not so that he can lose himself . . . It is the fetishised image of the
> Mother/Virgin that assists Joyce in getting beyond the referential,
> beyond the Father. But the reality of women remains ignored; fetishised
> disavowal allows textuality or free play even as it provides for the
> security of a dominant position – only the son's (disguised as the
> mother's) rather than the father's.[24]

This is the Lacanian 'lack' or unrepresentable, what Julia Kristeva calls 'the unnameable that one imagines as femininity, non-language or body'.[25] Discussing the controversy in the theory of homosexuality between 'social constructionism' and more essentialist views, Carole Vance remarks that while the social-constructionist approach frees us from 'a naturalizing discourse' tying us to folk knowledge and Victorian and Edwardian scientific ideologies (notions including 'spermatic and ovarian economies' or women's 'innate sexual passivity'), it may also unhelpfully obscure the material reality of the body: 'As sexual subjects, how do we reconcile constructionist theory with the body's visceral reality and our own experience of it?'[26]

There is a further difficulty which is located within more specifically literary theory and practice. Why should lesbians be presumed to be *ipso facto* free of stereotyping and the objectifying gaze – as if they occupied a world magically uncontaminated by the whole human system of cultural significations which is all that makes communication possible? As Mary Ann Doane points out in her consideration of whether the 'gaze' of film spectators can ever be 'female', 'the cinematic apparatus inherits a theory of the image which is not conceived outside of sexual specifications'.[27] Or in other words, there is no willed freedom from the given sign-system for any communicator within a culture. Kate O'Brien is obliged, like other writers however marginal or oppositional in aspiration, to work through the conventions within which social meaning is produced, and these are culturally given.

A possible way of proceeding might lie in a kind of compromise, a position negotiated something like this: that there is a moment of radical potential in 'sexual dissidence', in which marginalised people can by virtue of their marginality gain insights probably obscured (maybe mercifully so) from the 'normal' masses. This would be a kind of compensatory privilege, helping to make bearable the subordination and concealment of the marginal state.

But the achievement of such insights in no way amounts to or guarantees a liberation from the sexual signifying systems of the larger culture. Or, to return to the specific problem of Kate O'Brien's feminine and sexual representations, the eroticism of the domination-and-submission, subject-and-object pattern is only occasionally and imperfectly shed in O'Brien's fictional thought. Working within ideology may not disable covert resistances, making the semiotic message ironic or (either deliberately or unconsciously) contradictory. I have throughout my discussion been worrying away at such a recurring contradiction: we might identify its very presence as affording feminist interpretative leverage. While this stops short of attributing systematic *conscious* feminist critique to O'Brien, it opens the way to new readings and new uses of her work for the future.

## VI

I shall conclude by commenting on one remaining scene from Kate O'Brien's work. This is the passage in *The Land of Spices* where the heroine Anna Murphy, on the threshold of adult life, has a kind of epiphany in the gardens of the convent school which is the book's main setting. Anna has hitherto felt that her intelligence and personal energy rather lacked a theatre where they might operate in the future. In this passage she discovers a potential direction for her life in the form of a vision of one of her schoolfellows, becoming aware of the girl Pilar

> on a plane of perception which was strange to her, and which during its visitation she did not understand but could only receive – delightedly, but without surprise in fact, and as if she had been waiting for the lead it was to give. She saw her, it seemed, in isolation and in a new sphere. . . . (p. 271)

For all Pilar's schoolgirl silliness, Anna discerns her as

> yet herself a symbol as complicated as any imaginative struggle in verse; a common piece of creation, as exquisite challenge to creativeness; she saw Pilar as a glimpse, as if she were a line from a lost immortal; she saw her ironically, delightedly, as a motive in art. (pp. 271-2)

Anna is herself at that point without understanding of the significance of this 'translation of the ordinary'; the narrator describes
her ignorance of the visual arts, but for glimpses of 'old master
reproductions in the school library', but nevertheless mentions
Mantegna, 'a bright memory of Giorgione', and places Pilar explicitly in the aesthetic system:

> she was a girl of *La Vida Española*, a young girl in Goya, who dances
> and gathers grapes, and plays blindman's-buff; a small-waisted girl with
> shining eyes, eternally lifted off in joy from other Goya worlds. (p. 272)

This experience, however inadequately Anna grasps it herself,
identifies her as the possessor of an aesthetic sensibility; her vision
of Pilar is presented as a definitive, pivotal moment in her life.

> So Anna beheld her; something that life can be about, something with
> power to make life compose around it. She stared at her in wonder
> . . . realising her lustrous potentiality . . . that for her, the watcher, this
> moment was a long-awaited, blessed gift; that in seeing this transience,
> this grace, this volatility, flung in a sweet summer hour against . . .
> the evening star, she was encountering, alone and in terms of her secret
> need, a passage of beauty as revelatory and true as any verse of the
> great elegy. (p. 272)

In this scene, O'Brien presents Anna as an artist in embryo. Her
viewing of Pilar is an instance of the aesthetic gaze, part of a series
running through all the novels. The passage presents Anna as
witnessing something pre-existing, not for a minute as constituting
the aesthetic object by her look; the surrounding narration finds
Pilar quite unconscious of her own charms, and Anna smitten by
her, in a way which we can readily compare to Don Pablo's
shocked appreciation of Mary Lavelle, and many characters' admiration of Caroline in *Without My Cloak* (in particular that of
Denis, her artistic nephew, and Eddy, her connoisseur brother).
    There is a difference, however, in this scene: Anna views Pilar
actively, as 'an exquisite challenge to creativeness', 'a motive in
art'. In this, her fifth novel, O'Brien intimates, as hardly anywhere
else, the possibility of *female* creativity, an active aesthetic role for
a woman; and it is notable that she makes Anna's revelation arise
from the sight of another woman. This prefigures Luisa's love
of Clare as activity rather than as object, above all in the

performance of her art, and hence the sense in their sexual love of a mutual and equal subjectivity, in the later *As Music and Splendour*. Furthermore, this threshold scene in the late-adolescent Anna Murphy's life, which occurs near the end, forms a structural parallel to the earlier definitive moment in the life of the book's other protagonist, the Reverend Mother, Helen Archer. We are told in a flashback how Helen has become a nun in revulsion from the accidental discovery of her beloved father making love with a young male student friend. (This, incidentally, though narrated with extreme restraint in a single phrase, was the cause of the celebrated banning of *The Land of Spices* by the Irish censors.) That incident plays a major role in determining the course of Helen's life, as Anna's vision of Pilar, we are to realise, will play in hers.

There is no explicit indication in the Anna–Pilar scene that either Anna's perception of Pilar's beauty, or her apperception of its effect upon herself, is a sexualised one; nevertheless, it seems to me, to feel obliged entirely to edit out this aspect of O'Brien's usual construction of feminine beauty from the scene would be the reaction only of a reader determined at all costs to maintain silence on the issue of lesbian sexuality and the relation of O'Brien's writings to it. This again raises the question discussed above of O'Brien's conception of the aesthetic realm, and of its relation – or lack of a relation – to sexuality. Anna's vision of Pilar is a positive, celebratory one, in which Anna perceives a quality she thinks of as immortal underlying the surface frivolity of Pilar's personality. But the scene is also tinged with wistfulness. This is partly because, framed by Pilar's request to have Milton's *Lycidas* explained to her, it represents the completion of a stage in Anna's work of mourning for her beloved brother Charlie who has been drowned; but there is also the sense of an unspoken yearning, which we are perhaps meant to see as creatively unsatisfied: as at the end Pilar drops her and runs off to join her best friend, Anna is left alone, reading 'For we were nursed upon the selfsame hill. . . .' Her radiant glimpse of Pilar as an icon of aesthetic feminine beauty thus also entails a realisation of her own affinity with the other girl, a self-recognition in their common subjectivity. This triumphantly reverses Helen Archer's sad rejection of human bodily contacts, driven by her father's divergence from Freud's Oedipal master-narrative: Anna gets her chance at a life both affective and intellectual which Helen denied herself. In *The Land of Spices* Helen, a straight Freudian reading might say, suffers the loss — during her adolescent feminine father-attraction, renewed from infancy after childhood latency — of her 'Oedipal father', by her father's choice of a homosexual lover.[28] In Helen Archer, we may argue (as other critics have done, though from different perspectives), O'Brien is representing a figure of feminine power; I would add that she is also implicitly repudiating the Freudian narrative. Playing a displaced mother-role, but with a marked reversal of the passivity of the feminine stereotype, Helen makes Anna repeat cultural texts — a motif crystallised in the Herbert poem from which the book's title comes. She thus socialises her, introduces her to literary—intellectual culture and gives her access to the institution of aesthetic pleasure — the 'land of spices' — which is ultimately to offer her an adult, though secular, vocation. In this scene, then, the warmth of Anna's attraction to an incarnate creature of the same gender — whether emotional, sexual, or aesthetic, or a compound of all three, as, we might admit, real-world desire must generally be — palliates the isolation and chill of Helen's asceticism and holds out the promise of achieved human beauty and love. So perhaps after all we may locate, behind its delicate veil of discretion, the utopian moment, the instance of a projected freedom and joy, in Kate O'Brien's flawed, compelling texts.

## Notes and references

1   The banning of certain of her works in the 1940s indicates that the Irish authorities found her disturbing. The best general discussion of the culture and ideology of the period is Terence Brown's, in *A Social and Cultural History of Ireland 1922-1979*, London, Fontana, 1980.

2   Kate O'Brien, *The Ante-Room* (1933), Dublin, Arlen House, 1982, p. 152. Page-numbers will be cited in parentheses at the end of subsequent quotations from this text.

3   Laura Mulvey, 'Visual Pleasure and Narrative Cinema', *Screen*, vol. 16, no. 3, 1975; John Berger, *Ways of Seeing*, Harmondsworth, Penguin, 1972. My thinking about these matters in O'Brien was assisted at an earlier stage by discussions with Susan Kirwan; see her unpublished M.A. thesis: 'Feminist Project, Feminine Representation: An Interpretation of Women in the Novels of Kate O'Brien', University College Cork, November 1990.

4 See Peter de Bolla, *The Discourse of the Sublime*, Oxford, Blackwell, 1980.

5 *Mary Lavelle* (1936), London, Virago, 1984, p. 167. Subsequent page-references to this text will be cited in parentheses after each quotation.

6 Kate O'Brien, *As Music and Splendour*, London, Heinemann, 1958, p. 240.

7 Kate O'Brien, *Without My Cloak*, Harmondsworth, Penguin, 1949, pp. 30–1. Subsequent page-references will be given in parentheses at the end of each quotation.

8 See E. Ann Kaplan, 'Is the Gaze Male?' (1977), Ann Snitow, Christine Stansell and Sharon Thompson (eds.), *Desire: The Politics of Sexuality*, London, Virago, 1984, pp. 321–38, esp. pp. 327, 328, 328–9.

9 Kate O'Brien, *Mary Lavelle* (1936), Virago, London, 1984, pp. 33–4. Subsequent page-references will be cited in parentheses at the end of each quotation.

10 See Peter C. Sutton *et al.*, *Masters of Seventeenth-Century Dutch Genre Painting*, Philadelphia and London, Philadelphia Museum of Art, 1984, catalogue entries on several paintings by van Mieris and Molenaer of women before mirrors, pp. 259–63.

11 Luisa too is herself assimilated into the canon of works of art, in a passage focalised, rather preposterously when one examines it, through the (untravelled and provincial) Mary herself: 'Her hands reminded Mary of the hands of angels in Italian primitive nativities. She was dramatic and enchanting to behold, so happily did she harmonize mondaine with eternal beauty.' (p. 150)

12 The text clearly registers Juanito's orgasm, but so far as Mary's experience is attended to at all in the passage, it is characterised as one of pain (pp. 308–10); see especially the following: 'Mary, more than forgetful of the pain, underwent in her spirit, through sheer love and without physical response, the essential rapture that she gave' (p. 310). See below.

13 For an extremely illuminating discussion of the problem of pervasive patterns of domination and submission and their troubling mapping on to sexual relationships, see Jessica Benjamin, *The Bonds of Love: Psychoanalysis, Feminism and the Problem of Domination*, London, Virago, 1990.

14 And see p. 168: ' Pilar's protectress – he smiled – was so beautiful to-night as to seem again Medusa, or a flame-sworded angel at the gate of Paradise.'

15 This, together with other related issues, is discussed with great insight by Patricia Jagentovich Mills in *Woman, Nature and Psyche*, New Haven and London, Yale University Press, 1987; see especially the consideration of Marcuse's thought, pp. 149–70.

16 See Leo Bersani's classic discussion in *A Future for Astyanax: Character and Desire in Literature*, London, Marion Boyars, 1978, Chapter 2, 'Realism and the Problem of Desire'.

17 Seminar discussion at the Kate O'Brien Weekend, 1990, my recollection.

18 The extreme version of such critical positions as this is to be found in the thought of Pierre Macherey, who proposes that it is precisely the fissures and fractures in the smooth surface of writings which offer leverage to a truly productive criticism, and that the conditions of possibility of a text,

which by definition it cannot itself make manifest, are the ultimate object of critical inquiry. Pierre Macherey, *A Theory of Literary Production* (1966), trans. Geoffrey Wall, London, Routledge, 1978.

19  She always, however, retained a respect for the culture and customs of her class and milieu, however much she found herself placed outside them by her own self-development, intellectual, ideological and sexual. One may read this either as an honourable loyalty to and deep understanding of that social world which in material terms had produced and helped to form her, or as a lingering inability to free herself from class attitudes, a mixture of snobbery and provincialism.

20  This point was suggested to me by Anne Fogarty, in an earlier version, specifically concerned with O'Brien's other novel *The Last of Summer*, of her discussion below. See also Christine Van Boheemen, *The Novel as Family Romance: Language, Gender and Authority from Fielding to Joyce*, Ithaca, NY, Cornell University Press, 1987.

21  See Stimpson's pioneering 'Zero Degree Deviancy: The Lesbian Novel in English', Elizabeth Abel (ed.), *Writing and Sexual Difference*, Brighton, Harvester, 1982, pp. 243–59; Radclyffe Hall, *The Well of Loneliness* (1928), London, Virago, 1982.

22  This in turn raises the complex problem of butch/femme role-playing in lesbian relationships, and whether it can or should be left behind. See Martha, Vicinus ' "They Wonder to Which Sex I Belong": The Historical Roots of the Modern Lesbian Identity', and Saskia Wieringa, 'An Anthropological Critique of Constructionism: Berdaches and Butches', Dennis Altman (ed.), *Which Homosexuality?*, London and Amsterdam, GMP Publishers, 1989, pp. 171–98, for useful discussions of the issue.

23  At the 1992 Galway Conference on 'Gender and Colonialism', Terry Eagleton's placing of Oscar Wilde in this role of progressive dissidence by virtue of his gay orientation was vehemently and cogently contested by several other participants.

24  *Joyce and the Law of the Father*, New Haven and London, Yale University Press, 1989, pp. 175–6.

25  Julia Kristeva, 'Stabat Mater', Toril Moi (ed.), *The Kristeva Reader*, trans. Leon S. Roudiez, New York, Columbia University Press, 1986.

26  Carole S. Vance, 'Social Construction Theory: Problems in the History of Sexuality' (1989), in Altman, *Which Homosexuality?*, p. 23.

27  Mary Ann Doane, 'Film and the Masquerade: Theorising the Female Spectator', *Screen*, vol. 23, 1982, pp. 74–7.

28  See Sigmund Freud, 'Femininity' (1933), in *New Introductory Lectures on Psychoanalysis*, James Strachey, ed. and trans. Harmondsworth, Penguin, 1973, pp. 155, 162 ff.; see also his various feminist critics.

# Chapter 5

# The Ante-Room as Drama

*Anthony Roche*

Any account of my reading of Kate O'Brien's 1934 novel *The Ante-Room* must take as its starting-point the recognition that it might never have happened. The occasion was a day in Donegal in 1982 when I flicked idly through a paperback rack looking for some summer reading and came upon the then recent Arlen House reprint of *The Ante-Room*. None of O'Brien's nine novels had been in print from my early teens through the years when I was increasingly drawn to the study of Irish writing in English. Her writing figured on no syllabus of Anglo-Irish literature; her titles were not in the shops; even had one of my lecturers wished to concentrate on O'Brien, the lack of availability of the primary texts would have argued against it. It took the first Irish feminist press, Arlen House, to allow a succession of novels by Kate O'Brien (among other writers) to enter public and academic discourse at the very beginning of the 1980s. The result was a key moment in the development of Irish rather than London-based publishing, and a major step in the rewriting of the Irish literary canon.

Kate O'Brien's *The Ante-Room* took a surgical knife in prose

of great beauty and precision to areas of my Irish experience greatly in need of treatment: the situation of being a 'Catholic
agnostic',[1] of having been brought up in the language, forms and
rituals of thought and feeling of Irish Catholicism; of the conflict between duty and desire; of relations between mothers and
sons, men and women. The sense conveyed by the novel was of
working from within, of worrying at the forms it had inherited
and occupied, to issue in a truly subversive re-reading of Irish
experience. There is at least one belated and unintentional consequence to the silencing of Kate O'Brien. Her distinctive
achievements as a writer can now be read not only in terms of
her own time but re-read in the light of what has appeared since.

What the novel *The Ante-Room* most reminded me of was of
much more recent date and was of non-Irish provenance: John
Fowles's *The French Lieutenant's Woman* (1969).[2] When it first appeared, what was so striking about the Fowles book was the way
or ways in which it rewrote the classic nineteenth-century English
novel from the perspective of the late twentieth century. Fowles's
narrator reminds us on more than one occasion that exactly 100
years supervene between the writing of the book and the period
in which it is set. Kate O'Brien's *The Ante-Room* is set in Mellick
(Limerick) in the early 1880s and was written during the early
1930s. Her novel repeatedly sets both facts before us; measuring
the space between by what can and cannot be said. There is, for
example, the discussion between Dr Curran and Agnes Mulqueen
about her brother's syphilis: 'he decided that for everybody's sake
she had better know the facts. Briefly and accurately, then, he
gave them to her; but he was a conventional and puritanical young
man, she was a young unmarried lady, and the year was 1880.'[3]
At one level, there is in both novels a running commentary on
the sexual prudery of Victorian fiction and an exercising of greater
freedom of expression in representing relations between the sexes.
The title of Fowles's book is itself a euphemism; and his young
Victorian male Charles Smithson is startled when he first hears
her referred to not as 'woman' but as 'whore' (77). The 'syphilis'
whose symptoms are so evident and visible in Reggie can never
be named in the Mulqueen household. When Agnes meets with
her lover Vincent and refuses to go off with him, he argues: 'Listen.
I could take you now; I could rape you' (267), and the word is

still as brutal as the act it names. How much more so it must have been for an audience in the 1930s.

These passages make the point that, as Lorna Reynolds succinctly puts it, 'Such a novel could not have been written by a native Catholic author in the nineteenth century.'[4] She sees this as the novel's 'historical dimension'. Kate O'Brien's double perspective, on the 1880s and on the 1930s, is what gives *The Ante-Room* its real claim as a historical novel. Reading the past in the light of the present acknowledges the processes involved in writing a history and relativises the claims made in so doing. Both O'Brien and Fowles are not just inserting a gap of some decades to gain distance but are consciously reading one age against another. They are doing so not only or primarily to render explicit what the conventions of the Victorian age left implicit. The reading works both ways, revealing the extent to which the conventions and attitudes which helped form the twentieth century first established their hegemony in the nineteenth.

As Fowles's Charles Smithson and Sarah Woodruff play out their personal scenario, Karl Marx is writing *Das Kapital* in the British Museum and the movement for the emancipation of women is gathering momentum. Similarly, there are occasions in *The Ante-Room* when the troubled concerns of the household, gathered at the dying mother's bedside, and the romantic dilemma of its heroine are set against the momentous political events occurring in Ireland during the 1880s. The first occurs when the sisters' talk between Agnes and Marie-Rose is interrupted as the men come in talking politics. There follows a rapid succession of references to Gladstone, the Land Leaguers, and Captain Boycott. The second brings in Parnell, who 'looks too good to be true - or too true to be good - in politics' (209). This encourages a reading of the scene in the light of Parnell's downfall some years later, the scandal over his affair with Katharine O'Shea. These references do not need to be much elaborated, in O'Brien's fiction or in this analysis. They are characters from a familiar history, leading males in the narrative of Irish nationalism and the emergence of an Irish Free State. What the novel most often suggests in its comparisons between Ireland in the 1880s and the 1930s is that for all of the fifty-year gap and for all the political and revolutionary activity it witnessed, very little has changed.

Those matters which could not be mentioned in 1880s Ireland were no less taboo in the 1930s; indeed, they were undergoing systematic and explicit suppression during that period. The broken marriage between Vincent O'Regan and Marie-Rose Mulqueen is described as a 'desperate situation to have to conceal from the sharp and prudish eyes of Irish society in 1880' (105). And in the discussion of Parnell, Vincent and he are aligned as sulky gods, with the arena of sexual relations regarded as the true, if occluded, site of conflict.

Had *The Ante-Room* been written in the period of its setting, some sense of what might have resulted is given through the late entrance of Sir Godfrey Bartlett-Crowe, the visiting London surgeon. He is called in to give an expert medical opinion, or rather to give the metropolitan seal of approval to the views of the colonial backwater; but equally he is there to facilitate Kate O'Brien's acerbic comment on nineteenth-century Anglo-Irish fiction. From the Act of Union on, dozens of novels were written to represent, explain and justify Ireland to England (the better to secure the imperial relationship). The form they most often took was that of melodramatic romance, with England figured as a male suitor and Ireland as a beautiful maiden. As Sir Godfrey approaches the Mulqueen household, he anticipates that he is to meet a pair of wild and barefooted Irish 'colleens' (202); and is rather taken aback when he encounters two elegant, cultured, independent young women. But he is equal to the challenge of representation and soon has the two sisters pleasingly metaphorised, the 'dark' Agnes as the sea and Marie-Rose as 'the foam' (204). Sir Godfrey is determined, as he later puts it, to find Ireland 'the sanctuary of the old ideal feminine' (206), and resists and resents the notion that Agnes could be 'a new type'. Instead, he will flirt with Marie-Rose, and work on the symbolic connotations of her name and beauty. The satire is sharp, concentrated; and comprehends the Anglo-Irish novels of the nineteenth century and the Yeatsian pastoralism which succeeded them.

A novel that *was* available in the 1880s is consciously inserted into the dialogue, Henry James's *Washington Square:* 'They had been talking of 'Washington Square', which everyone was reading in the *Cornhill*' (123). Vincent is pressing Agnes to admit that James's heroine Catherine Sloper 'is utterly uncharming. . . . Unless there's charm in a kitchen dresser, say, or a set of fire-irons?' Agnes makes the comparison between herself and Catherine when she replies that if, as the men seem to be insisting, fire-irons can neither be charming or frivolous, then neither can she. The characteristic most shared between Agnes Mulqueen and Catherine Sloper is that of being overlooked. The two young women at the centre of James's and O'Brien's novels are reticent, shy, inward, formal, reserved. Neither are much given to parading themselves for social exhibition and male evaluation. And both become animated by a passion which the social order can neither contain nor fulfil. When Morris Townsend is drawn by the prospect of an inheritance to woo Catherine Sloper, she discovers a sense of her own self that is finally sensitive to the low esteem in which her father holds her. When Agnes discovers a passion within herself to be with Vincent, the relationship most illuminated thereby is that with her sister, Marie-Rose. Kate O'Brien alters the power relations of romantic comedy by making Agnes and her consciousness central to the novel and subordinating the various male discourses to her dilemma. But there is a debt to James in the treatment of the social scene to which the heroine's condition is related. It may be measured in terms of 'exactions' and the sense of what remains unsaid, as in Agnes's 'cold amazement . . . that a house ostensibly surrendered to one sorrow should all at once give roof to so many unmentionable intense and contradictory emotions' (130).

O'Brien had begun her career by writing plays before moving more successfully into fiction. Henry James had his own disastrous flirtation with the theatre. And *The Ante-Room* failed when it was dramatised and staged in 1936.[5] But as with James, and Joyce's experience with his one play *Exiles,* the lessons learned as a dramatist by Kate O'Brien found their way into her writing of prose narrative. She provides a further critique of the Irish Literary Revival and aligns herself with Joyce by the degree to which she draws on the plays of Ibsen in *The Ante-Room.* To the extent that the Irish theatre had admitted Ibsen, it had Celticised him by taking the character Nora out of a contemporary drawing-room and removing her to a lonely peasant cottage. Kate O'Brien restores Ibsen's original setting, the claustrophobic living-quarters of the upper middle-class bourgeoisie, and with it much of his social critique. The setting of this Irish novel is Roseholm, a name which

echoes that of a late and difficult Ibsen play, *Rosmersholm.* The
Mulqueen house also contains within it a version of Ibsen's *Ghosts*
in the suffocatingly Oedipal relationship between the dying Mrs
Mulqueen and her syphilitic son, Reggie. But *Rosmersholm* centres on a young woman, Rebecca West, who is companion to the
widowed John Rosmer. Their relationship is shadowed by the
man's dead wife, Beata, who committed suicide by throwing
herself into the mill-stream; and by Beata's living brother, Dr
Kroll, who wishes to win his old friend Rosmer away from the
radical influence of this young woman. Like Catherine Sloper and
Agnes Mulqueen, Rebecca West is a relatively undramatic figure
in conventional terms. But like them she too has suffered 'a blinding sickening passion'[6] which has transformed her sense of self
and made her obdurate in resisting the traditional patriarchal
weight of the house she occupies. She is finally trapped into
emulating Beata and killing herself in order to show her 'belief'
in Rosmer; and can only retaliate by drawing him with her in a
suicide pact. Only through a joint suicide do they 'marry' and
so resist the status quo. The ending of *Rosmersholm* clearly lies
behind that of *The Ante-Room,* as does that of *Hedda Gabler,* where
the pistol shot and Hedda's suicide provoke the comment, 'People
don't do such things.'

With Ibsen in mind, we can set the last chapter of O'Brien's
novel as the strong finish of nineteenth-century drama, with the
character who strains after a utopian alternative to his or her everyday circumstances finding it through self-annihilation. But the
suicidal figure in *The Ante-Room* is a man, not a woman, unlike
the Ibsen plays; and he has not succeeded in drawing the heroine
after him into a suicide pact. Instead, Kate O'Brien has provided
a double ending, as John Fowles was more self-consciously to
do in his novel. Fowles posed the technical problem thus: 'I cannot give both versions at once, yet whichever is the second will
seem, so strong is the tyranny of the last chapter, the final, the
"real" version' (349). O'Brien has countered this tendency by offering us in the final chapter an ending which most readers reject
as too melodramatic. This reaction throws us back on the alternative ending in the previous chapter. Agnes re-enters the house
to reflect that 'They are all alive, even Mother. But I'm dying.
Vincent, if I could only die – oh, Vincent, darling – ' (301). Agnes's

last statement in the novel strives towards full orgasmic expression, but breaks off into fragmented, incomplete utterance. The effect is desolate in the extreme, grotesque, an anticlimax, since all of the other characters have found some form of fulfilment: Vincent, by pulling the trigger on himself; Teresa, by accomplishing the 'miracle' she has sought in the proposed union of Reggie and Nurse Cunningham; and the others, by seeing the prospect of Teresa dying happily. What remains for Agnes is unclear. None of the options she has been offered, especially that of marriage to Dr Curran, appear satisfactory. Where Vincent undergoes the classic fate of the late nineteenth-century heroine, Agnes's ending is truly modernist or post-modernist in its open-endedness and incompletion. As Fowles's narrator remarks: 'The conventions of Victorian fiction allow, allowed no place for the open, the inconclusive ending.'

The paradox of Fowles's novel is that the tendencies of the Victorian age are most laid bare by a progressive reader of Darwin like Charles Smithson than by the more conventionally minded characters. His equivalent in *The Ante-Room* is Dr William Curran, who prides himself on being progressive. But what Curran's charged encounter with Agnes Mulqueen reveals, like Charles Smithson's with the French lieutenant's woman, is the central Victorian split between mind and body.

Through the figure of Charles Curran, Kate O'Brien examines the pathology of male romanticism in the late nineteenth century with at least as much skill as John Fowles. What emerges in the portrait of Curran is a conflict between outer control and 'inner frenzy' (57). As long as he regards Agnes from the viewpoint of a doctor, she is inessential to his life, simply one of 'so many decorative toys' (55). But once they have regularly conversed during the weeks he is visiting Roseholm, she threatens to become real, and in so doing to complicate his rational male world. Curran's response is to represent Agnes as chaotic, as an irresistible force of nature threatening him with delicious self-destruction. He derives pleasure and 'power' from this project, and renders it in self-consciously poetic terms: 'But he was not a poet. He was a Victorian bourgeois, rationalist in the idiom of his mind, Catholic in tradition and practice, a man eager to harness feeling into usefulness. This unlooked for love once quick in him, he must examine his chance to satisfy and domesticate it.' (57). When he reveals his passion to Agnes, Curran describes her as a *femme fatale*. This is the form in which he is most pleased to represent and view her. When he realises that she cares more for Vincent, he longs to get 'away from her and the madness she put on him' to where 'he would see it all and get control of it' (150). In moments of icy clarity, he can recognise the simple fact that she prefers someone else, but this alternates with the fixed view that she is his fate. Throughout these alternations between reason and romanticism, it becomes clear that these two world-views do not so much supplant as support one another. They conjoin in a male-centred view of an ordered universe undermined by a chaotic world of the emotions centred in and represented by woman.

Where Kate O'Brien's novel goes beyond John Fowles's is that this position is placed in question in her novel to a far greater extent than it ever is in his. For all of the additional cultural material from Freud, Marx and the twentieth century that Fowles consciously imports in constructing his narrative, the view, the fixed direction of the male gaze on the woman as object, remains unaltered from start to finish. Sarah disappears and only re-enters the story when she is 'found' at the end of Smithson's quest for her. But Dr Curran's view does *not* exclusively determine the narrative of *The Ante-Room*. Kate O'Brien's novel offers more than one perspective. Her conscious textual quotations and references are not reinforcements of a dominant patriarchal position but multiple questionings. In the scene where Curran proposes to Agnes, the obstacle that she represents to granting his request is described as 'nothing': 'It's only a maggot in my brain' (75) (coincidentally the title of a later Fowles novel). Curran confidently declares that he will 'cure' her condition. But this claim is undermined by an earlier passage which reveals that 'in the dark regions of her essential self he had no light by which to grope' (59).

In these exchanges, the novel goes beyond signalling the limits of Dr Curran's understanding to developing its sense of Agnes Mulqueen. What prevents her from accepting the offer of marriage from an eligible suitor is 'nothing' that can readily be put into words or described in conventional terms. The relation of Agnes to Dr Curran reveals the extent to which *The Ante-Room* is anything but the conventional romance it has sometimes been taken as, the extent to which it challenges rather than indulges the romanticism with which it engages:

> 'It was no part of my plan to fall in love with a *femme fatale!*' How angry his voice had been! Sane he might be and adult and all the rest of it, but he was fool enough to make a *femme fatale* of her. How long ago it seemed since he had said it — that almost irresistible phrase! (122-3)

By quoting from and commenting upon Curran's discourse, Agnes appropriates and reverses the relationship of power it is seeking to exert upon her. She also exposes the image of the *femme fatale* as something constructed, male. But finally she admits its attraction, that it is almost irresistible, that it offers her a flattering image which she is encouraged to imitate. In the immediate context, the fatal attraction of Agnes as *femme fatale* is countered by the discussion of James's *Washington Square,* where she resists being drawn into characterising Catherine Sloper negatively as uncharming and non-frivolous. Any identification between Agnes and a heroine in a novel will never entirely work or match up, however, since the beginning of *The Ante-Room* makes clear how little Agnes's experience can be identified with the lives she has read about in novels:

> She sometimes reflected coldly upon the unrelated phases of her life, through which the only unifying thread was Marie-Rose. The lives she read about in novels were not like that. There one thing always led to another, whereas what struck her about her own span of experience was that no section of it seemed to have offered preparation or warning for the next. (9)

This passage, at the very beginning, explicitly raises and confronts the issue as to what kind of novel Kate O'Brien's *The Ante-Room* is. As I have tried to suggest through the extended comparison with John Fowles, it offers a fully-fledged revision and subversion of the classic English nineteenth-century novel (another more recent comparison would be with Angela Carter's 1985 novel, *Nights at the Circus,* set in 1899 and offering a more theoretically feminist re-reading of the same terrain). Crucial to O'Brien's procedures is the lack of alignment between the plotted outcome and the dilemma of her central character. The conventional closure of a marriage, in which the heroine's desire is reconciled with the social order, is resisted throughout *The Ante-Room*. Agnes's attraction to her sister's husband must remain adulterous, since she is living in a country where then, as now, the possibility of divorce is not available. Agnes *does* receive an offer of marriage and is likely to consent to it; but neither she nor the reader is left in any doubt as to the degree of compromise and self-betrayal involved for her in such a (re)solution.

The novel takes its title from a statement by Vincent O'Regan, when he is buoyed by 'expectancy' over his desire for Agnes. "Today is an ante-room," he said dreamily' (213), and reflects later that all of the 'useful abstracts' to which the doors lead are incarnated for him in Agnes. 'And she was all of them' (236). But when the ante-room is more truthfully applied to Agnes, it serves as metaphor for her dilemma in the novel, on the threshold of a variety of male discourses, with no proper place of her own. The most striking use of an ante-room as symbolic locus for a young Irish woman is presented by O'Brien's near-contemporary Elizabeth Bowen early in her novel of 1929, *The Last September*, when her heroine Lois is discovered there:

> Personally, she [Lois] liked the ante-room, though it wasn't the ideal place to read or talk. Four rooms opened off it; at any moment a door might be opened, or blow open . . . People passed through it continually, so that one kept having to look up and smile. Yet Lois always seemed to be talking there, standing with a knee on a chair because it was not worth while to sit down, and her life was very much complicated by not knowing how much of what she said had been overheard, or by whom, or how far it would go.[7]

Much has been made of the differences between Kate O'Brien and Elizabeth Bowen in relation to their different social and religious traditions (Catholic Irish, Protestant Anglo-Irish). And yet I sense in passages like the above the common features of a shared dilemma confronted by Irish women writers undertaking a novel in the late 1920s and early 1930s. *The Last September* is one of only two Bowen novels set in Ireland rather than England, as *Washington Square* is a rare fictional excursion by Henry James into his native America rather than the European social scene. The figure of the ante-room raises the metaphoric place of a woman writer in the Irish house of fiction. It raises also the question of the narrative structure their Irish heroines are going to inhabit.

Agnes, as a member of a well-to-do Catholic family, is in certain respects well placed, since her class is the one that is going to succeed historically in the fifty years between its setting of the 1880s and writing of the 1930s. But Kate O'Brien is at one with the other writers of the 1930s in writing about and diagnosing the failure of a revolution, the betrayal of the promise of Ireland to gain a full and meaningful independence. She is distinctive in bringing her political critique to bear on the exclusion, not of the Six Counties, but of women from that promised liberation. Hence *The Ante-Room's* inversion between what constitutes normative politics, with the men referring to Parnell, Captain Boycott, the Land League, and so on, and what is normally excluded by such talk: the sexual politics of the household.

On the surface, Roseholm would appear to indicate a matriarchy (Mul*queens*). The father, away from his business and at home, is a mere shadow, shuffling around, given to muttering clichés and consoling phrases. The dominant figures in the household are mother and daughter, the dying Teresa and the living Agnes. But their centrality is more apparent than real, in a novel where superficial unity serves as a mask for underlying separateness and difference. Agnes cannot draw close to her mother because of a similarity of character and because she has to function as Teresa's living counterpart in the daily running of Roseholm, while her mother's spiritual needs are attended to by Sister Emmanuel and her physical ailments by Nurse Cunningham. This leaves Teresa free to prefer and to idealise Marie-Rose as her true daughter. But even allowing for such personal differences as the distaste Agnes feels towards the calculating nurse, the differences have more to do with an attraction towards and a dependence upon male power. In this regard, Teresa Mulqueen and Nurse Cunningham represent the most idealised and the most material or bodily extremes. The main reason why either Agnes or Mr Mulqueen has trouble communicating with the dying Teresa is that her own gaze is fixed on her son, Reggie. Teresa Mulqueen is denied access to the larger world of power in which her husband participates. He enjoys the added benefit of working for his wife's family firm, the

Considines; so that he inherits his position by marriage to his wife.

It is in the wasting away of Teresa's body that her symbolic power is greatest and that she is able to induce guilt for the denial of that body for so long. The classic compensation in Irish Catholic terms is the woman's withdrawal from the husband after marriage and the transfer to the son, the male body over whom she may (as mother) exercise power. The Oedipal nature of the relations between husband, wife, mother and son in the Mulqueen family is explicitly identified from the start in the husband's 'jealous(y) of the lifted look that Reggie could bring to the tortured woman's face, and he could not' (9). In her final delirium, Teresa addresses her husband as her son and imagines that she is giving birth to Reggie all over again, endlessly re-enacting the role to which she has been confined. Only when Nurse Cunningham agrees to take her place can Teresa bear to relinquish her lifeline. Her motherhood has served as cover and denial of Reggie's sexual delinquencies. The syphilis in turn means that Nurse Cunningham will marry him mostly in name, and come to enjoy the property; that she will in effect continue as mother and minder to him, and that the patriarchal order will thus be saved and sustained.

Agnes appears to enjoy a position of power and authority in Roseholm: by seeing to the running of everyday affairs, by being the one with whom Curran consults about Teresa, by effectively presiding at table. But as with Ibsen's Rebecca West in *Rosmersholm*, the position is more apparent than real. In both dramas, as Deirdre Madden writes of *The Ante-Room*, 'the great power . . . lies in the contrast between external appearances and internal realities'.[8] The bourgeois surface is exposed to reveal a stark condition of impossibility for the woman. She is posited between a sacrifice of her integrity to the espousal of patriarchal power or a willing consignment to the void of non-being. The role which Agnes is forced to play is doubly displaced, since she has taken it over from her dying mother, who in turn exercises it on behalf of the male Mulqueens. A much greater exacerbation for Agnes is the split between the surface tranquillity and unity of the household role she plays, where she is construed as 'steady and level and good' (233), and the inner desires by which she is riven, grief for her mother and desire for Vincent. The relationship with

Vincent is probably the most problematic of the novel, mainly because in Agnes's desire for her sister's husband and the narrative developments it raises, *The Ante-Room* would seem to come closest to a conventional romance. But this would be to deny and dismiss the legitimacy of romantic fiction to a cultural feminist analysis, and also to ignore how it is one of the discourses mobilised and explored by the novel, as my analysis has sought to show. Such a view would seek to deny the presence and reality of female desire (by construing it as romance), and to suppress the physical in the economy of exchange, as Agnes herself has tried to do: 'She was frightened by her need to touch that hand; she was terrified to think that to-night, in its flesh, it would lie within her reach' (34). When Agnes goes to bed that night, she does so in 'a mixed state of pity and desire', with her feeling for Vincent verbally acknowledged as desire. Two powerful forces stand in the way of the realisation of her desire. One is her allegiance to the Catholic Church. The other is her profound attachment to her sister Marie-Rose, the object of the 'pity' that complicates and confounds her desire for Vincent.

By basing its structure on the three successive feast-days of the Eve and Feast of All Saints, and the Feast of All Souls, *The Ante-Room* derives a structure from the rituals of the Catholic Church and so provides a challenge to the inherited plot structures, of the nineteenth-century English novel. The marriage that it looks forward to is not envisioned primarily in terms of the external social order. Rather it points towards an inner struggle that has more to do with inherited forms of belief and a search for spiritual self-realisation. The problem faced by Agnes in bringing herself to attend Confession is akin to that faced by Stephen Dedalus: how to translate her conflicted desires into language. Agnes's 'final fear was of words' (81); and their capacity to deny and misrepresent her lived experience; after Confession, she concludes that 'she was not herself. She was part of a formula' (84). Joyce and Stephen's iconoclastic engagement with Catholicism is to forge a counter-ritual to the imperium of the English language and the English novel. The danger for Joyce has to be faced in turn by O'Brien: that such a move may simply replace one oppressive colonising empire with another, the British with the Roman. But Catholicism is the language in which Agnes Mulqueen has been schooled and as an Irish woman she, like her author, is driven both to draw on that powerful tradition and to subvert it. The act of confession provides her with some relief; but the solution is only a temporary one. A gap remains and is finally seen as a failure of translation, between the words of consolation offered by the Church and the language of her human needs and heart.

Externally, Catholicism would appear to provide the language and structure of the novel's resolution. The concentrated prayer of the Mulqueen household, to which Agnes has contributed, has been asking for a miracle; and this miracle is effected by the proposed marriage between Reggie and Nurse Cunningham which enables Teresa to die. Confronted with the news, Agnes can only whisper: 'I think it's horrible' (295); and she feels absolutely excluded from the tableau that forms around Teresa's bed: 'They are all alive, even Mother. But I'm dying' (301). Nowhere more than in this conclusion is *The Ante-Room*'s mordant and unrelenting hollowing-out of its structures more apparent. The form of the 'miracle' has been achieved at the climax: but the result is a hollow parody, a triumph of the letter of the law (of the father) over the spirit of the vanished Agnes, the excluded other.

The prohibition placed by both the Church and the State is not, finally, that which interposes between Agnes and Vincent. As she reveals in their last meeting: 'I would never be *safe* from sin just because you're married – . . . And whatever the law is, it doesn't matter a scrap to me that I'm your wife's sister - ' (263). The novel has a great deal to say about displaced desire, about how actual relationships are shadowed by the ghosts of others. Teresa may be married but much of what should have been channelled towards her husband is redirected towards her son. And in the encounter between Agnes and Vincent, two other persons are present: Marie-Rose, in the double relation of wife and sister; and Vincent's own mother. It turns out that his actual wife is only a screen for Vincent's unresolved Oedipal attachment to his mother, a subtler version of that between Teresa and Reggie. He still needs his mother as someone to give substance to his dreams, to embody them. The key characterisation of Vincent is as 'a dreamer' (101). Agnes comes to see that what he has represented for her through their imagined liaison is a fantasy, a dream of escape from the conditions of their actual existence into some country where they could live together.

Given her dissatisfaction with the conditions of Ireland in the 1880s, it is tempting for Agnes to imagine such a future and such a state of possibility. Her final statement that it is 'impossible' not only acknowledges an affair with Vincent as a fantasy, as a flight from the conditions in which she must live and which must be transformed, but discloses it as a male fantasy. She recognises the doubleness by which both she and Marie-Rose are substituting for Vincent's mother and that all three beautiful women 'gave an unsought chance to give reality to dreams' of another life (102). Agnes's rejection of this male-oriented narcissistic realm is enabled through her sister, Marie-Rose, and the betrayal of her such an act would represent. Not that her sister would thank her, as Vincent is quick to point out. But Agnes is finally doing it for herself, asserting a sisterly allegiance that is not finally reducible or answerable to the demands of either biology or family.

When Vincent O'Regan commits suicide, his final vision is of the longed-for union with the image of his mother: 'Darling mother. He pulled the trigger, his thoughts far off in boyhood' (306). Agnes and Marie-Rose enjoyed their happiest period in childhood and Agnes's final decision might seem a parallel retreat for her, following Vincent into the consolations of nostalgia and fantasy. But to the end Agnes refuses to simplify her conflicted emotions, the 'pity' for Marie-Rose and the 'desire' for Vincent. Her final words resist the easy resolution of death and as a final statement are broken off, incomplete. Throughout *The Ante-Room* we have been told how inadequate words and language are to representing the truth of the central character.

The novel and its heroine draw close to and draw upon a wide variety of discourses – the traditional English and Anglo-Irish nineteenth-century novel, the rituals and prayers of Catholicism, the construction of woman as m/other or *femme fatale*, without being drawn into and dominated by any of them. None of them are adequate to representing Agnes Mulqueen. The final effect of her exclusion from a series of interrelating systems which she is forced to endure makes a nonsense of the conventional happy ending. In leaving so painfully open and unresolved the question of what is to become of Agnes Mulqueen in the future, *The Ante-Room* raises the question of the place of woman in the Irish context as the most urgent and troubling of personal, literary and political issues. As a novel of endless re-reading, it shows how that question can only be addressed by submitting the prevailing discourses to the scrutiny of what they have misrepresented and excluded. Agnes Mulqueen does not commit suicide; she does not go away. She re-enters the Mulqueen household as a silent living witness of what it is trying to deny, a continuing rebuke and contradiction of the consensus secured by a supposed miracle.

## Notes and references

1  'She was, as long as I knew her, an agnostic, but a "Catholic agnostic", as the Dublin saying goes.' Lorna Reynolds, *Kate O'Brien: A Literary Portrait*, Irish Literary Studies No. 25, (Gerrards Cross, Bucks, Colin Smythe, 1987), p. 118.

2  John Fowles, *The French Lieutenant's Woman* (1968), London, Picador, 1992. All page references are to this edition and will be cited in parentheses at the end of subsequent references in the text.

3  Kate O'Brien, *The Ante-Room*, London, Virago, 1989, p. 55. All page references are to this edition and will be cited in parentheses at the end of subsequent references in the text.

4  Reynolds, *Kate O'Brien*, p. 56.

5  ibid., p. 57.

6  Henrik Ibsen, *Plays: Three*, trans. and introd. by Michael Meyer, London, Methuen, 1980, p. 101.

7  Elizabeth Bowen, *The Last September*, London, Penguin, 1987, p. 9.

8  Deirdre Madden, 'Afterword', in O'Brien, *The Ante-Room*, p. 309.

*Chapter 6*

# 'The Business of Attachment' Romance and Desire in the Novels of Kate O'Brien

*Anne Fogarty*

In an essay reviewing the work of George Eliot, Kate O'Brien comes to the, at first glance, surprising conclusion that 'it is in the nature of the idea of a novel that it be imperfect, unsatisfactory.'[1] On these grounds, she announces that the 'unreadable' *Romola* is her favourite work by this English writer. It is its awkwardness which for Kate O'Brien constitutes its primary charm. While her reassessment of George Eliot is in itself refreshing and full of insight, her arguments acquire a further resonance if one considers the extent to which they may be read as self-commentary.

The literary output of Kate O'Brien, as this essay will argue, is of interest because of its flawed and hybrid character. Her novels are compelling because they are misshapen, open-ended and lacunary. It is their imperfect meshing of the conventions of women's romance with social critique which leaves the reader both with an impression of the probing acuity of O'Brien's fictions and also with an abiding sense of their imbalance. In entering the literary domain of Kate O'Brien, one makes the acquaintance of a social world permanently out of kilter and at odds with itself.

101

Yet the author seems as intent on commemorating the pretensions and prejudices of this unaccomodating world as on unmasking them. Just as James Joyce may be said never to have left Dublin behind him, so too Kate O'Brien appears to be tied eternally to Mellick, the refashioned Limerick of her imagination. In the main, her protagonists define themselves in opposition to the stifling and conventional Irish society from which they stem. It is the purpose, then, of this essay to examine both the formal and thematic tensions in Kate O Brien's novels. My exploration will indicate that these conflicts are at once enabling and inhibiting. Her characters shape themselves through a quarrel with their social environment. In particular they are given impetus to question received values, due on the one hand to the cleft between their familial identity and their private longings and desires and on the other to the divergence between their vocation and their *Bildung* or moral growth. Very few, however, succeed in progressing beyond these conflicts which define them. Escape lies in an indeterminate sphere at which the texts can only gesture. Like Rose in *As Music and Splendour,* O'Brien's central figures are often left in the closing moments of her novels in a 'polite twilight', torn between their private unease with the world and their need for the security and happiness of human fellowship.[2] In the end neither vocation nor *Bildung* provides a satisfactory answer to the restless desire which impels them.

In his analysis of the particular propensities of the novel as a mode of writing, Edward Said isolates two important moments. He argues that in its early history the novel is marked by a concern with beginnings and with continuity.[3] Thus, many traditional plots trace the progress of the hero in the light of his origins and birthright. In works such as *Tom Jones* and *Great Expectations,* relationships between fathers and sons act as a means of indicating the trajectory of the central protagonist's development. Genealogy and patrimony function as the principal axes around which these narratives are organised. Indeed, in both of these instances the final identification of the hero's father or paternal benefactor becomes a mark of closure. However, in its second phase, according to Said, the novel becomes preoccupied not with filiation, that is the passing of identity and power from father to son, but with what he terms the rule of the brother.

Instead of hierarchy and progression modern narratives are typified by disjunction and adjacency. In the reading of Kate O'Brien's writing which this essay will propose, it will be suggested that her work conforms in part to these two fundamental patterns identified by Said. Her novels may indeed be seen as beginning fictions, but they also strive to find an alternative to the founding but imprisoning myths of family. For many of her heroines emotional salvation is found in what Giacomo in *As Music and Splendour* refers to as 'coldness' and 'sisterliness' (175). The debilitating and oppressive structures of feeling fostered by the family are dislodged by acts of renunciation. They are undermined too by the discovery of the more sustaining and nurturing relationships which can exist between consanguine and sisterly selves.

As many critics have noted, O'Brien's work furnishes us with some of the first fictional representations of the *mores* and emotional dilemmas of the Irish Catholic middle class in independent Ireland. Moreover, like a *Möbius* strip, her entire *oeuvre* folds back on itself. Her first novel, *Without My Cloak,* which provides us with an almost Galsworthyan portrayal of the fortunes of three generations of a provincial but none the less ambitious Mellick dynasty is complemented by her final finished piece of writing, namely her autobiographical account of her childhood and of the history of her family in *Presentation Parlour.* Thus, however much the author may question the emotional constraints of domestic life, the family romance remains an abiding theme of her work. As my later discussion will show, O'Brien's involvement with family structures may be seen not only as an attempt on her part to explore the plight of women who are fated to be trapped in domestic relations but also as a reflection of the particular historical era in which these texts were produced. The familism of her novels acts as a commentary on the closed and hierarchical nature of Irish society in the initial decades of the Free State.[4] It is depicted at once as a resource and an impediment. Martin Kernahan in *The Last of Summer* comments that Ireland is 'Heaven's ante-room'.[5] For O'Brien this intermediary and dilatory state which sums up the insularity of Irish cultural and political life is paralleled by that zone of suspension in which many of her chief protagonists find themselves. Divided between thought and action and between passion and ascetic withdrawal they too seem forever caught in an ante-chamber of existence. Within terms of the narratives in which they feature, they are torn between the *fabula* of Irish socialisation and the *sjužet* of their own quest for freedom and self-determination. The plot of desire never releases them from the story of the family romance.[6]

Kate O'Brien's novels may be described as a fusion of the conventions of romance and realism. Uncomfortably, they straddle these two modes. While they generally outline the moral progress of a central protagonist on the road from innocence to maturity, they ultimately refuse fully to accede to the rules of coherence and transparency which underwrite the structures of the *Bildungsroman* and of the romance novel. It is in overlaying these two modes of fiction and writing beyond the customary endings associated with them that O'Brien highlights the perennial dissatisfaction of her principal characters in their quest to redefine their identities. In addition, by bringing the *Bildungsroman*, a literary genre which is a product of high culture, into contact with women's romance, a form of popular fiction, O'Brien creates an idiosyncratic literary space of her own. The eclectic web of intertextual references which pattern her texts indicate the alternating allegiances of their author. *The Last of Summer* is, for example, punctuated by references on the one hand to the poetry of Baudelaire and Racine's *Phèdre,* and on the other to Margaret Mitchell's best-selling novel *Gone with the Wind.* Similarly, *The Ante-Room* contains allusions to the sensation novels of Mary Elizabeth Braddon, Henry James's *Washington Square*, and the music of Schubert. Mary Lavelle, for her part, is as much altered by her attendance at a Spanish bullfight as she is by her visit to the Prado museum. O'Brien's novels seem to draw indiscriminately and wilfully on a self-constructed artistic canon, thereby ignoring any traditional separation of so-called high art from the domain of popular entertainment. While allusions to specific works are ultimately used in order to pinpoint the social pretensions and aspirations of a particular character, the free-ranging references to a wide variety of cultural artefacts and events in O'Brien's novels indicate the decentred and often oppositional nature of her leading figures.[7] If, as Georg Lukács argues, the novel depicts the world in terms of the 'transcendental homelessness' of its protagonists,

then the struggle on the part of her characters to define themselves
in relation to a shifting and varied cultural legacy may be seen
in part as an indication of their spiritual neediness, inchoateness,
and lack of fixity.[8] However, it must also be recognised that
their responsiveness to aesthetic experience acts as an index of
their middle-class sensibilities and their concomitant need to embrace what Moretti refers to as the 'comfort of civilization'.[9]
While their ability to judge and think for themselves helps them
to extricate themselves from a society which they find too con-
fining, the ambition which propels them is an emanation of their
Irish middle-class milieu.

It is her use of the conventions of women's romance that constitutes the most unsettling aspect of Kate O'Brien's novels.
However, Nicola Beauman suggests why this mode of writing
is a necessary aspect of her portrayal of women's lives. In employing the familiar strategies of popular romance, O'Brien is signalling
her allegiance with the traditions of women's writing.[10] The
very marginality of the romance which is frequently dismissed
as a trivial form of mass entertainment for women allows her to
create a literary ante-room of her own which is outside of and
in part runs counter to the literary mainstream.[11] In daring to
compose those apparently 'silly' novels which George Eliot was
so quick to dismiss, O'Brien thus is putting into effect her belief
that lack of orthodoxy is one of the qualities of the novel which
may be of advantage to the writer.[12] More importantly, her
adoption of the romance enables her to broach those themes which
have been its perennial concerns. Foremost amongst these is the
problem of female desire. As Bridget Fowler points out, traditional
romance narratives trace the difficulties of co-ordinating the requirements of family alliance with the uncertainties of desire.[13]
In the end, sexuality must be brought into alignment with the
social imperatives which dictate how family names and wealth
should be circulated. Hence typical romances depict the quest of
lovers to overcome the obstacles to marriage or the restoration
of order once a threat to family harmony has been removed. In
addition, while they explore the difficulties caused by female
dependency, they ultimately bow to the necessity of their subordination. The recalcitrant and resistant Pamela, for example, docile-
ly marries Mr B. at the end of Richardson's novel and promises

faithfully to accept his authority. Jane Eyre's search for autonomy is also curtailed and abandoned in favour of the higher good of marriage to Mr Rochester.[14] Indeed, marriage may be said to function as the ultimate indicator of resolution and of narrative closure in romance novels. No matter how much they may probe women's anxieties and sexual fantasies, romances finally subscribe to the patriarchal stereotypes of the passive and submissive heroine and of the active and dominant hero.

The inherent conservatism of the romance is a problematic aspect of this genre. It remains the most vexed topic of debate in recent investigations which set out to establish why the romantic novel continues to fascinate women readers and to satisfy their imaginative needs. The ideological freighting of this mode of fiction seems to preclude any attempt on the part of the author to rewrite the heroine's plot, which issues inevitably in self-abnegation and surrender. In short, there appears to be little likelihood that romantic fiction could accomodate any counter-hegemonic tendencies. However, feminist reappraisals of the genre have modified this view in important ways. Both Tania Modleski and Cora Kaplan argue that the reactionary politics of the romance is often undermined, or at least partially opened up to question by a 'concealed order' in the text which reveals various unresolved conflicts and intransigent problems.[15] They also point to the way in which romances act as wish-fulfilment fantasies. Their plots enable women to resolve the problems and banish the dangers to which they are exposed in patriarchal society. Thus, for example, male brutality is converted from a sign of contempt to one of love in romantic fiction.[16] The abrasive and violent hero is transformed into a reassuring and desirable lover in the end.

Bridget Fowler assesses the transformative powers of the romance in the light of Ernst Bloch's account of the social function of works of art.[17] For Bloch literature never simply panders to ideological interests. He claims that it always contains in addition a 'cultural surplus'.[18] This surplus he sees as an indication of the utopian appeal of art. Like the daydream, literature for him produces anticipatory images of world-improvement.[19] In such a reading, the romance may be deemed not just to act out oppressive fantasies but also aspirations. In the interpretation which follows of the novels produced by Kate O'Brien during the initial phase of her career, namely *The Ante-Room, Mary Lavelle,* and *The Last of Summer,* it will be proposed that she has recourse to the mode of romance not only because it allows her to depict the predicament of women and the immobilising effect of female social roles, but also because it furnishes her with a literary form which may be used to voice an anticipatory desire for change. While her heroines rarely succeed in remoulding themselves completely or in locating a solution to the predicament in which they find themselves, they derive consolation from that ante-room or forward-looking space of longing in which they find themselves. It remains crucial to the contradictions of O'Brien's texts, however, that this anticipatory space of desire shares aspects of the false enclosure of romance. Her protagonists are left poised between entrapment and escape. Utopianism, as Bridget Fowler reflects, is not synonymous with subversion.[20]

Kate O'Brien's first novel, *Without My Cloak,* contains her most despairing account of the family romance.[21] It is also her most traditional novel, issuing as it does in that conventional sign of narrative resolution, namely the announcement of the prospective marriage of the hero. For Freud, the family romance describes the divided emotions of children who are torn between regard for and hatred of their parents.[22] These contradictory responses are, in the Freudian view, a direct legacy of the conflicts involved in the Oedipus complex. He argues that this ambivalence manifests itself in revenge fantasies about their parents and siblings in which children act out their sexual rivalries. These negative romances compete in their imaginations with positive images which seek to aggrandise and elevate the family. Ultimately, for Freud, this process of overvaluation continues during adulthood and remains the means by which antagonistic feelings generated during the Oedipus complex are held in check.

*Without My Cloak* is a beginning fiction which chronicles the gradual rise to prosperity of the Considine family. The novel provides us both with an admiring account of their emotional unity and material wealth and a critical portrait of the sacrifices exacted by this imperious dynasty. Just as the Shakespearian sonnet from which the novel derives its title implies that anger and emotional pain may be converted and contained, so too the embittered conflicts which score the history of the Considines are suppressed and allayed. The plot concentrates on the relationship between fathers and sons. The account of Honest John's love for his son Anthony is matched in turn by the story of Anthony's obsession with his son Denis. Thus, O'Brien suggests that the family romance is a means by which male power is promoted and sustained. Although this paternal rule is shown to be vulnerable and corrupt, none the less it succeeds in perpetuating itself. The Oedipal bond which unites father to son by virtue of their shared power supersedes all other ties. Even the frictions which occur between them appear simply to reinforce these links. Consequently, the novel ends with a reinstatement of the myth of the family romance with its blinding insistence on univocality and harmony: 'Anthony stared at his son; his brilliant eyes blazed love on him'(469). Denis, the object of his approving gaze, has, by falling in love with Anna Hennessy, the daughter of a local magnate, brought the family romance into alignment with the potentially aberrant plot of private desire. In the closing moments, the demands of passion and the dictates of the family concur.

However, the novel suggests that the continuous relay of paternal love and power is achieved only at great cost. The story of the family romance suppresses and overrides all of the plots of desire which run counter to it. *Without My Cloak* abounds in tales which cannot be told. These unspoken or impeded plots revolve around the unfulfilled hopes of various subsidiary female characters and of the solitary homosexual figure in this family circle. All of these secondary personae prove the otherness of their desire by sacrificing themselves. While they strain against social and sexual norms, they ultimately insist on self-restraint rather than abandonment. Thus, Molly resigns herself to the burden of numerous pregnancies in exchange for her improper enjoyment of the sexual pleasures of marital love and Caroline resists the temptation of a passionate liaison with Richard by ceding to 'her filial and maternal and herd instincts' (194) which demand that she return to a loveless marriage in Mellick. Similarly, Eddy sacrifices his love for Richard in an attempt to rescue his sister from her despair while Christina forgoes her love for Denis in order to save him from public opprobrium. The desire that 'dare not speak its name' and which refuses to fit into the linear and orderly patterns of the heterosexual and patriarchal family romance is associated by Kate O'Brien in *Without My Cloak* with self-denial and unspokenness.[23] As the following discussion will show, reticence and asceticism continue to be its enduring features in her later novels, but these qualities slowly acquire a more disruptive and also more positive force. Eve Kosofsky Sedgwick, in her exploration of literary representations of gay and lesbian identity, notes that they are founded as much on silence as on open declaration and admission.[24] She concludes that these silences play as pointed a role in contributing to the epistemology of the closet as any enuciations made about the nature of same-sex love. Desire in *Without My Cloak* is depicted in terms of revelation and censorship. The transgressive longing of all of the figures whose actions imperil the continuity of the family romance is ultimately silenced and cloaked. While the actions of self-renunciation may endow these marginal characters with a momentary power they are in the end immured in the negative space assigned to them by the family. Molly dies in childbirth, Christina chooses unhappy exile in New York, while Caroline and Eddy live on in a state of permanent unrest and dissatisfaction. The plot of desire produces either rupture or narratives which resist the pat endings of the family romance.

Kate O'Brien's next novel, *The Ante-Room,* which was published in 1934, represents an important revision and deformation of the beginning fiction of the family romance.[25] Indeed, as my examination will show, all of the works produced during the initial phase of her writing career attempt to disrupt and dislocate the patriarchal power inscribed in the novel of filiation. The story of domination and surrender is now counterposed and challenged by an anti-Oedipal story of defiance and escape. The family becomes now not an inevitable destination but a point of departure.[26] Moreover, the focus shifts from the hierarchical relationships between fathers and sons to the interdependencies and mutuality of siblings, lovers, and cousins. Sexual dissidence and the transgressions of desire become linked not with difference and domination but with sameness and adjacency.[27] In *The Ante-Room* the reader encounters a family in disarray. It is presided over by the dying Teresa Mulqueen and her ineffectual husband. Teresa's fatal illness and her obsessive love of her syphilitic son Reggie are emblematic of the life-destroying effects of the family romance.

In opposition to this rigid and deadly linearity we are introduced
to a plot of desire which focuses on Agnes Mulqueen, the daughter
who has been condemned to act as caretaker of the family in lieu
of her mother. Agnes bears many of the hallmarks of the heroine
who becomes a recurrent figure in Kate O'Brien's later novels.
Restless and beautiful, her progress is mapped out in terms of her
transgressive and doomed love for her brother-in-law, Vincent
O'Regan. Thus, the heroine's desire defiantly resists the demands
of the family romance which stipulates that love must end in marriage. Agnes herself reflects on her own sense of incoherence. She
realises that the 'private wound' (p. 9) of love from which she
is suffering constitutes an anti-narrative:

> Still, in the hour of waking, she sometimes reflected coldly upon the
> unrelated phases of her life, through which the only unifying thread
> was Marie-Rose. The lives she read about in novels were not like that.
> There one thing always led to another, whereas what struck her about
> her own span of experience was that no section of it seemed to have
> offered preparation or warning for the next. (p. 9)

The discontinuity of Agnes's life is an index both of her powerlessness and of her strength. Because of the impropriety of her
love, her story, it is intimated, cannot be told. Her internal conflicts can be rehearsed and momentarily exposed but they do not
permit of resolution. In the climactic scene at the end of the novel
in which Agnes describes her feelings to Vincent, it becomes clear
that one of the reasons why she can never act on her desire for
him is because it is entangled with her equally passionate love for
her sister. The initial sisterly bond supplants any later attempts at
liaison. Similarly, Vincent's passion for Agnes turns out to have
a double basis. He cross-associates his love for her with his devotion to his mother. He portrays this interweaving of emotion
as follows:

> "The only way I can explain mother to you," he said, "is this. She used
> to make me feel something that you do too – a kind of finality of ap-
> preciation – a stillness, as if her mere being alive justified everything.
> It's a lovely, cool sensation, and though it's love, I suppose, it had nothing
> to do with the other feeling, of wanting to touch you". (p. 254)

Like Agnes, Vincent too is torn between the 'finality' of the family romance and the turbulence of desire. However, unlike him,

she succeeds in locating a mode of affection which perpetuates rather than destroys desire. Indeed, it is intimated that the bond which links her with her sister saves her from the limitations of what she terms 'the business of attachment' (255). Moreover, it is also evident that her heterosexual passion for him is a displaced version of the equally vibrant desire which she feels for Marie-Rose. Her loyalty to her sister allows her to discover what Marilyn Farwell describes as the 'disruptive space of sameness'.[28] Vincent's love, by contrast, is depicted as regressive and death-dealing. It issues inevitably in his suicide, which proves to be a parodic re-enactment of the Oedipal bonds of the family romance: 'Darling mother. He smiled. He could see every detail of her smile. Darling mother. He pulled the trigger, his thoughts far off in boyhood' (p. 306).

It is striking that *The Ante-Room* redistributes the endings which typify the traditional novel. The two competing fates of death or marriage which usually round out the heroine's plot are assigned in this instance to men.[29] While Vincent commits suicide, Reggie is saved by the promise of marriage to Nurse Cunningham. However, while Agnes evades the conventionalities of the heroine's text, she is left in an indeterminate space of unrelenting and painful longing: '"Du bist die Ruh," Marie-Rose sang under her breath. Agnes thought: They are all alive, even Mother. But I'm dying. Vincent, if I could only die – oh, Vincent, darling –' (p. 301). The romantic yearning of the song by Schubert silently sung by Marie-Rose in the above passage in which the singer wishes to be subsumed into her lover's identity is dispelled by the excessive effects of passion in the Considine household.[30] Agnes's survival must ultimately be seen as a dubious victory. The desire which saves her puts her back in the stranglehold of the family. She escapes the finality of Vincent's fate but remains trapped in the 'irrelevancy' (p. 201) of the domestic sphere and of daily life in Mellick. Vincent at least can have recourse to action, albeit a negative and self-cancelling one. His *Bildung* propels him to carry out a concrete deed in the external world whilst hers confines her inside herself.[31] The plot of her inner development is a circular one. While the novel grants her an ante-room for her desire, it does not permit her any agency beyond a self-denying gesture of love.

*Mary Lavelle* raises similar questions about the limitations of the heroine's power and the status of female sexuality. Like Agnes and Marie-Rose, Mary's potential for change and moral growth is linked problematically with her beauty and femininity. However, unlike the two earlier figures, Mary's *Bildung* comes about as a result of her ill-defined but nonetheless purposeful aim 'to be free and lonely' (p. 27). It is this inchoate ambition which rescues Mary from Mellick and the safety of marriage. However, her desire is set free by a reinstatement of the family romance. Mary swaps the narrowness of her domestic world in Ireland for the romance of the eminent and wealthy Areavaga family in Spain. Her job as a governess provides her with the 'tiny hiatus' or possibility to develop and grow. As her attachment to her fiancé John wanes to be replaced by her passion for Juanito, it becomes evident that her sojourn in this Spanish family allows her to act out the contradictory impulses of the family romance which Freud outlines.[32] The Spanish household proves to be in part a sublimated version of the home she has left behind and from which she wishes to escape. Her uncaring and narrow-minded father is replaced by the intellectual and sympathetic Don Pablo. Likewise, the forceful and sexually aggressive Juanito provides a counterweight to her feeble and asexual Irish lover. Moreover, the death of Don Pablo who passes away while Mary makes love to Juanito may be construed as a revenge fantasy. Not alone does Mary's new family create a space for her illicit desire, but it also enables her to act out her feelings of antagonism. Even the benign patriarch, Don Pablo, must be jettisoned to make way for her new-found passion. The anti-narrative of her desire, that 'lame and hopeless story' (p. 344) to which she refers in the final pages of the novel, undermines the structures of the family romance. Yet it does so by embracing another exotic version of this romance.

Her story, we are told, is 'as real as the bullfight' (p. 344). In admitting to her fascination with the bloody beauty of this latter event, Mary appears to appropriate the symbolic force of male violence in order to free herself. In this way, she escapes the fate of the traditional heroine. That androgyny which, we are told, is a peculiar aspect of her beauty, manifests itself also in her ability to use a male ritual of slaughter in order to remake herself. However, as in the case of Agnes Mulqueen, her struggle to free herself releases her into an indeterminate and ambiguous sphere. Her reshaping of her identity by means of her masochistic passion for Juanito makes it uncertain whether she can ever fully extricate herself from the imperious demands of patriarchy and of family structures. Her affections now centre not on her inadequate fiancé but on her dominant and aggressive lover. While she has escaped the dismal inevitabilities of bourgeois marriage, she appears to have submitted to an equally limiting version of the family romance in which power still remains in male hands. Mary's *Bildung*, like that of Agnes Mulqueen, seems as a consequence to involve a form of counter-investment. The novel ends with a description of her anticipatory mood of departure which is at the same time a gloomy realisation of the necessity for return. Mary travels back home with her 'brutal story' (p. 344). The question remains open as to whether the potent but contradictory fantasy of female desire outlined in the novel will succeed in dispelling the oppressive authority of the family romance.

Angèle Maury in *The Last of Summer* is the female protagonist in Kate O'Brien's early novels who succeeds most effectively in routing the family romance. Following the death of her parents, she pays a visit to her father's family in Mellick. By falling in love with Tom, her eldest cousin, and also awakening the devotion of Martin, his brother, Angèle finds herself caught up in the regressive and destructive cycles of the family romance. The seeming involutarism of her desire for Tom, we discover, is reinforced by the fact that it is a re-enactment of history. Just as her two cousins vie for her attentions in the present so too her uncles and her father fought in the past for the affections of her aunt, Hannah Kernahan. The latter in turn perpetuates the destructive regime of the family romance through her overprotective love for Tom, her eldest son. While it is clear that Angèle succumbs fully to the pleasurable attractions of the family idyll, she ultimately is able to give this immuring fate the slip.

Chief amongst the reasons enabling her to break away from the immobilising comforts of bourgeois life are her unfulfilled ambitions as an actress. Angèle is haunted throughout the novel by fragments from the heroine's speeches in Racine's *Phèdre*. However, the lines which she recalls from her mother's rehearsal of this play appear to support the view that female desire is

necessarily criminal and destructive. Thus, Angèle repeats Phèdre's
fatalistic premonition of her doomed love for her stepson,
Hippolyte: 'Athènes me montra mon superbe ennemi.' She also
intones Phèdre's admission of helplessness when it appears that
her illicit love will be discovered: 'Dans le trouble où je suis je
ne puis rien pour moi.'[33] Yet for Angèle the wish to play the part
of Phèdre, an ambition her mother was never able to fulfil,
distances her from the potentially tragic effects of the family
romance and of her own self-undermining desire. In *The Last of
Summer* the link is severed between female passion and patriarchal law. While it is suggested that a congruence between female
*Bildung* and desire will never be achieved, Angèle at least is given
the autonomy to escape the death-grip of the family and the
stagnation of a backward-looking and repressive Irish society. The
parting irony of the novel is that the place of refuge from the oppressions of the Irish family romance is a Europe poised on the
verge of war. The political crises of the summer of 1934 form
the backdrop to the narcissistic concerns of the family romance.
Angèle thus escapes from Mellick into the turmoil of history.
Unlike Mary Lavelle or Agnes Mulqueen, her bid for freedom
brings with it the reward of love as she is accompanied by her
anti-bourgeois cousin, Martin. The repetitive cycles and exactions
of family domination give way to the anticipatory celebration of
freedom and of anti-Oedipal relationships at the end of the text.
As with the heroines of the preceding novels by Kate O'Brien,
Angèle's future is uncertain. However, this indeterminacy the text
suggests is preferable to the suffocating security of her abandoned
dream of romantic love with Tom. *The Last of Summer* depicts the
dangerous attractions of the family romance for Angèle, but it
proves that the heroine is no longer fated to replicate her predis-
posed part in this fantasy. Momentarily at least, the conflicts between romance and desire and between *Bildung* and vocation
appear to have been resolved.

However, Angèle's escape seems as much to depend on the
vagaries of fate and the social prohibitions which prevent her marrying her first cousin as on any act of will of her own. Like Mary
Lavelle and Agnes Mulqueen, she breaks free from the family
romance only by submitting to its masochistic and self-denying
pleasures in full and then rejecting their considerable force and

allure. Thus, her love for Tom is described in terms of self-abnegation and submission: 'But now she was committed. She had pledged her love and faith, and if she was surprised by the peace that brimmed from a surrender so vast for her and so absurd, the surprise was only instinctive, for she was without experience' (p. 122). It appears to be their very lack of volition which is the salvation of Kate O'Brien heroines, rather than any internal strength which they can muster to rebel against a restrictive society. The purposeless, accidental and amoral nature of desire propels them beyond the scenarios in which it is enacted. The quandary for the reader remains that O'Brien's heroines realise themselves by capitulating to the fantasy of the family romance rather than by combating it actively. Its ability to transform them appears to parallel its power to enthrall and ensnare them. The account of their liberation is simultaneously the story of their entrapment.

O'Brien indicates that the closeted space of the family romance can become an ante-room or utopian space of longing. She harnesses the familiar stories of romance fiction in order to show how they occlude and in part contain those transgressive stories which run counter to them. As a consequence, the plot of desire remains always on the purlieu of the family romance. Its unspokenness and otherness mean that it can only be pointed to but never fully actualised. It is the strength of this plot that it falls through the net of narrative and occupies a space of resistance beyond the ending of the text. However, at the same time it is a sign of the resilience of the family romance that it foils any attempts to dislodge it. O'Brien is as much at pains to advertise its compelling force as to show how it might be counteracted. Her nostalgia for the comforts of civilisation and the pleasures of bourgeois family life rests uneasily with her wish to liberate her central female protagonists from the oppressive and destructive psychobiographies of romance.

Clare Halvey in *As Music And Splendour* appears to be the only Kate O Brien protagonist fully to escape the contradictory impulses of romance and desire. Her liaison with Luisa, a fellow opera singer, allows her to enjoy a relationship which is founded on sisterliness and proximity rather than difference and conflict. However, she too feels the countertow of her original identity:

One does not change, she thought, one does not escape. The heart grows and learns indeed - gladly, gladly, Luisa. But so do other parts of soul and thought and reason - and they grow as had been expected, along the taught and foreordained direction; not away and outward from sequestered life, as feeling, feeling in imperious charge insisted she must travel. And travel she did - she could do no other — yet so far, it seemed, without being able to get entirely out of sight of herself. (p. 253)

No matter how much Kate O'Brien's heroines succeed in dissociating themselves from the story of the Irish family romance, they remain lodged within its confines. Like Clare they can never manage to lose sight of themselves entirely. The business of attachment constantly thwarts their desire to break free and remake themselves. Their fates bespeak an impossible yearning for escape rather than an outright attempt at rebellion. In the end, the sentimental lure of 'the foreordained direction' of the family romance proves to be stronger than the 'imperious charge' of their private desire.

## Notes and references

1   Kate O'Brien, 'George Eliot: A Moralizing Fabulist', Sir George Rostrevor Hamilton (ed.), *Essays by Divers Hands, Transactions of the Royal Society of Literature,* Vol. 27, Oxford University Press, 1955, pp. 34–46, p. 41.
2   Kate O'Brien, *As Music and Splendour,,* London, Heinemann, 1958, p. 346.
3   Edward W. Said, *Beginnings: Intention and Method,* New York, Columbia University Press, 1985, pp. 83–188.
4   For an account of the cultural and political stagnation of Ireland in the early years of the New State, see Terence Brown, *Ireland: A Social and Cultural History 1922-1985,* London, Fontana, 1981, pp. 141–211.
5   Kate O'Brien, *The Last of Summer,* Dublin, Arlen House, 1982, p. 48. All further references to this text will be noted in parentheses.
6   For a discussion of the concepts of *fabula* (story) and *sjužet* (plot), see Peter Brooks, *Reading for the Plot: Design and Intention in Narrative.* Oxford, Clarendon Press, 1984, pp. 12–14. In the distinction proposed by Russian Formalist theory, the *fabula* is the order of events referred to by the narrative while the *sjužet* describes the order in which the reader becomes acquainted with these events in the text. Ultimately, as Brooks points out, it is only possible to infer the *fabula,* 'what really happened', from the text; it can never be known directly. However, at the same time there are points of coincidence between them. Franco Moretti argues, for example, that the endings of traditional mystery stories and of the plots of the classical

*Bildungsroman* allow for the convergence of the *sjužet* and *fabula* by resolving the problems which have dominated the narrative. See Franco Moretti, *The Way of the World: The Bildungsroman in European Culture*, London, Verso, 1987, p. 70.

7   Pierre Bourdieu argues that cultural taste is a means of stratifying societies. Taste thus becomes a measure of class status. However, my reading of Kate O'Brien proposes that taste may also be used as a way of rebelling against class and gender identity. See Pierre Bourdieu, *Distinction: A Social Critique of the Judgement of Taste,* Trans. Richard Nice, Cambridge, MA, Harvard University Press, 1984.

8   See Georg Lukács, *The Theory of the Novel,* trans. Anna Rostock, London, Merlin Press, 1978, pp. 60–2.

9   Moretti, *The Way of the World*, pp. 15–16.

10   See Nicola Beauman, *A Very Great Profession: The Woman's Novel 1914-39,* London, Virago, 1963, p. 1. Tellingly, Kate O'Brien is the starting point for Beauman's exploration of a forgotten history of women's fiction.

11   Many recent discussions of popular romance comment on the way in which it has been regarded as a suspect form of writing because it appears to act as a vehicle for oppressive female fantasies. See Tania Modleski, *Loving With a Vengeance: Mass-Produced Fantasies For Women*, London, Methuen, 1982, pp. 11–34. See also Diane Elam, *Romancing the Postmodern*, London, Routledge, 1992, pp. 1–25.

12   George Eliot, 'Silly Novels by Lady Novelists', Rosemary Ashton (ed.), *George Eliot: Selected Critical Writings,* Oxford University Press, 1992, pp. 296–321.

13   See Bridget Fowler, *The Alienated Reader: Women and Popular Romantic Literature in the Twentieth Century,* London, Harvester, 1991, pp. 7–8.

14   Samuel Richardson, *Pamela; Or, Virtue Rewarded,* ed. Peter Sabor, London, Penguin, 1980. Charlotte Brontë, *Jane Eyre,* ed. Q.D. Leavis, London, Penguin, 1966.

15   Modleski, *Loving with a Vengeance*, pp. 110–14. Cora Kaplan, '*The Thorn Birds:* Fiction, Fantasy, Femininity', in *Sea Changes: Culture and Feminism,* London, Verso, 1986, pp. 117–46.

16   For a discussion of the way in which the wish-fulfilment of romance 'inoculates' its female audience against the problems of patriarchy, see Modleski, *Loving with a Vengeance*, pp. 35–43.

17   Fowler, *The Alienated Reader*, pp. 45–8.

18   Ernst Bloch, *The Principle of Hope*, trans. Neville Plaice, Stephen Plaice, and Paul Knight, Oxford, Blackwell, 1986, vol. 1. For a similar account of the utopian function of transformations in romance, see Fredric Jameson, *The Political Unconscious: Narrative as a Socially Symbolic Act*, London, Routledge, 1981, pp. 103–50.

19   Bloch, *The Principle of Hope*, pp. 91–5.

20   Fowler, *The Alienated Reader*, p. 48.

21   Kate O'Brien, *Without My Cloak*, London, Heinemann, 1931. All further references will be noted in parentheses.

22  Sigmund Freud, 'Family Romances', *The Pelican Freud Library, Volume 7: On Sexuality,* trans. James Strachey, London, Penguin, 1977, pp. 221–5. My use of the notion of the family romance is indebted to Christine Van Boheemen-Saaf's explorations of the history and development of the novel. See Christine Van Boheemen-Saaf, *The Novel as Family Romance: Language, Gender and Authority From Fielding to Joyce,* Ithaca, NY, Cornell University Press, 1987.

23  Alfred Douglas, in his poem, describes homosexual liaisons as the 'Love that dare not speak its name'. See 'Two Loves', *The Chameleon,* 1, 1894, p. 28. For Oscar Wilde's impassioned speech on the meaning of this censored love, see Richard Ellmann, *Oscar Wilde,* London, Penguin, 1987, p. 435.

24  Eve Kosofsky Sedgwick *The Epistemology of the Closet,* London, Harvester, 1991, pp. 3–4.

25  Kate O'Brien, *The Ante-Room,* London, Virago, 1989. All further references to this edition will be noted in parentheses.

26  Gilles Deleuze and Félix Guattari provide an illuminating account of the constrictions of the family and argue the case for the development of anti-Oedipal structures to counter its pernicious effects. They point out that in the Freudian family 'in the aggregate of destination, in the end, there is no longer anyone but daddy, mommy, and me, the despotic sign inherited by daddy, the residual territoriality assumed by mommy, and the divided, split, castrated ego'. See Gilles Deleuze and Félix Guattari, *Anti-Oedipus: Capitalism and Schizophrenia,* trans. Robert Hurley, Mark Seem and Helen R. Lane, London, Athlone Press, 1984, p. 265.

27  Jonathan Dollimore makes the important point that the outlawing of homosexual love is due to a fear not of difference, but of sameness. See Jonathan Dollimore, *Sexual Dissidence: Augustine to Wilde, Freud to Foucault,* Oxford, Clarendon Press, 1991.

28  Marilyn Farwell, 'Toward a definition of the Lesbian Literary Imagination', Micheline R. Malson, Jean F. O'Barr, Sarah Westphal-Wihl and Mary Wyer (eds), *Feminist Theory in Practice and Process,* University of Chicago Press, Chicago, 1986, pp. 201–19.

29  For analysis of the twin alternatives of the heroine's text, namely the choice constructed for the female protagonist between death and marriage, see Nancy K. Miller *Subject to Change: Reading Feminist Writing,* New York, Columbia University Press, 1988, pp. 125–61.

30  This *Lied* by Schubert which is hummed by both Vincent and Marie-Rose provides an ironic counterpoint to the events of the novel as it describes the lover's yearning for harmony and unison with the beloved. See *Schuberts Liedertexte: Band II,* ed. Maximilian and Lilly Schochow, Hildesheim, Georg Olms Verlag, 1974, p. 484.

31  For a discussion of the circular patterns of the female *Bildungsroman,* see Marianne Hirsch, 'Spiritual *Bildung:* The Beautiful Soul as Paradigm', (eds) Elizabeth Abel, Marianne Hirsch and Elizabeth Langland, *The Voyage In: Fictions of Female Development,* Dartmouth, University Press of New England, 1983, pp. 23–48.

32  It is no accident of course that her two lovers, John and Juanito, have similar names.

33  Jean Racine, *Phèdre,* ed. Jean Salles, Paris, Bordas, 1963. For an analysis of the play which sees it as revolving around a conflict between male authority and female transgression, see Francesco Orlando, *Toward a Freudian Theory of Literature With and Analysis of Racine's Phèdre,* trans. Charmaine Lee, Baltimore, Johns Hopkins University Press, 1978.

# Chapter 7

# Kate O'Brien
# and the Splendour of Music

*Fanny Feehan*

Music, being the representative art of Germany, was a natural choice for Thomas Mann to use in *Dr Faustus* in order to decry that country's decadence at a certain time: with hindsight it now seems that the novel could be said to define the collapse of a civilisation evolved over 500 years. Thomas Mann's knowledge of music was also of sufficient width to allow him to use the medium emblematically in *Death in Venice* where it represents a dark and uncontrolled Aschenbach who has turned his back on definite images. Hans Castorp in *The Magic Mountain* conveys a fine analysis of *Aida*, of *Carmen*, of *Lieder* (Schubert), *Faust* (Gounod) and *L'Apres-midi d'un faune* (Debussy). Thomas Mann occupies the dark side of the moon. J. B. Priestley, Brigid Brophy, Boris Pasternak, Frank Wedekind, James Joyce and Ernst Schabel, to name a few – and qualitatively very different – writers at random, occupy a different plane: but though they love music, none of them used it as intuitively as, say, Charles Dickens – or our own Kate O'Brien.

It has always surprised me that Flann O'Brien, apart from describing a clarinet as a very black class of an instrument or speaking of Trellis in *At Swim Two Birds* as listening to noises in his head did not make greater use of music in his writing, because he above all Irish writers had the knowledge. Kate O'Brien and Charles Dickens give their characters an extra arm, and in doing so show how firm is the musical ground on which they walk. Dickens's father-in-law was a music critic, and his wife a good singer. Micawber was susceptible to music and chose his wife because she not only sang 'The Dashing White Sergeant' well but she made an impression with 'Little Taflin', an aria from Storace's opera *Three and the Deuce*. Mr Wegg in *Our Mutual Friend* was a balladmonger, while Mr Morofin in *Dombey and Son* could hum Beethoven's cello sonata. Mr Morofin also 'produced dismal and forlorn sounds from his cello before going to bed, and frequented a certain club-room hard by the Bank where quartets of the most tormenting and excruciating nature were executed every Wednesday'. Little Dorrit's Uncle Fred played a clarinet in a theatre orchestra 'and never raised his eyes above his book'. With those few words Dickens reveals how very much he knew about musicians, and in similar small ways Kate O'Brien gives ample evidence of her knowledge in *As Music and Splendour* (London, Heinemann, 1958).

When I came to know Kate O'Brien well, long after I had read her books, we had many arguments about music. Unlike Sir Arthur Bliss and J. B. Priestley she did not discourse at me, but encouraged me to voice my ignorant views about music, and even though I was a professional musician I marvel now at her tolerance. However it was only when I was roped in to play the harmonium at a country wedding that I came to appreciate her instinctive grasp of music. I can still see her throw back her head, roaring with laughter at my bizarre choice of wedding music. The only tunes which I could play by ear on the harmonium were 'Sheep May Safely Graze', 'Jesu, Joy Of Man's Desiring', and 'For Unto Us A Child Is Born'. In that nightmare situation I felt confident that no one in the congregation would know or care what I was about . . . I had reckoned without Miss O'Brien.

In *As Music And Splendour* we are not blinded by science, nor is the reader bullied into reading about a subject couched in terms which he cannot understand; the expertise is admirable. In Chapter II the student singers are spoken of as listening to one another, and by these simple few words the author shows, just as Dickens did when he spoke of the orchestral player in the orchestra pit not lifting his eyes from his music, how much she understood about musicians. Nothing of music can be conveyed in symphony, aria, sonata or quartet unless those taking part know what each is playing or singing. They must be able to sing or play every note of each other's part, and it is only when this jigsaw falls into place for them after hours of rehearsal that excitement and satisfaction of unparalleled proportion is experienced. It all takes great patience.

This is a tantalising book for musicians, especially for Irish ones, because much time will be spent trying to decide which fictional character conceals a real-life performer. No less than Thomas Mann, with Schoenberg, Nietzsche, Schumann, or Mahler, Kate O'Brien keeps us guessing. Are Clare Halvey, Rose Lennane, Luisa Carriaga, in fact, Margaret Lydon, Margaret Sheridan and Cathe rine Hayes? My own feeling is that Clare Halvey might well be Lydon, who sang oratorio so beautifully and, according to her contemporary Margaret Sheridan from Mayo, was 'the only first-rate singer that I have ever heard who didn't come to the top, and who only wanted to go back to her mother in Galway'. Rose Lennane, that golden girl, is probably Sheridan herself, but the most shadowy character, that of Luisa Carriaga, could be either Catherine Hayes of Limerick, who was born in 1825 and who died on 11 August 1861, or Violet Pickering, who studied with Sheridan in Italy, and knew her well. *As Music And Splendour* is the story of six young musicians and three older ones, and while in her other novels there are plenty of references to music, ballad singing of the drawing-room variety and piano-playing, it is in this one that the so-called professional musician is examined under a microscope. His terrors, few joys, and satisfactions are laid bare as a body on the dissecting-room table. The bombshell which hits the two young aspiring singers Clare and Rose, that they are to be despatched forthwith from the shelter of Rue des Lauriers and the benevolent if jaundiced eyes of Mère Marie and Mother Superior to Rome, is a fitting preparation for them in that at once they are shown that personal likes and dislikes must always take second place to their art. In future they will be summoned by intendants of opera houses at short notice, so they can't learn early enough.

A few hours is often all that a singer receives by way of warning that he or she must pack and get off to Rome, Paris, Covent Garden, Vienna, New York, where they may need a Violetta, a Norma, a Lucia or an Elvira. Intendants always accommodate one another no matter how outrageous the demand because they never know, singers being human, when they will be in the same boat themselves.

Private loves and fears are nothing in the mad and savage operatic world, so without batting an eyelid Kate O'Brien shows the reader what a difficult life has been chosen for the Irish girls by Rose's Committee and Clare's Uncle Matthew. In opera there is bitterness hand in hand with simplicity. 'What's wrong with Ireland?' asks Rose. 'Nothing, child, save its total ignorance about music', replies Mère Marie.

The girls arrive in Rome, at the house of Professor Buonatoli, a singing maestro whose wife had been an opera diva, but who now spends most of her time behind a haze of alcohol. Occasionally she permitted herself to make pointed comment, or floated off an aria from an opera *sotto voce*. For instance, the entire household of students, professor, signora and servant went on a picnic to the Alban hills on the day following the girls' arrival. This harmless adventure leads to a discreet unveiling of one of the writer's sub-plots, relating to the professor and his wife.

After lunch Maestro Giacomo, replete, muses about the new opera *Otello* and hums the aria *Gia nella notte della dansa*. He thinks of the 'unusually written duet in Act I' and Tamagno's treatment of it. The reader therefore knows at once that the writer is aware of Blanche Roosevelt's lively account of the first night when she speaks of Tamagno 'bleating' his way through the opera. Verdi himself chose Tamagno for the part, and he was regarded by most as the *prima tenore forza* in Italy at the time. So why was his treatment of the duet so intriguing? Was Tamagno a rival of Giacomo's? Had the Signora been in love with him? Obviously something other than music had reduced her to her present state, and the tolerant good-natured love of Giacomo, not to mention that of Assunta, her servant.

*Gia nella notte* appears again just before the end of Chapter X when Clare and Thomas, the young Welsh singer-turned-conductor, are talking about Rose's debut in La Scala as

Desdemona. They are looking out on to a Roman night, full of stars and the warm smells of cooking. Thomas launches out into *Gia nella notte,* Clare tells him to continue, that she'll try 'to come in' at *Vien questo immenso amore.* The writer reveals once more how well she appreciated the problem of pitch for the soprano who sang Desdemona, and the difficult entry.

This chapter makes an excellent preparation for Rose's debut in La Scala as Desdemona (p. 216). In Chapter XI we are given the best account I know of a first night in a great theatre. I think of it often, and it applies equally well to Covent Garden or the Bolshoi, and is as relevant today as it was of the time Miss O'Brien was writing.

> As usual in La Scala, there were far too many flowers, there was too much fuss. Too many rich people, too many diamonds and loud voices. Yet why all this social brilliance to-night? He (Thomas) acknowledged as he moved (in ill temper) through the over-perfumed and self-confident crowds that the commotion meant that lovers of opera, lovers of the human voice . . . dreadful though they might seem as he pressed among them . . . were here with their inexplicable wits on edge to-night, to listen attentively to a new singer . . . once Faccio mounted the podium they would fall still, lose their individual vulgarities a while, and simply, and mercilessly listen.

Today, 29 December 1979, I have just read an account in *The Guardian* of a riot in the opera house at Parma where *La Traviata* was being presented. The crowd did not like the soprano, conductor, or tenor, and the commotion was so great that the opera had to be stopped during Act III, and taken off altogether.

Rosa d'Irlanda's career, which we have followed from the time that she arrived as an ignorant schoolgirl in the Rue des Lauriers to this opening in *La Scala* singing Desdemona in Verdi's greatest opera, give or take *Don Carlos* or *Falstaff,* was carefully mapped and planned. If only that other Irish, real-life singer Margaret Sheridan had been as fortunate in her mentors or her leading men! Unlike Rose, Sheridan was the foil for the debuts of Gigli, Martinelli and Pertile at Covent Garden . . . her clear, beautifully true voice was unable for their enormous *tenore forza.*

When Rose makes her debut in *Otello* at La Scala we are told that she 'grew to live and work in a condition of cold joy and colder terror'. She was like a sleepwalker, a condition well

understood by her teacher Serrano and the director of La Scala,
Signor Faccio, who 'observed her with satisfaction' (p. 226). Earlier
it has been remarked that La Scala had chosen 'Otello' with great
wisdom. 'Giovanni Maroni was a handsome man in his mid-
thirties who had never either succeeded or failed, but whose voice
remained clear and pure, who knew his work and was a good
actor. . . . An excellent background voice, strong and moving, for
our Irish Desdemona' (p. 217).

Somebody on the inside must have told Kate O'Brien about
the procedure at La Scala for the final rehearsals the *répétition générale*
from which Signor Faccio excluded all but the internal members
of La Scala; Sheridan herself or someone who had been through
the hoop perhaps, anyway it all rings as true as Waterford glass.
The chapter about *Otello* keeps me on the edge of the seat. We
don't know after Act I whether Rose is going to be success or
failure, even though she has sung beautifully. Two critics talking
in the bar after Act I are cautiously hopeful, but one of them fears
that she won't have the stamina for Act IV. But by the end of
Act II it becomes clearer that 'Rose was in charge of her work;
and every note she sang was true, charged with meaning.
Desdemona's last hour of fear for ever after to be famous.' Shades
of Sheridan in *Madame Butterfly* at La Scala, which was also a
famous interpretation. Interestingly, when Sheridan lay dying in
a Dublin nursing home, Veronica Dunne was singing *Un bel di*
('One Fine Day') from the then broadcasting station in Henry
Street. Sheridan heard the broadcast which the nurses were afraid
to turn off, but the dying woman's eyes were glued to the kimono
she had worn as Butterfly lying across the end of the bed.

On page 106 we read of 'the miseries and senseless terrors which
a public performer must undergo each time his hour draws up'.
The deathlike loneliness that hits a singer or violinist or pianist
as he or she waits for his or her entry cannot be minimised.
Beethoven's Violin Concerto with its long introductory *tutti* is
agony for every violinist who plays it. Some can see their whole
life drifting in front of them as does a drowning man, while others
feel like turning and running wildly off the platform. Only training
and discipline keep them standing there listening to the timpani
which is like a heartbeat.

*Orpheus and Eurydice,* Gluck's opera, figures considerably in the

book. Clare and Luisa sing it with Duarte conducting. His calm
beat helps the singers, but once more the writer gives a twist to
her story-line which is at once ironical and compassionate. Luisa
had had an affair with Duarte, but she was also in love with Clare,
her Eurydice. The characters of Orpheus and Eurydice take the
girls over, so that it is difficult to separate the myth from the reality.
This counter-theme runs beneath the story proper, but it is a theme
which is handled with great compassion by the writer; there is
no shame nor prurience. But it provokes a musician to wonder
why the author hadn't chosen *Der Rosenkavalier*. The thought
vanishes, because no music in *Rosenkavalier* offers the simplicity
of *Chè faro*. Once again Kate O'Brien makes an unerring choice.

As the lifeline runs across the palm of a hand, so does an aria
*Dite alle giovine* ('Say to your daughters') from *La Traviata* become
associated with the Signora. This aria hovers always like a dark
bird over the bright heads of the young singers. There is the example of the Signora, now fat and alcoholic; it jangles their nerves
and is a terrible warning of the future.

Signora Vittoria jangled nerves early on in the book when, with
her throat full of cake crumbs and gulping a glass of wine she
sings, softly, *Dite alle giovine.*

> She seemed to make no effort, hardly it seemed, that she used her lungs,
> yet each note came in its place, gently taking part in what the song
> said. Her audience knowing the Opera, followed her closely, but lost
> sight of the ageing woman who sang; they only heard the voice or
> what they accepted momentarily as the voice of Violetta. What they
> heard in truth was interpretation, understanding memory and art . . .
> art neglected, flung aside, but when as now for a lazy whim picked
> up, still gold, pure gold. (p. 62)

This passage is very reminiscent to me of a fortunate hearing of
Sheridan when I was young and she was in her fifties or early
sixties. It occurred in the Aula Maxima, 86 Stephens Green, when
HMV persuaded the great soprano to make a series of records
for them and a few of us were roped in to play the orchestral parts.
I shall never forget it, because we heard snatches of the great ar-
tist which even now I can hear in my head. But of whom was
O'Brien thinking? I never had the courage to ask of the basis for
Vittoria, but 'her intoxicated arrogance, her sensitive brilliant
drunkenness' is somehow familiar.

On page 132 we find Rose contemplating her first performance in Bellini's *I Puritani*. She knows the music well, but hasn't sung it before, nor does she know the conductor. She realises that it is difficult to portray madness, and more troublesome still to portray madness *legato*. Later on we discover her to be even more nervous because her friend and contemporary is to be in the audience. Clare will know only so well what she is or is not doing. It is typical of musicians that the only people they ever worry about are other musicians. The tenor, René Chaloux, is in love with Rose, and very ambitious for himself. He is not such a good musician as she, as an experienced singer points out to Rose: 'He seems to think that *Creadasi* is a sort of steeple chase.' This lady is far wiser than young Rose in the ways of tenors, and says 'The matter with your French darling is that he's shocked at your brilliance and determined to tone it down!' René has asked Rose to slightly alter the *tempo* of *Creadasi*. Nothing changes in the opera world.

Music is an art, and is full of tricks, says Luisa, a remark that had enraged the Spanish conductor Duarte. He is faithful to the composer, and represents a different type of musician, one who will take no liberties. He prefers oratorio to opera, and his discernment is no finer than that of his creator. Kate O'Brien knows music and musicians inside out. One is never inclined to squirm when reading *As Music And Splendour*: on the contrary, the musician is mortified that a non-musician should show such awareness and intuition. No writer on music that I know of has demonstrated such feeling or sensitivity, since the death of Neville Cardus, for the art on which so many critics feed like parasites.

The great American composer Charles Ives has said 'the beginning of the art process lay in the artist's consciousness of spiritual and moral truths'. Very few have as yet grasped that message, but Kate O'Brien gave ample evidence that she was well aware of its implications.

*Chapter 8*

# The Art of Writing
# Kate O'Brien's Journalism

*Michael O'Toole*

On the one occasion that I met her, Kate O'Brien said to me: 'I am a journalist too, you know. It was by journalism that I first made my living and I still practise the art every week.' This was 1972, when she was living in Kent and writing an occasional column for *The Irish Times.*

The 1960s were difficult years for her. Her creative talents had long been on the wane – there had been no novel since *As Music and Splendour* in 1958 – and she was making little headway with *Constancy,* the novel that had long been promised to Heinemann and which she would never finish. In between there had been two non-fiction books – the travel book *My Ireland* in 1962, and *Presentation Parlour,* an affectionate memoir of family life in Limerick, in 1963. By the 1970s all her books were out of print. She had become, she was fond of telling her friends, unfashionable, and there was nothing she could do about it. Attempts by friends and well-wishers to revive her career as a writer of fiction came to nothing. Her nephew, John O'Brien, tells of an embarrassing interview with the then artistic director of the Abbey Theatre, Hugh Hunt. Kate O'Brien had been under the impression that the

Abbey was interested in reviving an adaptation of one of the novels and began to make some suggestions. Hunt cut her short. She should forget about raking over old coals, he said, and write something original for them. She was silent for several moments and then said wistfully: 'If only I could.'

*Long Distance* had been suggested by Douglas Gageby, the then editor of *The Irish Times,* who has been a benefactor and of whom she spoke most warmly during our brief meeting. Gageby had also been indirectly responsible for *My Ireland*, which originated as a series of travel articles for the paper. During her worst of times, when she was ill and unable to meet the deadlines, Gageby kept the modest cheques coming and she was on her deathbed when she endorsed the last *Irish Times* cheque.[1]

Kate O'Brien's first job after graduating from UCD in 1919 was as a translator on the foreign page of *The Manchester Guardian Weekly,* then edited by C. P. Scott.[2] When that folded she went to London, where in 1926 her play *Distinguished Villa* was produced and where she spent the years 1926-29 on the periphery of professional journalism as the editor of *The Sunlight Magazine,* the journal of The Sunlight League which endeavoured to impress upon the English race the benefits of ultra-violet rays.

Miss O'Brien was proving to be one of those aspiring novelists who took Henry James seriously when he advised them to be people on whom nothing is wasted. The play, produced at the Aldwych Theatre, was based on her experience of boarding-house life in Manchester. Its production coincided with the General Strike and it suffered accordingly. But it was widely reviewed and the critics were, generally, sympathetic. Its principal benefit to its author was that it brought her name to the attention of editors, many of whom invited her to write for their publications.[3]

In one of these early pieces she takes the opportunity of repaying a debt of childhood. Contributing to a series in *The Daily Chronicle* called 'The Loveliest Place I Know,' she waxes lyrical — and purple — about the O'Brien family's summer playground, the zigzagging line of rock and strand that runs from Loop Head to Lahinch.

The piece starts with a typical enough display of the travel writer's boastfulness, telling of 'those wide-flung beautiful play grounds of the world which it has been my luck to see.' She has not, she writes, forgotten 'the thousand coloured Pyrenees, or the

long, grave, twisting Rhine, or the blue Virginian mountains; I
am remembering the Cornish seas, the winey morning air of the
English downs and the muted melancholy of Norman strands at
dusk when the fishing fleets go down'.

> And then the description of that road . . . a dangerous road which twists
> itself crazily along the cliff-line. But on [an] August day when the Irish
> sky is blue and tender and bees are loud above the thymy grass, when
> the Aran Islands are visible on the north horizon and you can spy a
> seal sunning himself on the rocks below you, when a donkey and her
> foal are trotting contentedly two inches ahead of your bonnet, and
> when a barefoot child with soft eyes and a voice so shy that you can
> only barely hear it has told you that that semi-circle of pink and blue
> houses clustered round a yellow strand is only Kilkee.

Kate O'Brien's journalism ranges from the long, scholarly essay
*English Diaries and Journals*[4] — which she begins with the premise
that the best English diaries have been written by bores, and goes
on to claim that women would not have taken to diary writing
at all if they had had the opportunity of being more self-
expressive[5] — to some very ephemeral pieces dashed off at speed
for newspapers and magazines. The lighter pieces could be sparked
off by a chance encounter, such as the 1959 *Evening Press* piece
on contemporary manners. Kate O'Brien had gone into a bank
in O'Connell Street, Dublin, to cash a few small cheques where
an unsuspecting cashier, youthful and brash, addressed this formidable lady with the aristocratic sense of hauteur as 'love'.

While it is obvious that many of these lighter pieces were undertaken solely as a means of earning some ready cash, her approach
to literary criticism was at once serious and generous. Professor
Lorna Reynolds, her biographer and friend, has spoken of the
great seriousness with which she approached this aspect of her
work.

> She always tackled her reviewing assignments with great seriousness
> and never allowed her natural ability to be easily bored to affect her
> reviewing. Her fine critical faculties had been sharpened by Professor
> Roger Chauviré at UCD and she frequently acknowledged her debt
> to him. She paid him the great tribute of declaring that it was while
> listening to him lecturing on 17th and 18th century French poetry
> that she grew up. It was Chauviré who revealed the study of literature
> to her as a serious adult occupation.[6]

Kate O'Brien's first reviews appeared in *The Sphere* in the early 1920s. There was also an early association with *Time and Tide* of which the novelist E. M. Delafield (Mrs A. P. Dashwood) was a director. There was a lively literary circle attached to *Time and Tide* and the young Irish writer recently arrived from Dublin, via Manchester, was soon absorbed in it. A friendship developed between the two novelists and in 1942 Kate O'Brien went to live as a paying guest in the home of E. M. Delafield in Cullompton, Devon. It was here that she wrote *The Last of Summer,* which came out in 1943 — the year of E. M. Delafield's death at the age of fifty-three.

Four years later, when Kate O'Brien wrote the foreword to the compilation of the four 'diary of a provincial lady', pieces which had originally appeared in *Time and Tide* and were now titled *The Provincial Lady,*[7] she forecast the likelihood of immortality for Delafield 'not because I do not see her weaknesses and uncertainties, but because those virtues which are peculiar to her as a writer are surely those which must override time and fashion'. The first of these, she insisted, was

> her precise and if you like fussy observation of one small, narrow ledge of the complicatedly graded English society of her own time. . . . In her writing she appealed to no fixed set of rules, invoked neither ideology nor faith, embarked on no special pleadings; in short, she was no kind of propagandist or sociologist — but only that much greater thing, a natural satirist.

By the late 1930s Kate O'Brien had established herself as one of England's most prominent and most prolific critics. She was now reviewing five novels a fortnight on a regular basis. The 1930s was the most productive decade of her life; it produced four novels as well as the courageous travel book *Farewell Spain* — courageous because, as she must have been well aware, it would cause her to be banned for many years from a country she loved probably more than any other because of her comments on General Franco and his fascist followers.

Across the divide of more than half a century most of the titles of the books she reviewed in the pages of *The Spectator* appear quaint and strange. Her list for 25 March 1938, for example, contained: *The Mountains and the Stars,* by Valentin Tikhanov; *The Time of Wild Roses,* by Doreen Wallace; *The Larches,* by John Hampson and L. A. Pavey; *Kanthapura,* by Rajo Rio – and *Murphy* by Samuel Beckett.

Although *Murphy* received several sympathetic reviews, most of the reviewers (they included Dylan Thomas, Edwin Muir and Dilys Powell) had been reticent and cautious. Kate O'Brien took the opposite approach. '*Murphy,* at least to this humble examiner, sweeps all before him,' she declared.

> Rarely, indeed, have I been so entertained by a book, so tempted to superlatives and perhaps hyperboles of praise. It truly is magnificent and a treasure – if you like it. Quite useless, quite idiotic, if you don't. It is a sweeping, bold record of an adventure in the soul; it is erudite, allusive, brilliant, impudent and rude.

Rejoicing in 'Beckett's bright, clear lyricism', she goes on to describe him as

> a magnificently learned sceptic, a joker overloaded with the scholarship of great jokes. There are two ways for the man in the street to read him – the one, which has been mine at first reading, is to sweep along acknowledging points lost by lack of reference in oneself, but seeing even in darkness the skirts of his tantalising innuendo, and taking the whole contentedly, as a great draught of brilliant, idiosyncratic commentary, a most witty, wild and individualistic refreshment. If he takes it so, with modesty and without fuss, the sympathetic reader will be amply rewarded by the gusts of his own laughter, by the rich peace of his response to Murphy's flight from the macrocosm into the microcosm of himself in his own truth. . . . There is no plot, as novel-readers mean plot, but there is a glorious, wild story and it is starred all over with a milky way of sceptic truths. And read once simply and sportingly as it flies, this book is then to be read again, very slowly, with as many pauses as may be to pursue the allusions and decorations which may have had to be guessed at in first flight. There is no more to be said. One can only hope – being eager for the gladdening, quickening and general toning up of readers' wits – that a very great number of people will have the luck and the wit to fall upon *Murphy* and digest it. For the right readers it is a book in a hundred thousand. My own great pleasure in it is not least in the certainty that I shall read it again and again before I die.[7]

Beckett, who according to his biographer Deirdre Bair, was generally displeased and depressed by the reviews of *Murphy,* said in a letter to his friend George Reavy that he was 'very obliged' to Kate O'Brien.[8]

Although meticulous in regard to her critical work, she was easily bored. Professor Reynolds says:

> Certainly Kate O'Brien, when she chose, commanded all the aptitude for boredom and hauteur any aristocrat could desire. She did not suffer fools gladly. . . . She lost interest very quickly and made no attempt to hide the subsequent exhaustion. Merely not to be bored is such a relief, she would say. She found most people's way of entertaining themselves inexplicable. It is pitiful, she often said, what people will do to amuse themselves, pitiful.[9]

When it came to literary criticism these proclivities were kept under tight rein. One assumes that she was bored and irritated by Daphne du Maurier's *Rebecca* which she reviewed in *The Spectator* five months after her glowing account of *Murphy* in 1938. The message is clear — but gentle enough. Daphne du Maurier's novel, she wrote,

> is a Charlotte Bronte story *minus* Charlotte Bronte but *plus* a number of things which the latter would not have paused for. Descriptions of meals and comforts, sentimental passages about scenery or dogs, little passages of dialogue which either misfire, or, more unfortunately, illustrate character in ways unforeseen by the author. But Miss du Maurier's plot is undoubtedly the kind of thing which the three girls of Haworth Parsonage would have liked to thrash out as they paced the dining-room arm-in-arm after Papa had gone to bed. . . . Horrors and misunderstandings are piled up courageously and the author has a very neat surprise up her sleeve for the moment when you may be growing a little weary.

Towards the end of her career Kate O'Brien revealed something of her philosophy of literary criticism when she reviewed Elizabeth Coxhead's biography of Lady Gregory [10] in *The Kilkenny Magazine*.[11] 'Let us return for our own sakes to the Lady of Coole,' she wrote, 'and study her again — learn from her to be serious in art, to be humble and to be generous towards talent — generous, instead of eternally malicious, as it is too often our curse to be.'

*Generous* is a key word in the Kate O'Brien canon. Generosity was one of the virtues she most admired in others and, as her friends attest, she was herself richly endowed with it. Nowhere is her own generosity towards new talent more transparent than in her review of John McGahern's first novel, *The Barracks*, in 1963. As with *Murphy* twenty-five years earlier, here was an unerring eye for a major new talent:

> Seldom do we read a first novel, and a novel by a writer still in his twenties, in which we find true maturity of thought allied to unbroken certainty of direction. But John McGahern, it can be readily said from the evidence of this first book, is an endowed and gifted writer of prose fiction; and it is with a sense of real safety that one reads this book, page after page, from the anxious beginning to the lonely end. . . . It is difficult to find words exact enough to express my admiration of this subtle, close-woven, tender, true poetic work. Mr McGahern's prose fits with exquisite rightness of sensitivity and colour to his subject matter, and his eye and his ear for character are wonderful also, though finely controlled; his human understanding, his sense of compassion, seem measureless.

Kate O'Brien's non-fiction is headed by five books: two travel books (*Farewell Spain,* Heinemann, 1937, and *My Ireland*, Batsford, 1962); a memoir of family life in Limerick (*Presentation Parlour,* Heinemann, 1963); a short portrait of St Teresa of Avila (*Teresa of Avila,* Max Parrish, 1951), and the monograph in the Britain and Pictures series *(English Diaries and Journals,* Collins, 1942). Next comes the great mass of book reviews (five books each alternate week) over a period of almost thirty years in *The Spectator.* There is some important critical work in *The University Review* between 1956 and 1963 which includes the text of a lecture to the Graduate's Association, *The Art of Writing* (vol. 3, no. 4, 1963) and the essay *UCD as I Forget It* (vol. 3, no. 2, 1962). There is a 1951 lecture to the Royal Society of Literature, *George Eliot: A Moralising Fabulist*, in which she says that she is all in favour of the graphs and compasses that chart the course of artistic fame and greatness, adding: 'and I think that the responsibility of those who hold the measuring sticks and lead judgements in matters so eternally important as the creative arts is immensely grave and honourable'.

The newspaper journalism has not been systematically collected and most of it is lost in the files of Fleet Street papers. That is a pity, because the fragments that do survive often provide fascinating insights into her thinking at a time when she was at the height of her powers. A 1938 article *Why the Rage for French Films?* in the London evening newspaper, *The Star,* for example, demonstrates her great interest in the cinema, her views on its development and her admiration of French films. Although only one of her novels (*That Lady*) was filmed, Kate O'Brien wrote at least two original film scripts, neither of which were successful.[12] In the *Star* piece she declared that simplicity and humility were the approach virtues of true cinema, as they were of every other art. The average Hollywood film was 'purse-proud, slick and rule-of-thumb' and dominated either by snobbery ('America's defence in handling the artist') or by a jovial assertiveness of glossy, materialistic, non-reality which derived straight from the world of advertisements. British cinema, she declared, had failed because nothing good was ever created in condescension. 'In British films we are expected to be surprised, over and over again, on (sic) how the other half lives – it never strikes a British film maker that we who pay to see his films are the other half.'[13]

Although Kate O'Brien's journalism was occasionally addressed to social topics – in *Hibernia,* in 1959, she suggested that the way to curb emigration was to encourage would-be emigrants to try living in the smaller Irish cities rather than heading for London, Manchester or even Dublin – she remained journalistically silent on the issue that concerned her very deeply – the development of what Benedict Kiely described as 'the grocer's republic.' This she addressed through fiction in *Pray for the Wanderer* and again in *The Last of Summer.* That she was hurt by the banning of *Mary Lavelle* and *The Land of Spices* and disgusted by the illiberal and puritanical society that was flourishing in the 1930s and 1940s is certain,[14] yet she failed to respond journalistically. Likewise, during the period when her native city was enduring a consistently bad press she failed to join the ranks of the tormentors, electing instead to dedicate *My Ireland* to 'Limerick – my dear native place'.

## Notes and references

1  Mary O'Neill, literary executor, in an interview with Michael O'Toole.
2  Lorna Reynolds, *Kate O'Brien: A Literary Portrait*, Irish Literary Studies, No. 25, Gerrards Cross, Bucks, Colin Smythe, 1987, p. 36.

3   Mary O'Neill, interview.
4   London, Collins, 1943.
5   *English Diaries and Journals,* p. 48.
6   Professor Lorna Reynolds, in an interview with Michael O'Toole.
7   *The Spectator,* 25 March 1938, p. 546.
8   Deirdre Bair, *Samuel Beckett: A Biography,* London, Picador, 1980, pp. 243, 570.
9   Reynolds, *Kate O'Brien*, p. 28.
10  Elizabeth Coxhead, *Lady Gregory: A Literary Portrait*, London, Macmillan, 1961.
11  No. 4, Summer 1961.
12  Mary O'Neill, interview.
13  *The Star,* 1 February 1938.
14  See Reynolds, *Kate O'Brien*, pp. 75, 76.

*Chapter 9*

# Moving Pictures
# Kate O'Brien's Travel Writing

*Michael Cronin*

## Introduction

On her first trip to Dublin in 1907, the young Kate O'Brien is taken to the Bioscope theatre in Grafton Street. The seats inside are arranged like those of a tram or a Pullman train and the author declares, 'in them we travelled by screen, far and high and dangerously, over mountain passes and by rocky shores, through gentle lanes and along busy streets. I remember only all the marvellous travelling. There can have been no story-telling, no human interest.'[1] Kate O'Brien's experience was not unique. The travel genre was one of the most popular in early cinema and the fusion of the railway and cinematography in Hale's Tour Car at Kansas City Amusement Park in 1905 was immediately successful. The Tour Cars were simulated railway carriages that functioned as movie-theatres with the audience seated in passenger seats and the screen replacing the view out of the front or rear window. The Grafton Street Bioscope with its Pullman seating is a sober version of the extravagant literalism of Hale's Tours but it does point up an aspect of Kate O'Brien's own 'marvellous travelling' that makes for the particular quality of her travel writing.

Charles Musser in his essay 'The Travel Genre in 1903-1904: Moving Towards Fictional Narrative' claims that the railway sub-genre in travel films, for example, Edwin S. Porter's *What Happened in the Tunnel, Romance of the Rail* or *The Great Train Robbery*, was crucial to the development of fictional narrative in early cinema. Musser drawing on the work of Wolfgang Schivelbusch stresses the affinities between rail and screen:

> The traveller's world is mediated by the railroad, not only by the compartment window with its frame but by telegraph wires which intercede between the passenger and the landscape. The sensation of separation which the traveller feels on viewing the rapidly passing landscape has much in common with the theatrical experience of the spectator. The allusion of train window with the screen's rectangle was frequent within this travel sub-genre.[2]

Trains and films frame the world and in a profoundly ambiguous sense (departure/distance), travel becomes an act of separation.

It is this awareness of travel as a form of distancing, a frame around the anarchy of experience, that informs Kate O'Brien's two books of travel, *Farewell Spain* published in 1937 and *My Ireland* which appeared in 1962. Both books are highly self-conscious in their recognition of the specific prerogatives and constraints of the travel genre in literature. In her critical assessment of women's travel writing and colonialism entitled *Discourses of Difference* (1991), Sara Mills comments on the biographical reductionism of much of the critical literature on women's travel writing and argues, 'I want to take these texts seriously, not simply to reduce them to biographical studies of exceptional spinsters, as some critics have done.'[3] The intent in this essay is similar. The focus will not be on the biographical clues scattered throughout the travel books or on the travel writing as a colourful, secondary if instructive backdrop to novels of O'Brien such as *Mary Lavelle* or *That Lady*. Kate O'Brien's travel writing deserves recognition in its own right, both in terms of its distinction and as part of a larger tradition of Irish travel literature which is only belatedly receiving due recognition.

## Sentimental Travel and Guide Books

In *My Ireland* Kate O'Brien wonders what brings foreigners to Ireland:

> Only because it is always impossible to imagine how that which is familiar to oneself strikes on sensibilities foreign and new to it. And also, because I am a great one for liking to stare about in new and foreign places – and often amid strange pleasures and palaces I question if I am seeing at all what they in fact are, in their own right and in the accustomed sight of their inhabitants.[4]

The sensitivity to the limitations on her own vision of other places and the tendentious exclusiveness of ethnocentrism sharply differentiates O'Brien's travel writing from the contemporary, postcolonial writers examined by Mary Louise Pratt in *Imperial Eyes: Travel Writing and Transculturation*. The monarch-of-all-I-survey scene that is standard in travel accounts of the Imperial Age where the (usually male) colonist climbs to a high place and in one panoramic sweep takes in the landscape emptied of people and filled with scientific/political/commercial possibility is now translated to the dystopian commentary of late twentieth-century writers perched on the balconies of third-world hotels. Taking examples from the work of Alberto Moravia and Paul Theroux, Pratt claims, 'Despite the fact that they too are on unfamiliar territory, these writers . . . claim authoritativeness for their vision. What they see is what there is. No sense of limitation on their interpretive powers is suggested.'[5] O'Brien, on the other hand, continually questions her own discursive authority and repeatedly reminds the reader in both her Irish and Spanish travel books that they are strictly personal, individual accounts with the idiosyncrasy and partiality that such accounts imply.

She situates her writing within the sentimental tradition that would emerge in the mid-eighteenth century, partly in reaction to the encyclopedic aridity of the natural science paradigm dominant in travel writing of the period.[6] In the opening pages of *Farewell Spain* O'Brien declares, 'I write as a sentimental traveller' but immediately qualifies this statement by adding 'in a country long-suffering at the hands of such.'[7] Sentimental travel writing places the subject-narrator at the heart of the narrative in opposition to the putatively objective self-effacement of the manners-and-customs narrator who dutifully lists plants, trees, annual rainfall and the morphological traits of observed peoples. Sentimental travel is firmly located in the private sphere of the bourgeois world, defined by Pratt as the 'home of desire, sex, spirituality, and the Individual'.[8] O'Brien in the first chapter of *Farewell Spain* entitled 'Adiós, Turismo' stakes the claim for the individual imagination and explicitly invokes the private sphere, 'Let us praise personal memory, personal love.'[9] The commitment to the sentimental mode of travel writing must explain in part O'Brien's antipathy to guidebooks.

In her Spanish account the relationship with the primary intertextual source of information, the *Blue Guide,* is uneasy. The guidebook can be seen as the twentieth-century successor to the respectful empiricism of the Renaissance and Classical Age, presenting historical facts and details in an apparently neutral and impersonal fashion.[10] Though books such as the *Rough Guides* in English or the *Guide du routard* in French show the latter-day encroachment of sentiment, the French *Guide bleu*, like Baedeker's famous guides in German, by and large observed the decorum of the genre, assiduously detailing buildings, dates and important historical figures. When O'Brien goes to Santillana del Mar, she foregoes any elaborate, physical description of the town, arguing: 'It would be pointless to describe the place in factual detail here. Every guide-book explains the crumbling armorial bearings over every door.'[11] Similarly, the cathedral in Santiago de Conpostella is not the subject of any meticulous description, the author advising any prospective visitor to the Cathedral that an efficient guidebook would be more than adequate in providing the necessary architectural and historical information. However, when guidebooks exceed their brief and venture into the realm of the sentimental, offering an opinion, the result for O'Brien is an unhappy one. She is sardonic in her dismissal of the *Blue Guide's* claim (which she quotes in French) that her beloved Avila has 'un aspect conventuel, sombre et froid'.[12] She is unconvinced by the guide-book's description of the location and climate of Burgos and confesses, 'It seems as if the guide-book writers and I can never agree.'[13]

This disagreement illustrates the dilemmas of travel writing in general and the specific aesthetic choices of Kate O'Brien in particular. Firstly, if travel writing sought the imprimatur of fact in the Renaissance period because of its previous associations with fantasy, in the modern period, the guidebook has effectively occupied the high ground of the factual. To justify its continued existence as a genre, travel writing must, therefore, distance itself from a form that has appropriated one of its previous functions, to provide circumstantial information. Kate O'Brien is significant in that she both signals this generic crisis and radically breaks with a tradition of incorporating intertextual guidebook detail (not completely however as both the Irish and Spanish books bear traces of guidebook borrowings). Secondly, imagination and memory are motivating forces behind O'Brien's travel writing and not the linear, chronological positivism of the didactic travel text. In *My Ireland* she declares that the reader does not want to be bored with a history lesson on the Treaty Stone in Limerick and, after a very brief description of the European rather than Irish consequences of the signing of the treaty, O'Brien states, 'That is all the imagination needs to know about the awkward piece of stone that Sarsfield and the Williamite used as writing table.'[14] The emphasis is on imagination not factual intelligence or knowledge.

It is memory, not the sequential order of the calendar that will structure *Farewell Spain:*

> But my journey will be a composite one, made of many, and without unnecessary chronological reference. The route will be a plaiting together of many routes; seasons and cities will succeed each other in reminiscence as almost certainly they did not in fact; companions or chance acquaintances of travel will crop up, disappear and return without sequential accuracy, and with no justification from all those useful diaries which I never keep.[15]

When O'Brien considers the genesis of *My Ireland* she claims that the idea came to her when she was abroad and 'the writing of it has indeed engaged me in much and varied travel, travels of memory, of imagination and, of fact'.[16] Fact is a poor third and *My Ireland* is even more radically digressive than *Farewell Spain*. Her travel accounts are reflections on travel, expressions of personal and political opinions, occasions for autobiographical anecdote, brief historical interludes dictated by personal interest, all tenuously held together by the different geographical locations (Bilbao, Madrid, Armagh, Limerick, Belfast, Dublin, and others) that provide the rationale for chapter divisions. The endless digressions are almost a defining characteristic of the sentimental travel account in its proximity to fiction and the peripeteia perpetually delaying the arrival of the picaresque hero. O'Brien resists a 'natural' presentation of this textual constraint by ignoring its existence and draws the reader's attention to the explicit mode and tradition within which she is working as a travel writer.

## Virgin Landscapes

Mills, in her discussion of women writing in the colonial period, alludes to Kay Schaffer's work on travel writing in the Australian cultural tradition:

> What Schaffer has shown is the difficulties attendant on women attempting to write within a colonial context where the figure who generally writes about the other countries is male and adventurous, supremely masculine and where the land to be conquered or in the process of being conquered is represented as feminine and passive.[17]

It is not surprising that Kate O'Brien would have difficulty with the androcentric, adventurer-hero tradition of travel writing with its passivisation and restrictive feminisation of the landscape. However, O'Brien does predicate countries, people and landscape on gender but in a tellingly different manner. She dedicates *My Ireland* to her father but the Ireland that she describes in her lyrical opening passage is a woman who can go through a series of possible incarnations as a Reverend Mother, a swan, a street girl, Anna Livia, a serpent or a saint. In the Burren, O'Brien senses a 'kind of sisterhood' between Ireland, Spain and Palestine. The sisterhood is a spiritual association between the three lands based on a likeness in 'virginity' and 'austerity'.[18] County Clare is described as 'a fair, rippling land, feminine and virginal in suggestion – at ease with all the elements'.[19]

Further on in the text the female inhabitants of Ireland are conflated with the landscape when O'Brien warns visiting philanderers that Irish women are chaste by habit. She adds, 'I suggest to exploratory Don Juans that no matter their global experiences in brothels and palaces and shady lanes, they move carefully over Ireland's virgin territory (I use the adjective with conviction).'[20] The landscape, like Irish woman, is not passive but inviolate. The landscape is feminine but it resists: it is not the site of an easy conquest for the predatory traveller but displays an austere indifference to the blandishments of would-be conquerors. O'Brien's insistence on virginal sisterhood can be caricatured negatively as naive *post hoc* rationalisation of a prevalent Catholic discourse on sexuality and sin but that is to miss the point. Firstly, because her presentation of landscape runs directly counter to repressive, gendered images of landscape that assume male violation and female passivity. Secondly, her insistence on virginal territories is arguably bound up with her antipathy to traditional travellers' stereotypes of the Irish colleen. As late as 1950 Gary Hogg, an English traveller, in *Turf Beneath My Feet*, laments the scarcity of 'colleens' in his Irish travels: 'I could tell myself that I had seen a leprechaun, but I could not tell myself that I had seen that other product of Ireland: a colleen.'[21] O'Brien dismisses the idea of the colleen as an infantile, Victorian fantasy that is gainsaid by the powerful, independent figures of Niamh, Gormlait, Gráinne and Máire Rua O'Brien in Irish history and mythology. She asserts, 'For let the uninformed believe me that in Irish recorded literature – legend, history and verse – the colleen is missing. In a plenitude of women, the most of whom were somewhat alarming and unlikely to be found peeping out of little hoodshawls, she is not there.'[22] Ireland as Virgin rather than Mother is independent, disruptive and strong-willed and is unrecogisable in the simpering innocence of red-haired donkey drivers.

The private sphere of the sentimental traveller is also, as mentioned earlier, the site of desire. Indeed, the references to landscape and virginity must be placed in the larger context of travel and sensuality in O'Brien's writing. As a traveller she is sensitive to questions of physical beauty, and in both travel books O'Brien comments on the appearance of the inhabitants not in the taxonomic terms of the ethnographer listing distinctive physical traits but as a sexually mature adult might. She finds the women of

Spain shrill and disappointing. On the other hand, Spanish men
are presented as undeniably handsome on the grounds that Spanish
male beauty is deeply related to the Spanish landscape.[23] In
Ireland, it is the 'girls' of Cork who are especially pretty, 'in a
civilised, individualised way of prettiness, in which speech and
smile and movemnent partake'.[24]

Thus, in both Spain and Ireland we find an eroticisation of the
landscape where the natural world becomes the focus of an-
thropomorphic desire. The attention to beauty and the sensual
is also, of course, at another level part of the eternal *raison d'être*
of travel. The solitary traveller as a wanderer does not have the
sexual ties or commitments of members of settled communities
in a conjugal relationship. Hence the countless stories and ballads
where it is the traveller passing through a town, village or castle
who proves to be fatally attractive and where after a night of exalted passion the traveller leaves to remain the object of unrequited
love. This pattern of what Pratt calls 'loving and leaving' makes
travel at once the locus of desire and the traveller alternately
welcome as a sexual saviour or feared as a sexual menace. The
commodification of travel in mass tourism and the unholy trinity of sea, sun and sex has merely foregrounded an immutable
element in the practice and narrative of travel.

## Moors and Modernity

Travellers, like the countries they visit, change so that the genre
is inexhaustible, the threat of extinction is remote. How the
traveller views others is determined by the social, cultural and
emotional history of the observer. Hence no one person experiences a place in exactly the same way as another and no one
place is experienced in exactly the same way by the same person
because of the intrusion of history, personal and public. Kate
O'Brien's travel books depict two countries that have changed
in a dramatic fashion since her accounts were published. The
changes, indeed, have been so dramatic that both Ireland and Spain
continue to draw travel writers to their familiar territories. The
Spain of Kate O'Brien is markedly Castilian. It is a country of
exquisite good manners and its native good taste, sober, functional

and lovely, is unequalled anywhere. The Spanish figures that are to the fore, St Teresa of Avila and Philip II, fascinate O'Brien, through their uncanny combination of workaday pragmatism and an exalted passion for other worlds. The enemies of this Spanish distinction are modernity and the Moor.

In a writer sensitive to questions of national stereotypes and the paralysis of cliché, O'Brien rather strangely adopts a standard Eurocentric discourse on the Moorish presence in Spanish history and architecture that is closely allied to negative Orientalist discourses on Spain. She does not like Toledo because she feels the Moorish influence is excessive. The good taste of Spain that is so admired by O'Brien almost perished, she argues, at the hands of the Moor, and she goes on to state: 'The Moor long ago imperilled Spanish judgement with his arty-and-craftiness. Imperilled and infected, but mercifully did not dominate. Still, his legacy remains a menace, and I, for my part, detest all signs of the Moor in Spain.'[25] For O'Brien the latter-day successors to the Moors are Franco's supporters, new Moors whose brutal indifference to individualism and democracy endangers the Spain that occasions so much of the book's praise and introduces the valedictory note into her account expressed in the telling ambiguity of the book's title. Though O'Brien, writing at the height of the Civil War when much Catholic opinion backed Franco, is generous in pointing out the basic similarities between Catholicism and Communism and staunchly defends the embattled Republic, she cannot go beyond Christendom's traditional mistrust of the Crafty Moor, the Dark Other.

Modernity in the form of the 'cosmopolitan' is the other agent of aesthetic dissolution in Kate O'Brien's Spain.[26] Spanish women destroy their beauty by falling victim to the ravages of the modern cosmetics industry and Spanish hotels forfeit their Spartan loveliness when they opt for radios, strip-lighting and new furniture. Johannes Fabian and Sara Mills have both commented on the phenomenon of 'temporal distancing' in travel writing where the host country is projected backwards in time to emphasise the culturally and politically superior position of the traveller from the major imperial centres.[27] O'Brien's travel writing on both Ireland and Spain invokes the notion of temporal distance but this is deemed to be evidence of virtue rather than an admission of backwardness and failure. In *My Ireland* she thanks God that in Ireland 'we are not really into the future yet'.[28] Dublin is happily in a time-lag and at the end of her account O'Brien freely confesses that she is slow to 'welcome conceptions of tomorrow'.[29] It is the rejection of the modern that guarantees the preservation of specificity, thwarting the homogenising impulse of American consumerism (Spain/Ireland) or a potentially triumphant Communism (Spain). However, for O'Brien that rejection is increasingly impossible.

Modernity will triumph and everywhere will become the same so that the 'Farewell' is not only to Spain but to Ireland and all those areas of distinctness that play host to the interpretive curiosity of the travel writer. O'Brien's predilection for the past might be seen as profoundly conservative in presenting the Spaniards and Irish as noble savages who, unmade-up and gracious, are happily suspended in an ahistoric limbo. On the other hand, the preoccupation with the modern world and its attendant economic and cultural changes could be interpreted as resulting from a keen awareness of history and socio-political circumstances that entertained no illusions about pastoral permanence. As she wrote her Spanish travel account, the cities and towns and villages Kate O'Brien described were being torn asunder by a violent civil war. Good manners had given way to irresponsible acts of criminal sadism on both sides. The temporal distancing makes the enormity of the change all the more striking: its impact is, therefore, paradoxally *historical* rather than *ahistorical*. Similarly, in the case of Ireland, Kate O'Brien's travel book appears in 1962, when Ireland is beginning to experience the convulsions of the economic and social modernisation of the Whitaker/Lemass years. For a reader of *My Ireland* today the country Kate O'Brien describes in the book has changed beyond all recognition. In fact, one of the book's virtues is to highlight the extent to which Ireland has been utterly transformed by its very recent past. Again, the Irish travel account, like the Spanish, is situated on a historical fault line, a moment when the past would become irredeemably the past as the result of fundamental shifts in the political culture. In a sense, Kate O' Brien's stated aversion to the modern in her travel accounts is more to do with a prescient sensitivity to the dramatic and imminent changes in the societies she describes rather than a reactionary, atemporal nostalgia.

## Monks and Utopia

The French road to Santiago de Compostela is seen by O'Brien as the highway of influence, in successive periods of Spanish history carrying styles, skills and knowledge from elsewhere. One of these skills was lettering and illumination brought, she claims, by Irish theologians. This Irish gift is part of the much larger cultural munificence that O'Brien describes in *My Ireland* as originating from Irish monasteries in the Dark Ages. The Early Christian period in Ireland demonstrated 'art, sanctity and civilisation' and the monks made in Ireland a kind of Utopia within its stormy life and held it there, active and exemplary, for an extremely long period in European history'.[30] Their contribution is more admirable and enduring than that of the chieftains, warriors and their stone keeps and endless conflicts. It is possible to see the attraction of the Saints and Scholars period for O'Brien in its appeal to her innate pacifism and to a belief in the aristocracy of the intellect – in Early Christian times, Ireland established, O'Brien argues, 'a society of pure aristocratic form'.[31] On the other hand, one can anticipate a more contemporary argument in O'Brien's claims for the period, claims that were advanced by many, not just Irish, travel writers of this century. A central thesis of Mary Louise Pratt's work on travel writing is that the transcultural dimensions of notions such as Romanticism that are seen to be quintessentially European are ignored. She declares: 'Westerners are accustomed to thinking of romantic projects of liberty, individualism, and liberalism as emanating *from* Europe to the colonial periphery, but less accustomed to thinking about emanations *from* the contact zones *back* into Europe' [author's italics].[32] In the Irish case, for O'Brien and others, the contribution of Irish monasticism to the preservation and growth of European civilisation is an emanation from the periphery back into mainland Europe. It is the reversal of the metropolitan-centred readings of cultural history and influence. Just as Kate O'Brien accords the Spaniards the right of reciprocal vision in *Farewell Spain*, where she and her companion Mary are occasionally portrayed through the eyes of the Spaniards, so too she demands this reciprocity from histories of European culture by placing the Irish periphery centre-stage. The Irish objects of the foreign travellers' gaze *look back* (in both senses of the phrase).

## Marvellous Travel

Like much Irish travel writing this century, Kate O'Brien's travel accounts merit close attention. Their attempt to negotiate a peace between private travel and mass tourism without succumbing to the Patrician condescension of the romantic traveller is instructive. She is aware that though most Irish and English people speak and write about travelling in the same language, they travel differently (though here again, she does not exaggerate). O'Brien takes a genre that had a tradition of distinguished women authors in Ireland (Somerville, Edgeworth, Delaney, Herbert) and enlivens it with her distinctive and imaginative contribution. Des Esseintes, the hero of J. K. Huysman's novel *À rebours*, wonders why one should bother travelling when one can travel magnificently on a chair.[33] Huysmans's eccentric dandy would have delighted in the moving pictures of Kate O'Brien which allow the sedentary reader any amount of 'marvellous travelling'.

## Notes and references

1   Kate O'Brien, *My Ireland,* London, Batsford, 1962, p. 111.
2   Charles Musser, 'The Travel Genre in 1903–1904: Moving Towards Fictional Narrative', Thomas Elsaesser (ed.), *Early Cinema: space - frame - narrative,* London, British Film Institute, 1990, p. 127. See also Wolfgang Schivelbusch, *The Railway Journey: Trains and Travel in the 19th Century,* New York, Urizen Books, 1980.
3   Sara Mills, *Discourses of Difference: An Analysis of Women's Travel Writing and Colonialism,* London, Routledge, 1991, p. 6.
4   O'Brien, *My Ireland,* p. 163.
5   Mary Louise Pratt, *Imperial Eyes: Travel Writing and Transculturation,* London, Routledge, 1992, p. 217.
6   ibid., pp. 69–85.
7   Kate O'Brien, *Farewell Spain* (1937), London, Virago, 1985, p. 3.
8   Pratt, *Imperial Eyes,* p. 78.
9   O'Brien, *Farewell Spain,* p. 6.
10  For the emphasis on the factual in Renaissance travel writing see Jenny Mezciems, ' "Tis not to divert the Reader": Moral and Literary Determinants in Some Early Travel Narratives', Philip Dodd (ed.), *The Art of Travel: Essays on Travel Writing,* London, Frank Cass, 1982, p. 2.
11  O'Brien, *Farewell Spain,* pp. 58–9.
12  Cited in ibid., p. 114.

13  ibid., p. 193.
14  O'Brien, *My Ireland*, p. 23.
15  O'Brien, *Farewell Spain*, p. 21.
16  O'Brien, *My Ireland*, p. 16.
17  Mills, *Discourses of Difference*, p. 44. See also Kay Schaffer, *Women and the Bush: Forces of Desire in the Australian Cultural Tradition*, Cambridge University Press, 1989.
18  O'Brien, *My Ireland*, p. 32.
19  ibid., p. 35.
20  ibid., p. 57.
21  Gary Hogg, *Turf Beneath My Feet*, London, Museum Press, 1950, pp. 231–2.
22  O'Brien, *My Ireland*, p. 54.
23  O'Brien, *Farewell Spain*, p. 120.
24  O'Brien, *My Ireland*, p. 158.
25  O'Brien, *Farewell Spain*, p. 183
26  ibid., pp. 182–3.
27  Mills, *Discourses of Difference*, p. 89.
28  O'Brien, *My Ireland*, p. 30.
29  ibid., p. 186.
30  O'Brien, *My Ireland*, p. 25.
31  ibid., p. 135.
32  Pratt, *Imperial Eyes*, p. 138.

*Chapter 10*

# Lock Up Your Daughters
# From Ante-Room to Interior Castle

*Eibhear Walshe*

They shut me up in Prose
When as a Little Girl.
They put me in the closet
Because they liked me 'still'.
                    Emily Dickinson.[1]

## Introduction

In 1938, in something of a panic, Kate O'Brien published her most polemical, least mediated and, in a sense, weakest novel, *Pray For The Wanderer*. Her 1936 novel *Mary Lavelle* having been banned in Ireland and her 1937 travelogue *Farewell Spain* banned in Spain, O'Brien construed these threats to her own creative freedom as manifestations of a broader destabilisation of 'civilisation' as she saw it. 'The warm personal principle now about to die, perhaps the individual thing, the piled-up memory, the piety, the long-held, bitterly wronged sweetness of personal liberty now going out everywhere.'[2] At this historical moment, not only did O'Brien feel personally marginalised, she feared the obliteration of the European cultural context that had informed and supported her own fiction.

150

All the thoughtful world a thing of ruins and archaisms; Scholarship and art in prison or in the pay of politicians. . . . Spain, – one of Europe's eternal glories – tearing herself apart, being helped to do it, not being hindered. Man's courageous heart, individual heart, undiscoverable anywhere. Even at last the poets in vocal flight – to absurd and terrible obedience. Hugging their chains. Singing the new theme of captivity.[3]

In this essay, I wish to examine the consequences of this moment of panic and crisis in O'Brien's writing. Specifically I want to delineate the process by which she moves away from direct confrontation with this threatened patriarchal hegemony towards the establishment of a counter-hegemony. This initial confrontation is seen most overtly in *Pray for the Wanderer* and is also at work in *Farewell Spain,* only achieving transformation into counter-strategies of female empowerment in her 1946 novel *That Lady.* It is the argument of this essay that, in a sense, *That Lady* represents the completion of a project partially attempted (and ultimately unfulfilled) in *Pray for the Wanderer,* that project being the realisation of a viable defence against censorship and, by implication, against the constrictions of a centralised and masculinist nationalism.

Essentially what the earlier novel attempts, and fails, to provide is a site for some sort of alternative resistance. What is sought is a locus for the beleaguered individual to reconstitute identity. What O'Brien feared was the rise of a devouring and controlling authoritarianism, which would lead to a usurpation of private morality. At the centre of her panic was a fear of the incipient destruction of 'man's courageous heart' and outrage at the rise of cultural fascism. I would argue that only in *That Lady* does O'Brien finally create a narrative wherein a female protagonist actualises radical dissent and achieves vital contradistinction from patriarchial control.

This successful realisation of alternative sources of personal identity and political identity comes not simply from the chronology of these works. It would be too simple to see these three novels as moving in a sort of teleological progression, time providing O'Brien with an opportunity to reflect and to rally. Rather I would contend that the completion of this project of resistance

in *That Lady* depends largely on O'Brien's use of the metaphor
of claustration and derives from her interpretation of the life and
the writings of Teresa of Avila.

O'Brien, in her 1951 monogram on Teresa, makes overt her
own particular reclamation of this emblematic figure:

> I write of Teresa of Avila by choice which is passionate, arbitrary, per-
> sonal. I am free here to speak of a great woman. But I am not writing
> of the canonised saint. I propose to examine Teresa, not by the rules
> of canonisation, but for what she was – saint or not – a woman of
> genius.[4]

Crucial to the ideological subtext of *That Lady* is O'Brien's
reading of Teresa's spiritual works, particularly *The Interior Castle*
and *The Life of Saint Teresa of Avila by Herself*, a reading that remakes
Teresa's concept of the woman mystic, the ascetic. O'Brien appropriates this figure of the 'holy woman' and transcodes her as
female radical, political dissident. By interpreting the spiritual as
the political, O'Brien finds a core of resistance, a denial of the
centre that allows her fiction to move beyond the merely reactionary and towards the actively subversive.

In particular she takes Teresa's concept of the *Interior Castle*, a
reflection 'on the soul's progressive discovery of the divine in
dwelling',[5] and recasts it as the prison, the closet, the cell. Thus
a radically refashioned interior castle now becomes the site from
which the female protagonist can produce a counter-hegemony,
facilitating disruption and inscribing the text with challenge.

Therefore in this essay, I will first consider *Pray for the Wanderer*
and *Farewell Spain* (O'Brien's situating of the individual artist as
marginal) where she defines both the threatened 'civilisation' and
the threatening oligarchies. Then, examining the writings of Teresa
of Avila and, in particular, O'Brien's reading of these works, I
will argue for a direct analogy with *That Lady*, O'Brien's most
fully realised anti-patriarchal novel.


## Pray for the Wanderer

This 1938 novel has, uniquely for O'Brien, a male protagonist,
Matt Costello, but a male protagonist who bears undoubted

resemblance to his creator. A distinguished novelist abroad but banned within the Free State, Costello, dubbed ironically 'Mellick's returned celebrity',[6] visits his old family home. He arrives in Ireland at a moment of crisis when political disturbance, both national and international, is being countered by de Valera in his proposed new constitution. As Matt ruminates:

> A dictator's country, too. But a more subtle dictator than most – though he also, given time, might have the minds of his people in chains. He did not bring materialism out for public adoration, but materialistic justice controlled by a dangerous moral philosophy, the new Calvinism of the Roman Catholic. . . . Subtle but dictatorial and obstinate. A clever man, Dev. Well, the Free state would vote on its constitution and Matt imagined and imagined that de Valera too imagined, that Ireland, newly patrolled by the Church, would be unlikely to vote solid against the Holy Trinity.[7].

Into this self-refashioning Free State comes Matt Costello, whose novels have been described as 'myth-creating, anti-social and unnecessary'.[8] In a key scene in the novel, Matt is called upon to defend his art by Father Malachy, a formidable young priest ('What is the function of such work as yours, I've often wondered?')[9] Malachi, respected by Matt for his integrity and the 'generosity of Saint Francis'[10] is, nevertheless, an advocate of censorship and suppression.

Here, in the figure of this austere priest, O'Brien presents a version of Catholic Ireland that is intellectually rigorous, impressively forthright in argument and well-versed in aesthetic debate. Matt, on the other hand, seems indecisive, indolent and without a centred artistic purpose:

> Any books, mine or Amanda Ros's or Virgil's exist solely to demonstrate the artist's desire or ability to write them. They are the fruits of the creative function, as irresponsible, if you like, as other fruits of creation. . . . I'm perfectly content that you others don't allow the likes of me our clear faith, our definite duty to – something or other.[11]

In a sense, O'Brien deliberately juxtaposes Matt's careless, apparently random defence of his art with the precise and measured censure of Father Malachi, as if arguing for a gradual formulation of an aesthetic code, to be discovered in the face of opposition.

Throughout the confrontation, it is Malachi who attacks, Matt who must defend, and from that defence comes a manifesto for 'individualism': 'If Father Malachi insists that I must have a function, a social duty, all right. I believe that now as never before it is the duty of those who can refrain from meddling not to meddle. I believe that it is useful at present to be an individual.'[12]

Father Malachi presents a conventional Thomist notion of art: 'I'm a practical man, concerned with the problem of good and evil here and now, as I think men like you should be'.[13] He rejects Matt's assertion of artistic individualism: 'It's they who are the instigators and inspirers of egotism, the handers-on of all the romantic and individualist nonsense that's made a shambles of the world. Artists are dangerous fellows.' . . . 'Plato thought so. So does Hitler', said Matt, 'So does Stalin. So does Dev, I'll be bound.'[14]

To this, Matt opposes with a Joycean belief in the innate integrity and organic self-sufficiency of the artistic imagination:

> My job is to re-create life, not as it is, Good God, but as the peculiarities of my vision and desire assume it. I give you life translated to my idiom. You take it or leave it. But if your leaving it makes me endeavour to force my eyesight differently, or to alter my reaction, then, Father Malachi, I am in danger of committing mortal sin.[15]

Thus O'Brien articulates, through the medium of a civilised after-dinner debate between the well-informed priest and the respectfully dissenting novelist, a clear rejection of the control sought by Church and State over creative autonomy. As Matt declares:

> I reject the censorship, lock, stock and barrel because it is a confession of failure. It is a denial of human judgement and understanding, and a gross intrusion on liberty. If you, Tom, or Nell Mahoney may read my books and sit in judgement on them – by what right do you decide that it is not for others to do so, sheer impertinence. . . . Too many negative regulations are a symptom of weakness in any authority. . . . I'm not prepared to be saved on Ireland's dictated terms.[16]

The problem with Matt Costello, and indeed with *Pray for the Wanderer* as a whole, is that, although there is a clear and argued attack on censorship and an impassioned and reasoned defence of the privacy of private morality, O'Brien fails to make this dissent manifest within the text. Matt articulates much of the same resistance to authoritarian control as Ana de Mendoza, but unlike Ana, can offer no viable counter-resistance to the dominant culture. He tries to marry Nell Mahoney, a devout Catholic and intellectual, who has dubbed his work 'unnecessary'. Instead she marries her cousin Tom, another Mellick man and one who has made his peace with De Valera's Ireland and is prepared to live under its terms and exactions. Matt finally quits Mellick, having been defeated in his efforts to settle, and leaving behind a community largely untroubled by its rejection of artistic freedom.

## Farewell Spain

In *Farewell Spain*, O'Brien's lament for a doomed civilisation, there is also a continuing subtext of panic, of threat, focusing on the rise of Fascism in her beloved Spain. In this spirit of alarm and at a moment when the Civil War was still unresolved, she writes 'as an escapist, of that which recedes and is half-remembered'.[17] In a sense, this travelogue is a plea for direct political support and indeed for moral approval of the Republican cause: 'A war such as General Franco's, openly aimed at the murder of every democratic principle – such a war strikes not merely at the death of Spain but at every decent dream or effort for humanity everywhere.'[18] However, it was a plea that resulted in her being banned from Spain when, as she feared, Franco became ultimate victor and the democratic impulse so cherished by O'Brien had been obliterated.

As with *Pray for the Wanderer*, there is a reassertion of the need for individual liberty and a fear of imposed political conformity: 'If there is anything at all in human promise, in political struggle, it will be uniform and monotonous. That is what the maddened world must seek now, the justice of decent uniformity.'[19] However, it is important to note that O'Brien's elegy for Spain and her championing of Spain's particular 'solitary' spirit are both precise and, at the same time, excluding, partial constructs. 'It is their secret to be highly vitalised yet detached from life. Warm and cold, generous and secretive.'[20] (In all these writings O'Brien deploys terms like 'solitary' and 'individual' to denote particular cultural valuations, investing them with specific ideological nuance.)

In seeking to resist the destruction of democracy, O'Brien presents a version of Spanish 'civilisation' that is, in actuality, solely Castilian and Catholic, and concerned with monarchs, mystics, painters and writers of that region. O'Brien excludes any consideration of the lively cultural identity of regions like Andalusia, Galicia and Catalonia, presenting Castile as cradle of an archetypal 'Spanish' spirit and culture. Furthermore, there is a complete rejection of any Moorish influence, when she declares: 'The Moor long ago imperilled Spanish judgement with his arty – and – craftiness. Imperilled and infected but mercifully did not dominate. Still his legacy remains a menace and I, for my part, detest all signs of the Moor in Spain.'[21] (There is a dangerous trifling by O'Brien with racist terms like 'infected' in relation to Moorish influence, throughout *Farewell Spain*).

Therefore, in this process of writing 'Spain', O'Brien chooses to concentrate, geographically, on places like Avila, Salamanca, El Escorial, Santilla, centres of Catholic worship, cathedral and university towns, bastions of Castilian aristocracy, key sites for Catholic belief and power. She devotes whole chapters to emblematic figures of Catholic Spain like St Teresa of Avila and Philip II, and evaluates painters like Goya, El Greco and Velázquez as prototypes of the liberal humanist artist. What interests O'Brien about these artists is their struggle to find ways of dialoguing with a personal God through the freedom of the solitary artistic vocation. Indeed her comparison between Teresa and her contemporary Martin Luther in many ways epitomises her vindication of proud, individual, Castilian conscience:

> I risk suggesting that the great reformer Teresa had gifts and attributes in common with her enemy, Luther. She was a Castilian lady and therefore had beautiful manners, which he sadly lacked; she also had a subtle kind of humour which was not his, and she was fine where he was coarse. But she was like Luther, passionate. . . . When Luther went to work, his intention was precisely what Teresa's was later to be. His temperament and his career, creating between them a certain set of accidents, carried him far from his first moorings. Teresa had the advantage of his – in breeding, let us say, certainly in social

training. Also she was a woman and conservative; also her impulse
for reform was backward to the old forgotten austerities – not forward to their overthrow and dismissal.[22]

Thus in *Farewell Spain* O'Brien posits a particular 'civilisation'
(Castilian, Catholic, aristocratic), providing a redefinition of the
individual, set against cultural paternalism. In a sense, what this
travelogue really allows for is the imagining, by O'Brien, of a
cultural and racial context for Ana De Mendoza, the crucial figure
in her parable of resistance and the controlling metaphorical element in her strategies against patriarchy.

## From Ante-Room to Interior Castle

Imprisonment, incarceration, claustration; a familiar literary device,
central in texts like *Little Dorrit, Jane Eyre, The Man in The Iron
Mask*. A metaphor for entrapment, a means by which repression
and curtailment could be covertly discussed. There is, however,
a distinct definitional separation to be made in modes employed
to depict male and female claustration, as noted by D. A. Miller
in an essay called 'Cage aux Folles': 'Male carceral representations
tended to be more consciously and objectively elaborated and were
thus metaphysical and metaphorical, whereas female ones tended to be social and actual.'[23]

Miller argues that in key texts male claustration is portrayed
as having wider implications. *Little Dorrit*, for example, figures
the imprisonment of the Dorrit family as metaphor for wider
cultural entrapment, the chains that bind them within the
Marshalsea ultimately reaching out to encircle an entire society.
Conversely, in the novels of Charlotte Brontë, claustration is
specifically identified with the interiority of the (female) protagonist. Brontë's 'madwoman in the attic' may represent aspects
of the protagonist's psyche and seems rarely to move into the realm
of wider metaphysical signification.

In terms of O'Brien's own narratives, the notion of the cell,
the room, the private space has a particular resonance but one
that confines itself to the interior and, with the exception of *That
Lady,* never implicates itself in the overtly political. I would argue
that, in general, O'Brien tends toward this gender-oriented use

of the metaphor of incarceration, and it is by transmuting Teresa's paradigmatic figure of the woman ascetic that she moves beyond interiority simply as interiority.

Before examining the workings of this transformation in *That Lady*, it is worth considering two other novels where O'Brien makes specific imaginative use of the chamber. In both works, the 'holy' woman's cell becomes a focus for implicit resistance to the dominant discourse of the novel's world. In *Mary Lavelle*, the room of Agatha Conlon foreshadows Ana De Mendoza's prison cell, and in a later novel *The Flower of May*, the private study of Eleanor Delahunty in her father's house at Glassala occupies a parallel position in the imaginative structure of the novel.

Both novels, bracketing *That Lady*, serve as fruitful comparison, as both Agatha and Eleanor bear a generic resemblance to Ana (severe, perceived as nunnish and referred to as 'mad' by those who surround them) and yet, essentially, O'Brien keeps both within the realm of interior conflict and exploration. Agatha's marginality is derived from her 'aberrant' sexuality, Eleanor's from her subversion of patriarchal control on female autonomy and education; yet O'Brien never politicises her figuring of these women as completely as she does Ana.

In *Mary Lavelle* Agatha's difference is expressed by the severity and rigour of her faith, reflected in the personal space she has created for herself in Spain: 'Her room was immaculate and im-personal as a monk's. She opened a long, lace-screened window that overlooked the square. Mary, looking out, saw the church facade and tower; saw the rigid masts of ships and the wine red mountain-side with evening light'.[24] Like Ana, Agatha is viewed in terms of her androgyny: 'The hungry, unbalanced face looked smooth and young, "You might take her for a boy now"'[25], but also aestheticised because of this strangeness: 'How beautiful the creature can seem.'[26]

In *The Flower of May* the focus is less on the 'Holy Woman' as sexual dissident than on the room, the cell, as the site for resistance to patriarchal control. Eleanor Delahunty's private room functions as her office in her father's old mansion, Glassala, and is depicted in terms of apartness from the rest of the house: 'Aunt Eleanor's office was a very small room at the back of the back hall, . . . the lighthouse beam did not strike this side of the house directly but its reflection swept past over the sky every minute.[27] (This lighthouse beam has already been used by O'Brien to signify an 'outer' world that Fanny, the protagonist, is learning to 'fraternise' with.) Eleanor's conscious separateness from the rest of her father's house is even more overt in the following:

> Fanny had very seldom been allowed even to look round the door of Aunt Eleanor's office, and certainly had never sat in it before. . . . This room expressed a part of Aunt Eleanor which she did not know . . . this room was a very private piece of self-expression and bore no relation to the rest of the vast, haphazard house. . . . In spite of all it contained, orderliness gave the little room an extreme austerity. . . . "I know what this room is like, Aunt Eleanor" said Fanny, "it's like Mère Générale's study."[28]

In this austere room, away from the main body of the house and the intrusive lighthouse beam, Eleanor plots to leave her property to Fanny (disinheriting her brothers) and thereby empowering Fanny towards education and autonomy.

Both Agatha and Eleanor are partial expressions of sexual and patriarchal dissidence in O'Brien's work, each representing particular aspects of counter-resistance, but only in her depiction of Ana de Mendoza does O'Brien conflate all these aspects of dissidence and confront her censors directly.

## That Lady

For O'Brien, the genre of historical fiction allowed some form of protection from the threat of censorship or from accusations of dissidence. Indeed, as she puts it in the preface: 'what follows is not an historical novel. It is an invention arising from reflection on the curious external story of Ana De Mendoza.'[29] She takes the 'mystery' of Ana's imprisonment by her friend and monarch, Philip II ('Historians cannot explain this episode'[30]), and reworks it as confrontation between this stubbornly independent 'holy woman' and her most Catholic and absolute sovereign. (In reality, historians have no difficulty in explaining this episode: the historical Ana De Mendoza was an arrogant and difficult aristocrat, whose family eventually had to beg Philip to put an end to her dangerous and treasonable intrigues with her lover, Antonio Perez. Philip responded by locking her up!)

*That Lady* investigates the 'criminality' of Ana's covert affair with Antonio, construed by Philip as an affront to his suzerainty over Ana as imperial subject. Ana De Mendoza, as O'Brien presents her, enjoys a dual relationship with her ruler; she is both loyal servant of her feudal master and, as an aristocrat herself, a firm monarchist and a believer in royal authority. She is also one of his oldest friends, widow of his loyal and beloved minister, Ruy Gomez, and popularly, if incorrectly, assumed to be his former mistress. It is this *frisson* of the scandalous, this unspoken, yet implicit, erotic charge that draws the puritanical Philip to casual, eccentric Ana and gives a particularly intense quality to their relationship.

However, this delicate balance between respect and flirtation, between public duty and private affection, is exploded when Philip learns of Ana's secret affair with his secretary of state, Antonio Perez. What alarms Philip is the implicit assumption of sexual and moral autonomy by Ana and he punishes her through incarceration, thus, he believes, neutralising the threat of insubordination. It is therefore important to consider the way in which O'Brien sexualises this 'criminal' act, this illegal affair. As with other imaginative constructs by O'Brien, she figures Ana De Mendoza and Antonio Perez in such a way that these imaginative values operate for subversion.

O'Brien presents Ana in terms that disrupt conventional gendering and aestheticises her in a manner quite outside her usual obsessive interest in conventional female beauty. Perez, her lover, initially derides her as 'one-eyed and thin',[31] noting that she is 'simple, almost to dullness and doesn't play the great beauty'.[32] However this physical difference, this disfigured, spare, androgyny begins to attract him and he finally admits 'her dangerous simplicity, her gaunt, almost ungainly beauty'.[33]

A significant element in Ana's representation is her lost eye, the badge of difference and disfigurement. Marked, significantly, during a youthful duel with a servant while defending the honour of Castile, Ana is jolted into a state of metaphysical isolation and apartness, made different both physically and spiritually. Her eyepatch, covering the empty socket, becomes fetishised in the course of the novel when, at moments of tension and defiance, Ana touches the dark, triangular piece of silk, her talisman of interiority.

Towards the close of the novel, when she has suffered the full rigours of imprisonment and alienation, her friend the Cardinal of Toledo finally raises the question: '"Your injured eye", he said gently, "has that distressed you much in your secret life?" "There is nothing to say now. I am old. But I think it decided everything in my life for me."'[34]

Set apart physically, Ana's difference is expressed in other ways, her distinct lack of maternal affection for some of her children, her disdain for material wealth and, most crucially, her intellectualising of the erotic itself, the erotic being the radical destabiliser for Philip's Catholic autocracy . She says of her decision to become Antonio's lover: 'I'm nearly thirty-seven and I'm said to have more power in my hands sometimes than any other woman in Spain. Yet this is only the second time in my life that I've decided anything for myself'.[35]

Consistent with this re-gendering of Ana is O'Brien's feminisation of her lover, Perez, encoded with images of womanly beauty, and initially dismissed by Ana as effete and sexually irrelevant. 'He seems to be just a little popinjay, almost a mignon.'[36] Her confidant, Bernardina, also dismisses him as effeminate: 'He smells like a woman.'[37] Significantly, when Ana decides to becomes his lover, it is because of the atypicality of his masculinity: 'He's odd. He runs quite counter to our usual male conventions.'[38] In the course of their liaison it is Ana who buys jewels as love tokens for her vain, pretty lover.

As a result of this affair, this covert mating of transgendered lovers, Ana and Perez make a mortal enemy of the puritanical Juan de Escovedo, Philip's other secretary of state, who violates the privacy of Ana's bedchamber to denounce the lovers directly. Thus, when Philip decides to have Escovedo secretly murdered in the interests of the state, Perez becomes an accomplice. This is against Ana's advice, knowing that Perez wishes to avenge the blasphemous attack on their intimacy. However, in the ensuing outcry, the demand for justice and a public investigation into the Escovedo case seems to alert Philip to the love-affair and he withdraws from Ana's life, playing a cruel waiting game with the lovers and refusing to allow the murder case to come to trial.

In the pivotal scene of the novel, Philip finally visits Ana after many months of silence, and at the height of public demand for a trial. In the course of this encounter between subject and autocrat, crucial issues of state authority and individual conscience are debated and confronted and two radically opposite interpretations of Ana's affair become the starting-point for a more profound difference.

> She outraged no claim of his in loving another man and her private life was her own. This was her secret argument and it was well founded and in that sense true. But it did not compass the whole of Philip and because in her innocence and mercy she thought it did, it was dangerous for her.[39]

Dangerously, honestly and naively, Ana presents Philip with a clear and unequivocal account of the inviolate sacredness of personal morality:

> There have been, Philip, as long as I can remember, thoughts, and even acts in that private life, which, presented to the world, would seem to injure this or that. If I do wrong in it, that wrong is between me and heaven. But here below, so long as I don't try to change it into public life, I insist that I own it.[40]

In a certain sense, O'Brien places Ana's forthright, if idealistic, defense of an autonomous personal life in contradistinction to Philip's world-weary political pragmatism, setting her up as an innocent adrift in complex and urgent matters of state. Yet Ana displays a precision and a directness in the final confrontation, when it comes, an understanding of essential conflict: 'You know that in everything of me that your office commands I am absolutely yours. But if you were ever to forget to be king, you know perfectly well that I'd refuse.'[41] Ana pleads with Philip for openness in government, for a public trial of the Escovedo murder, and, most radically, for a democratic judgement, 'the breathing and blowing of the larger world on that dilemma'.[42]

This is at the heart of Ana's impulsive and generous idealism towards Philip, this vision of a system of government drawing its power from a base of shared moral responsibility. Philip's sense of personal destiny, of intuitive and absolute knowledge of the priorities of statecraft, is what Ana is deconstructing. As he expresses it: 'I know what Spain is. And before the world and Heaven, I represent that Spain I know and so I cannot, cannot be subject to Castile's small moral judgements.'[43] It is to correct this paternalism, this usurpation of all individual and democratic impulses that Ana reminds Philip: 'Nevertheless, you are finally subject to "Castile's small moral judgements".'[44] She goes on to exhort him:

> Come back to govern us so that we can see what you are doing. Make this gesture of having a fair trial and facing the consequences. Let us feel the movement of government in Spain again; let us throw in our responsibility with you and lend you those moral judgements you so fear. Will you do it, Philip?[45]

For Ana, this is a crucial opportunity, an end to the devious concealments of closed government: 'She felt very happy and almost envied Philip the opportunity he had to seize.'[46] Political-ly, however, it is a blunder. Philip's response to her generous ex-hortation is panic at the audacity of her belief in equality and distrust in her individualism. He acts swiftly to neutralise her transgression. Ana is arrested, deprived of liberty, cut off from family and influence and brought near to death by the severity of her incarceration. The individual, it would seem, is without power when faced with totalitarian control.

However, it is the form that this imprisonment takes and the way in which O'Brien politicises this claustration that provides a counter-resistance to Philip's absolutism. Her ill-fated plea for democracy seems, initially, to be symptomatic of Ana's dangerous-ly simple naivety, but as her punishment progresses, O'Brien makes manifest the dissenting principles articulated by Ana and her radical opposition and stubborn individualism are hardened into direct resistance.

Earlier in the novel, Ana makes reference to an embarrassing episode in her life, an encounter with Teresa of Avila, when the newly-widowed Ana attempted, impulsively, to become a Carmelite nun. Teresa, head of a reformed and rigorously spar-tan community, rejects Ana, considering her vocation for a strict life of contemplation and absolute denial to be a false one. Now, at a later stage in her life, Ana finds herself, albeit unexpectedly, fulfilling the strict rule of Teresa, becoming, as it were, a discalcated 'holy woman', a protesting, reformed subject because of dissent from her Catholic king.

Ana's claustration, her 'shutting up', is made literal and absolute. Her ducal palace, formerly the symbol of her wealth and station, becomes her cell, her cloister:

> A great wall had been built to cut them off from the staircase which led to the garden. A small iron door was inserted in this, through which the wardress would come to see them henceforth. Ana's bedroom and dressing room were entirely deprived of daylight and ventilation. . . . She never saw the great staircase of her house. There was no window by which to sit and talk. There was no light any more in the drawing room at Pastrana. The great window had been built up and Ana would never again see the sky or the tower of the colegiata.[47]

Within this secular 'convent' Ana's physical well-being deteriorates rapidly, her increasing infirmity paralleled by a gradual removal of material comfort and an insidious erosion of mobility and of contact with the outer world. Already gaunt and different in appearance, she becomes a rheumatic cripple, her long, elegant fingers twisted and disfigured through illness, a middle-aged woman made old prematurely, all 'dangerous' erotic impulses obliterated by incarceration and ill-treatment in this living tomb.

However, what transforms Ana's shabby prison into a site for resistance is her gradual discovery of an 'interior castle', a growing certitude that sustains her gesture of defiance and is born of the extinction of the sensual and the consequent nurturing of the spiritual. From illness and solitude comes a more profound understanding of the integrity of her dissidence until as the Cardinal of Toledo observes at the end of the novel: 'She looks very distinguished and ascetic, he thought, like a very good nun who has been worked too hard.'[48] Ana finally realises her vocation as holy woman, creating, as it were, an alternative religious community in her prison cell, with her companion Bernardina and her daughter Anichu as fellow votives. The decision by Anichu to become a nun after her mother's death simply reinforces this.

There is, for O'Brien, a sense of triumph implicit in Ana's life and death, a belief in the validity of her gesture of defiance. There is also a lament for the moral bankruptcy of Ana's country: 'Spain is the mistress of the world and she is decaying.'[49] Although supreme controller of her physical fate, Philip proves ultimately powerless in his attempts to colonise her interiority. This, for O'Brien, supports and validates her attack on authoritarianism and realises a confounding and a countering of patriarchy.

This closure marks a departure for O'Brien as artist, this sense of a complete and distinct finality in the narrative. *That Lady* is her only novel that doesn't move towards a suspended note, an open ending, and this is because it is her only novel which can't be classed as family romance, but is, instead, a political fable.

Her parable of dissent achieves closure with the image of the aged, disappointed Philip, isolated and lonely in his tyranny and haunted by the spectre of the victorious and eternally vivid Ana.

> He rose painfully from the table and moved without purpose across the room. A bell was ringing from Santa Maria Almudena. He remembered how much more clearly one heard that bell in the Long Room of the Eboli Palace. He looked out at the sunlight towards her empty house and the glare hurt his eyes and the bell seemed to toll for his loneliness, and the sins that drove him on, for ever further into loneliness. [50]

Thus O'Brien gestures towards the powerlessness of autocracy and the enduring resistance of individualism and of political dissidence.

## Notes and references

1   Emily Dickinson, *Collected Poems*, T. Hughes (ed.), London, Faber and Faber, 1988.
2   Kate O'Brien, *Pray for the Wanderer*, London, Heinemann, 1938, p. 4.
3   ibid., p. 4.
4   Kate O'Brien, *Teresa of Avila*, London, Max Parrish, 1951, p. 10.
5   *Teresa of Avila by Herself*, London, Penguin, 1988, p. xi.
6   O'Brien, *Pray for the Wanderer*, p. 181.
7   ibid., p. 41.
8   ibid., p. 181.
9   ibid., p. 181.
10  ibid., p. 190.
11  ibid., p. 182.
12  ibid., p. 183.
13  ibid., p. 183.

14   ibid., p. 187.

15   ibid., p. 184.

16   ibid., p. 191.

17   Kate O'Brien, *Farewell Spain* (1937), London, Virago, 1985, p. 1.

18   ibid., p. 221.

19   ibid., p. 2.

20   ibid., p. 225.

21   ibid., p. 138.

22   O'Brien, *Teresa of Avila,* p. 68.

23   D. A. Miller, 'Cage aux Folles', E. Showalter (ed.), *Speaking of Gender,* London, Routledge, 1989, p. 189.

24   Kate O'Brien, *Mary Lavelle*, London, Heinemann, 1936, p. 97.

25   ibid., p 117.

26   ibid., p. 201.

27   Kate O'Brien, *The Flower of May,* London, Heinemann, 1953, p. 219.

28   ibid., p. 220.

29   Kate O'Brien, *That Lady,* London, Heinemann, 1946, foreword.

30   ibid.

31   ibid., p. 44.

32   ibid., p. 46.

33   ibid., p. 57.

34   ibid., p. 328.

35   ibid., p. 59.

36   ibid., p. 32.

37   ibid., p. 60.

38   ibid., p. 51.

39   ibid., p. 233.

40   ibid., p. 236.

41   ibid., p. 246.

42   ibid., p. 243.

43   ibid., p. 245.

44   ibid., p. 245.

45   ibid., p. 245.

46   ibid., p. 246.

47   ibid., p. 302, 317.

48   ibid., p. 328.

49   ibid., p. 316.

50   ibid., p. 378.

*Chapter 11*

# Something Understood?
# Kate O'Brien and *The Land of Spices*

*Mary Breen*

This essay is a reading of Kate O'Brien's *The Land Of Spices*. It considers the ways in which the novel has been read in the past and suggests possible alternatives to, or modifications of, these readings. Its concerns are firstly, the narrative techniques adopted by O'Brien and the ways in which they inform the meanings of the text, secondly, the possibility of reading the text as a feminist work, and finally, the stance adopted by the narrative on issues such as nationalism, homosexuality, family life and interpersonal relationships. The main contention in this argument is that *The Land Of Spices* is a radical and subversive critique of conservative patriarchal ideology, in particular that articulated in the Irish Constitution of 1937. The essay is divided into three sections. Section I discusses the banning of the novel in 1942, also considering Austin Clarke's contemporary appraisal of the novel. Section II explores the implications of reading the novel as a form of gynocentrism or woman-centred fiction, examining cultural representation of the woman and the psychological construction of female creativity. Section III outlines some of the central discourses of the novel: Irish nationalism, the family and

interpersonal relationships, discussing the representation of each
of these discourses, their limitations, and the alternative structures with which the text proposes to replace them.

# I

The Constitution of Ireland came into operation on 29 December
1937. Just a few years later, in 1942, *The Land Of Spices,* Kate
O'Brien's fifth novel, was published. In that same year it was
banned by the Irish Censorship Board for its 'immorality'.[1] The
Censorship Board 'understood' that this novel, which deals with
convent life in Ireland in the early years of the twentieth century,
was 'so repulsive' that it 'should not be left where it would fall
into the hands of very young people'. Homosexual desire was suggested in the line: 'she saw Etienne and her father, in the embrace
of love'[2] and was thus offered as irrefutable evidence of the
novel's immorality. What the Board chose not to understand was
that homosexuality is not necessarily approved of in the novel
and, furthermore, the word 'homosexual' is not in fact used, nor
is there any further discussion of same-sex desire in the text. Helen
Archer, profoundly shocked by seeing her father and Etienne
together, reasons: 'So that was the sort of thing that the most
graceful life could hide! That was what lay around, under love,
under beauty. That was the flesh they preached about, the ex-
tremity of what the sin of the flesh might be.'[3] This interpretation of what she sees as her father's aberrant sexuailty causes
such revulsion in Helen that she turns in disgust from human love
and undertakes 'the impersonal and active service of God' as a
nun in the Compagnie de la Sainte Famille.[4] Although Helen in
later life is reconciled with her father, this reconciliation is partial
and censors the fact of his homosexuality. Of course, even to mention or suggest the possibility of homosexuality could be read
by some as a promotion of it: whether or not homosexuality is
approved of in the novel was irrelevant to those who chose to
be offended by it.

The irony is, however, that at a more profound level *The Land
Of Spices* was indeed a subtle threat to the narrow isolationalist
and xenophobic politics that ruled Ireland in the 1940s. But it

was not explicitly a threat to what the Irish Censorship Board protectively considered was a vulnerable Irish morality. Far more seriously, it questions and criticises the whole ideology of that period in Irish cultural history. It does so in a number of ways: by its detachment from Irish nationalism, its emphasis on individual freedom and responsibility, its championing of religious and educational structures, detached from parochial concerns, its foregrounding of the viability of female identity outside patriarchial family units, and its determinedly outward-looking, European perspective. All of these concerns, I would contend, amount to a concerted and rigorous attack on key articles of the Irish Constitution.

The Censorship Board was correct in recognising that this novel was in some way dangerous, but wrong, I would argue, in its location of that danger. It is not difficult to understand why the Board misguidedly focused on this one sentence as the narrative itself foregrounds it. It is a disturbing and arresting sentence, not because of its 'immorality' but because it opens out wider disturbances within the text. The whole issue of Helen Archer's vocation is predicated on this moment, and is thus implicated in these wider disturbances. O'Brien presents obliquely this aberrant sexuality as an agent of vocation and disturbance. The words associated with Helen's vocation are 'hysteria', 'panic', and 'agonising pain'. There are sinister hints in sentences such as: 'She had worshipped as perfect the author of her destruction', and 'She trembled now in revulsion from his once dear kisses.' [5] The crucial scene is described in a very graphic but simple way: 'Two people were there. But neither saw her: neither felt her shadow as it froze across the sun.'[6] This is followed by the phrase which we may tend to find coyly euphemistic: 'She saw Etienne and her father, in the embrace of love.'[7] All the preceding chapters lead up to this moment and those following are shaped by it. The structural importance of the sentence is evident, but does it carry the weight required by the plot and the theme? Is it artistically credible?

Austin Clarke, one of the first people to review the novel, speaks for many critics of the novel when he writes: 'There seems to me to be one artistic flaw in this book, the nature of the shock which drove Helen Archer, the beautiful intelligent, young English girl into a Continental order in a mood of agonised revulsion.' He suggests that a 'more personal experience would have given more scope for analysis'.[8] He also questions the 'curious aloofness' of the novelist. (I will return to this 'curious aloofness' later.) Clarke's reading of this infamous sentence as an 'artistic flaw' is as interesting in its own way and, I propose to argue, as ill-informed about the novel as the Censorship Board's decision on the same sentence. A close reading of the novel suggests quite a different conclusion.

Helen Archer has two strong and competing attachments in her young life: her emotional and intellectual belief in her father and her intellectual understanding of and belief in her religion. Before her discovery of her father's homosexuality (which is, according to Catholic theology, a sin), Helen's love of and loyalty to her father far outweigh her admitted attraction to convent life. The conflict between these two beliefs is detailed clearly in the narrative:

> So, vaguely she argued herself away from the threat of vocation. But perhaps her soul always knew that these arguments were beside the point, and that the issue was quite simple – that it lay between him and the only thing that measured up to him in her mind – the religious ideal. But all her feelings gave victory to him – and the other thing remained only an intellectual temptation.[9]

Helen feels that the 'intellectual temptation' will pass but that 'her need and love of him could not'. But this does in fact pass in one blinding flash of insight and the 'intellectual temptation' of the religious life is all that remains. The 'embrace of love' reveals to Helen not simply her father's homosexuality but the lie which their apparently honest and wholesome lives concealed. She is forced to rewrite their whole lives together. She must reassess her father's relationship with her mother, with his pupils, particularly Etienne, and most painfully of all, with herself. In the course of this process she is overwhelmed by jealousy, hate and regret for a lost and now grotesquely distorted past. She turns in 'blind outrage from one collapsed house of her spirit to another standing by, intact'.[10] She is in fact driven 'mad', placed 'outside herself', a key phrase in O'Brien's fiction, which links her experience with that of Mary Lavelle and Ana de Mendoza.

To read the sentence, itself, as a flaw is to misunderstand the delicate and intricate narrative patterning that O'Brien has constructed in *The Land Of Spices*. The two central strands of this patterning are the handling of time and the variations in narrative technique. The novel is set in Ireland between the years 1904 and 1914, and Helen Archer's childhood and adolescence, which she spent in Brussels in the late nineteenth century, are introduced by means of flashback. Helen Archer, now the Reverend Mother of an Irish convent, is betrayed back into a petrified past, which she has for years refused to confront, by the news of her father's imminent death and the arrival of his last letter to her. O'Brien focalises the narrative through Helen in this scene. The phrase 'in the embrace of love' is not the narrator's but Helen Archer's; the euphemism is therefore psychologically credible, whether it is the young sexually innocent construction of the adolescent who witnesses the scene, or the celibate nun's reconstruction of the traumatic event from memory.

Austin Clarke is troubled by the 'curious aloofness' of the novelist. Here he comes closer to what could be described as an artistic flaw, but it is one of style, not of construction. The story is told by an omniscient narrator; it ranges from non-focalised to variably focalised omniscient narration, the focalised narrative varying primarily between Anna and Helen. But control of the narrative is never withdrawn from the omniscient narrator. The novel is at its best when using focalised narrative; the position of the non-focalised omniscient narrator is, however, more problematic.

O'Brien had very firm views on the position the writer should occupy. In her essay, *Imaginative Prose by the Irish*, she writes: 'It is essential for a writer to be detached; but the well-tempered ear knows the difference between the professional detachment of a Flaubert or a Mary Lavin and the from-above amusement of the jokey, look-how-clever-I-am writer of the Somerville and Ross mark.'[11] Though Kate O'Brien belongs with the former rather than the latter, at times in the novel the omniscient narrator does slip disconcertingly from 'professional detachment' into what is best described by O'Brien herself as: 'from above amusement'. I would distinguish this from Jane Austen and George Eliot and the other realist novelists who use narrator's irony at character's expense. This slippage or unevenness in O'Brien's text occurs only at specific times.

While the narrator is ruthless with her minor characters, their flaws and foibles being crudely held up to ridicule, the construction of her central characters, Helen Archer/Mother Marie-Hélène, Henry Archer and Anna Murphy is completed with professional detachment. Even Henry Archer, arguably the most flawed of all, is subtly constructed. In his case the narrator makes no intrusions or impatient asides. The central characters are allowed their complexity, the narrator's opinion of them is never forced on the reader, while the minor characters are not only treated with irony, but there is a deliberate attempt to make them transparent. (I will argue later that this construction of complex central characters and simple minor characters provides very useful insights.)

The narrator is at her most cynical in her treatment of Maud Murphy. She is described as having 'a heart which she believed to be unusually tender and maternal'.[12] The narrator, cuttingly remarking on her self-pity, goes on to explain how 'in dramatisation of her commonplace ineptitude Maud Murphy evaded the brief ordeal of a natural pang'. For an author whose touch is normally so delicate this is rather heavy-handed. Her touch is much more assured when dealing with Mother Marie-Hélène. In her case there is a space between the narrator's view and the character's, and this is filled with subtle approval. (Clearly the narrator thinks more highly of Mother Marie-Hélène than Mother Marie-Hélène does of herself.) But this approval is merely suggested, not laboured, as the disapproval of the minor characters is.

## II  'The Soul Selects Her Own Society'

Eavan Boland has described Kate O'Brien's writing as 'only incidentally feminist work'. She develops this assessment further: 'Because Kate O'Brien always takes womanhood one step further than the accepted conventions of the time, because she never defines it within conventional Romanticism, she has made a significant contribution to the excellence of literature and the understanding of women.' This assessment of O'Brien's work raises several questions that I would like to discuss in this section.[13]

There are several reasons why *The Land Of Spices* might be

classified as a feminist work: it explores gender-specific concerns which are centred around the problem of female identity; the narrative foregrounds the position of women and marginalises that of men; it sees women as individuals and not simply as members of a family unit. Relationships between men and women, between husbands and wives, fathers and daughters, and brothers and sisters, are portrayed as ultimately destructive. The only successful and lasting relationships in the novel are those between women, and these are neither familial nor sexual. Mother Marie-Hélène and Anna Murphy, the two central female characters, emerge at the end of the novel as independent, successful and detached individuals.

The novel offers an alternative to patriarchy, an all-female community which works for the good of all its members. The feminist perspective is implicit, 'something understood'. The introduction of Miss Robertson, a suffragette, who has been on hunger strike, and has been imprisoned for her feminist convictions, offers a very clear opportunity for feminist polemic, but this is not availed of by the narrator. She is used instead as a foil for the Bishop's nationalist stance and as an advocate of the Reverend Mother's philosophy of 'detachment of spirit'. There is no attempt made in the novel to engage in open debate on the rights of women: their equal, even superior status, to men is taken for granted. It is from this position that the novel explores the forces that conspire to deny Helen Archer and Anna Murphy their freedom.

*The Land Of Spices* is a novel of growth and development: a *Bildungsroman*. But the conventional format is complicated by the double plot structure. The novel traces the lives of the two central protagonists over a period of eleven years. The narrative structure is complex, but well balanced, so that their stories do not jostle for position in the text, nor do they emerge as competing narratives. On the contrary, they are both complementary and enabling. The novel opens and closes with Mother Marie-Hélène. Within her narrative are embedded both her own recollections of childhood and also the narrative of Anna Murphy. This narrative patterning has the effect of highlighting the many parallels and contrasts in their young lives and of comparing the mature Mother Marie-Hélène with her young self and with Anna Murphy. The successful relationship between the two narratives is mirrored by the successful and enabling relationship that develops between Mother Marie-Hélène and Anna.

Their successful relationship is based on freedom, not dependency, but it is preceded in the novel by many others which have failed. The most spectacular and most closely detailed of these is that between Helen Archer and her father. The young Helen depends on her father for everything, and finds in him 'an accidental delight which had no necessary spring in filial feeling, but rose from the privilege of intimacy with someone whom she found pleasing and satisfactory far beyond what was necessary in a father, or in any fellow creature'.[14]

The dependent nature of her relationship with her father is seen as the reason for its destruction. In psychoanalytic terms this is quite interesting. Helen is dependent on her father but, until she discovers him with Etienne, she also believes herself to be in control of him. She is certain of her knowledge of him, of their mutual love, and of her position in his life. It is not only disgust which alienates her from her father, but what she perceives as her loss of knowledge and power: she cannot accept her dependency on someone she no longer feels she knows, and over whom she can exert little influence. Her response is an attempt to take responsibility for her own life, and in turn to punish him. She chooses to do this by adopting a life that she knows will cause him great pain and keep him in doubt about her desertion of him, for the rest of his life.[15]

Helen Archer, no longer the one for whom decisions are made, is now the dominant partner in the relationship. Like the speaker in Emily Dickinson's poem she

> close(s) the Valves of her attention —
> Like Stone.[16]

She remains incapable of human emotion until she notices Anna Murphy and recognises something of her young self in her 'look of pure attention'.[17] Anna's recitation of Vaughan's poem 'Peace' breaks through the barriers that she has erected around her feelings and enables her to see 'this baby in herself, herself in those tear-wet eyes'.[18] Mother Marie-Hélène never tells her father that he is the reason for her sudden decision to enter the religious life: she denies him this knowledge and chooses to see it as a kind of protection of him. But she is puzzled by his failure in perception, although she herself is the author of it. Even in his last letter to her he returns to the subject: 'I wished another kind of life for you, and even now, after thirty three years of resignation, I still wonder, and so does Marie-Jeanne, why you turned away so sharply from that life.'[19]

Henry Archer dies as he lived, contented and totally unaware of the exacting price his wife and daughter had paid for loving him. They shield and protect him from the knowledge of his own destructiveness. This could be read as a stereotypical feminine response to what is experienced as the badly flawed male: the woman suffers in silence and isolation in order to protect the integrity of the man. Catherine Archer's only means of escape is death, the self-sacrificing task that she has undertaken becomes more than she can bear. 'She was broken inside; something was wrong which she must have understood only too well could not be put right — and she was content to die.'[20] Helen escapes from her father, but her flight to freedom can be seen as another form of imprisonment. However, it is only temporarily a prison. The only real prisons in the novel are over-dependent relationships. She makes a success of the life she chooses but in order to do so she must, for many years, deny the emotional side of her nature.

Anna's father, Harry Murphy, is a more crudely constructed version of Henry Archer. This doubling motif is apparent throughout the novel and is an example of O'Brien's skilled narrative planning. His relationships with his wife and his daughter mirror those of the Archers. The Archers are more polished and sophisticated but underneath this veneer the relationships are equally destructive. The narrator strips away the educated and civilised behaviour of the Archers and exposes the crude workings of their relationships in the Murphy family. Like Henry Archer, Harry Murphy can never recognise himself as the author of his children's pain 'He couldn't bear distress in his children, and he was confident, in his brief, casual way, that he was never its cause. When they cried he looked round in whirling rage for their enemy.'[21] Harry Murphy is unreservedly rude and slighting in his behaviour towards his wife, but his treatment of her is, if anything, more humane than Henry Archer's treatment of his wife Catherine. Catherine has no defences against Henry's politeness and civility; her great love for him disables her and leaves her helpless. Maud Murphy escapes into an all-embracing self-pity which renders her immune to Harry's opinion of her; in fact his treatment of her strengthens the role she has adopted for herself, that of long-suffering and abused wife, who shares her grief with a few close friends who indulge and even feed her need to be pitied. The relationship between Anna and her younger brother Charlie is the only potentially successful one between male and female in the novel. It is presented as some kind of ideal: Anna's emotional life is totally satisfied by Charlie, who is generous and thoughtful and, unlike other men in the novel believes in the equality of women. (When he dies he is wearing a suffragette ribbon as a tie.) But this relationship is not allowed to develop, as Charlie is drowned in a tragic swimming accident when he is only thirteen years old.

In *The Land Of Spices* men are seen as destructive, but they are also dangerously attractive and physically beautiful. Helen Archer likes to look at her father: 'In childhood she thought her father very beautiful, . . . She noticed that his face grew more beautiful as one drew near it.'[22] Harry Murphy is handsome and a competent horseman. Anna loves to look at her brother Charlie: 'She thought he had the nicest face it was possible to imagine. Sometimes his face pleased her so much that she did not know how to keep herself from hugging him.'[23] In this novel women look at men, but not in a sexual way: though it may appear to resemble the appropriating male gaze, women's gaze, although at times appropriating, is desexualised. This, I would suggest, also holds true for the lavishly detailed cameo at the end of the novel when Anna suddenly sees and experiences Pilar as beautiful. This gaze is an appropriating one, certainly, but the appropriation is artistic, not sexual. Pilar represents for Anna the possibilities in everyday life for the artist; the accidental and aesthetically empowering quality of beauty.

How does Henry Archer insulate himself from the knowledge of his destructive effect on his wife and daughter? Here again the character of his intellectually crude, but more open counterpart, Harry Murphy, offers some insight. Harry Murphy isolates himself from life by reasoning that:

> It was after all, the easiest way with women, whom he needed but could not understand. They did not like what men liked, and the only

way for a man to get on with his likings was to hand them the virtues, be dirt under their feet. It was a sell-out, but it secured a kind
of peace they would not befoul themselves by sharing.[24]

Maude and Harry Murphy are a graphic example of a binary
model of difference; here the two poles of masculinity and
femininity could not be more rigidly structured. His masculine
rationality and aggressiveness are contrasted with her irrationality
and chaos. But Harry Murphy's rationalisation of his position
ironises and questions this polarisation by making it an obvious
construction by Harry himself. This is not a given, or a natural
state, rather it is a structure which Harry consciously imposes
on his relationship with his wife. This questions essentialist views
of sexual identity which sugggest that men and women are
naturally opposite to, and in conflict with, each other. It also
highlights Simone de Beauvoir's concept of otherness. De
Beauvoir argues that the self establishes unified identity by defining otherness.[25] Harry Murphy invents something different to
himself: the feminine world represented by his wife Maud and
her mother, in order to construct his own identity. The point I
wish to argue here is that O'Brien shows how gender is socially
and culturally produced, and not simply biologically determined.

Henry Archer protects himself by keeping 'about him what he
called the decent, unpretentious rags of intellectual pride'.[26] His
impeccable public *persona* is kept intact throughout his life by the
willing self-sacrifice of his wife and daughter. 'The married state,
undertaken in darkness' is 'gracefully upheld, to the world at
least'.[27] Helen chooses to uphold the façade even though it hides
what is, in her terms, a corrupt interior. As with Oscar Wilde's
beautiful but corrupt Dorian Gray, Henry Archer retains his
beautiful appearance despite the passing years. Helen, searching
for some indication in his physical appearance of the life he leads,
is surprised that: 'Although he was fifty five at that date, her eyes
could discover almost no impairment in his physical beauty which
was always marked.'[28]

But unlike Wilde's story, this one lacks a denouement. Henry
Archer's duplicity is not uncovered, not even to himself: He retains his 'Innocence — to the very end — of all the woe and pain
that lay between them'.[29] Reverend Mother thanks God for the
ease and innocence with which her father approaches death. She

seals up his life so that it retains its perfection for the world and for him, if not for her. The men in O'Brien's fiction are often portrayed as naive. Henry Archer may be a gifted scholar and an accomplished teacher, but he has little insight into the feelings of those around him, particularly his wife and daughter. On the surface his life achieves the sort of perfection that Charlie's assumes with death. Reverend Mother sees Charlie's life as perfect, but the perfection is produced by premature death. His life 'was given its particular shape – as it happens, a lovely, untarnishable, poetic shape, unlike the outward shape of most lives'.[30] Reverend Mother herself is the author of the seeming perfection of the 'outward shape' of her father's life: there is a perverse form of control or power in her deliberate decision to keep secret the knowledge she has about the lie that is at the centre of Henry Archer's existence. In the end she does control her father's life, its outward shape and form, and his perception of it. One of the ironies of the novel is that Reverend Mother's own life is a cleverly constructed and controlled façade: not unlike her father, she too has a closely guarded secret. She enters religious life, not with the 'purity of intention' that would be expected of a religious vocation, but because intellectually and emotionally she has nowhere else to go.

This novel highlights the destructive nature of patriarchy. Having shown its limitations, O'Brien proposes an alternative model: matriarchy. The convent of the Sainte Famille is exclusively female: however, it does have a patriarchal figurehead, the Bishop, in whose diocese the convent is situated, but he is disempowered. Foreign teaching orders in Ireland were not subject to the authority of the local church hierarchy. This is a source of great frustration to the Bishop who, although an admirer of Reverend Mother's, gravely distrusts her stance on national issues but is unable to exercise any authority over her. Life in this matriarchical system is presented very favourably, but it is hierarchal: there is a clear authority structure, with Reverend Mother in command, followed by her two lieutenants. At the bottom of the system are the lay sisters, who work in the kitchen and gardens. Reverend Mother is a very competent leader: she is clever and just, even kind, in her rule. Life in the convent exists outside the patriarchal system: it is a comfortable alternative home for both nuns and pupils. But for the pupils it is an isolated and temporary place. In the convent Reverend Mother is the sole authority, but when it comes to dealing with problems which involve the world outside the convent her power is ineffectual and she has to rely on the Bishop, who wields power in the 'real' world. Anna's grandmother is also a matriarch: she shapes and controls the lives of those in her immediate family. Having usurped the patriarchal role, she uses all its traditional weapons: money, influence and her standing in the community. Manipulative and aggressive, her views on women are those of the patriarchy. She does not believe in higher education for women. Having decided Anna's future without consulting her, she only agrees to allow Anna to go to university when it becomes politically expedient to do so.

One of the problems with reading O'Brien's *The Land Of Spices* as a feminist text is the marginal position it occupies. This marginality occurs on a number of levels. It is, firstly, a novel written by a woman almost exclusively about women. Secondly, it is a novel which was banned, because of its suggestion of homosexuality, by an all-male censorship board. Thirdly, within the text women occupy a liminal position, physically cut off from the outside world by the walls of the convent, and emotionally removed from the orbit of patriarchal power. Patriarchy insists on an absolute divide or difference between men and women. O'Brien attempts, in this novel, to redefine and valorise this difference by placing her central female characters in their own counter-society. Its radical nature can easily be misread, as a convent is traditionally seen as a rather harmless and non-threatening community of women.

However a reading of the Sainte Famille as a counter-society would align O'Brien with such cultural feminists as Mary Daly and Adrienne Rich who, in an attempt to reverse binarism, would like to see women embrace difference to the full in order to build a separatist female culture.[31] It is from such a marginal and oppositional position that Julia Kristeva advocates that women should attack patriarchy.[32] But this leaves the novel open to the same criticism that could also be levelled at Kristeva. If women are to occupy a marginal position, then they are excluded from culture, and the polarisation of men and women and of male and female literature is further intensified. This argument is also problematic in that it tends to idealise, to see female experience as absolutely positive. (Incidentally, this is probably a criticism with which Eavan Boland would agree. Boland's writing has been a continuous attempt to redefine the position of women in patriarchy from within Irish culture, and not from some notional position on the margins.)[33]

### III    'To-morrow to Fresh Woods and Pastures New'

John Milton's pastoral *Lycidas* is structurally important in the concluding chapters of *The Land of Spices*: the central action of the poem and its resolution mirror those of the novel. The two main characters in the novel, Helen and Anna, experience great loss and trouble in their lives, but they resolve their problems and, strengthened by their struggles, go out to confront the future.

*The Land of Spices* witnesses the disintegration of the family, the absolute failure of even the most promising relationships, and the ineptitude and myopic vision of the exponents of Irish Nationalism. But for each failed situation detailed in the novel a promising and at times radical alternative is proposed. One of the great strengths of *The Land of Spices* is that each of these — the institution of the family, loving but dependent relationships, and Irish Nationalism — is presented as having at least some strengths. Helen Archer's relationship with her father is in many ways very beautiful. Anna Murphy loves her home, Castle Troy. As a young child she feels secure in her mother's warm embrace and in her father's ability to protect her. The positive elements of Irish Nationalism are presented through the character of the 'brilliant but dangerous' Bishop, who approves of higher education for women 'up to a point, or when they seemed worth it', and who allows Miss Robertson, an Englishwoman and a suffragette, to speak publicly in certain women's training colleges in his diocese, having first read and edited her speeches.[34]

Article 1 of the Constitution of Ireland states: 'The Irish nation hereby affirms its inalienable, indefeasible, and sovereign right to choose its own form of Government, to determine its relations with other nations, and to develop its life, political, economic and cultural, in accordance with its own genius and traditions.'[35]

*The Land of Spices* is set in Ireland in the years directly preceding
the 1916 Rising, a period when the country is seething with
cultural and political nationalism. The central action of the novel
is set within the confines of a convent, whose ethos is different
in every way from the culture that surrounds it. This is not the
Ireland of the peasantry or the down-at-heel gentry of the Big
House. The lifestyle of the nuns and girls at the convent of Sainte
Famille is far from austere. It is comfortable, even opulent: 'There
was a good French smell of coffee. At every footfall in the room
the chandeliers tinkled prettily.'[36] The majority of nuns and
pupils come from the upper-middle classes, and are far more concerned with their relative positions within that structure than they
are with questions of Irish nationality or culture.

'La Pudeur et la Politesse' are the two central aims of the education provided at Sainte Famille. This is a source of concern to
the chaplain to the convent, Father Conroy, who accuses Reverend
Mother of 'training Irish girls as suitable wives for English Majors
and Colonial Governors'.[37] Father Conroy is presented as commonplace and naive. His nationalism is crude and uncompromising
and is treated unsympathetically by the narrator. The Bishop is
a far more persuasive exponent of Irish nationalism. Clever and
articulate, he presents the nationalist argument as reasonable, even
irrefutable. This position is challenged by Reverend Mother and
by Miss Robertson, both of whom succeed in destabilising what
might otherwise seem an infallible argument. The Bishop holds
extremely strong views on education, he recognises its power and
consequently the power of the people who are in charge of the
country's schools. What the Bishop wants is 'a truly national
education'.[38] Reverend Mother, whose intelligence and pragmatism are constantly highlighted by the narrator, responds to
what appears to her to be a very narrow argument by suggesting
reasonably that 'When Ireland decides what she means by that,
my lord, the Compagnie de la Sainte Famille will try to provide
it.'[39] Reverend Mother believes that the business of the school is
not with national matters. What she hopes to provide for her girls
is 'choice of cultures', not something narrowly defined and crudely
adhered to. She is critical of Irish Nationalism, and constantly
highlights its inconsistencies: 'How odd were these Irish, who
believed themselves implacably at war in the spirit with England,

yet hugged as their own her dreariest daily habits.'[40] But the most distressing characteristic of Irish nationalism for her is that 'About Ireland . . . no detachment was regarded as just.'[41] In a novel that celebrates detachment of spirit, a more severe criticism of Ireland and the Irish would be difficult to make.

The Bishop, discussing nationalism with Miss Robertson, contends that the convent of Sainte Famille is 'too European for present-day Irish requirements. Its detachment of spirit seems to me to stand in the way of Nationalism.' Sinn Fein, he goes on to explain to Miss Robertson, 'means ourselves'. He believes that great deeds will be done in its name. Miss Robertson is not convinced. She likes 'detachment of spirit' and finds Sinn Fein 'an unattractive motto to give to young people'. But there is no place in this novel for great deeds of the kind the Bishop anticipates.[42]

Set on the brink of the First World War and the 1916 Rising and written and published during the early years of the Second World War, the novel excludes national and international crises, and concentrates on personal ones. The historical setting of the novel and its date of publication provide an interesting subtext, emphasising the isolation and confined setting of the novel, and acting as a contrast to the interior struggle of the main characters. In 1942 it was apparent to most politically aware people that the First World War had resolved nothing. Similarly, to many the 1916 Rebellion and its consequences had created an Ireland that was far from satisfactory. These failures are contrasted with the successful resolution of the internal warfare that takes place in Helen Archer and Anna Murphy.

Adèle Dalsimer, in her essay on *The Land of Spices*, suggests that O'Brien 'grants the nationalists a voice and they justify their self-absorbed concerns in equally sympathic tones. The result is a particularly balanced view of the Irish and their political attitudes during this historic period.' She stresses O'Brien's desire to 'present both sides fairly'.[43] Such a reading ignores the subtlety of the narrative. The nationalist point of view might appear to be fairly presented, but it is influenced dramatically by those who present these views and the narrator's view of them. Father Conroy, one of its chief spokesmen, is ardent, but politically stupid: Mother Mary Andrew is arrogant and cruel. Even the Bishop, although politically astute, is too narrow in his outlook and is tainted by his association with the more blind and xenophobic attitudes of his fellow nationalists.

The novel does articulate the nationalist position in its crude and even in its more sophisticated forms, but it is dismissed because of its intrusion on the spirit of individuality so important to the central character, Helen Archer. What is proposed instead is choice; primarily what is proposed is a choice of cultures. The Irish Literary Revival might never have happened as far as the nuns and girls of Sainte Famille are concerned. The literary scaffolding that supports the education system in Sainte Famille, and indeed the novel, is European in outlook. The novel is composed around the poetry of the English metaphysical poets of the seventeenth century: Donne, Herbert, Cowley, Vaughan, Traherne and Bishop King. The girls study Schiller, Shakespeare, the Spanish poet De Leon and Milton's *Lycidas.* The nuns and pupils of Sainte Famille speak French, not Irish, at mealtimes. Reverend Mother approves of 'the optional revival of the Irish language in Irish education', but she regards it as a 'local incident, and not as the mission of her Order'.[44]

What the novel does propose is an education system that trains girls for their own sake, not to be the wives of British majors or colonial governors, nor indeed of Irishmen. In this scheme of things nationalism is not important, it is merely a 'local incident'. It must be considered, even offered, as an option, but it is not central. In the novel the concept of nationhood is examined and found wanting. So too is the family as the basic unit in society. What survives at the end of *The Land of Spices* is the individual, standing independent and alone.

Article 41 of the Constitution of Ireland outlines the position of the family in the new state:

> i The State recognises the Family as the natural primary and fundamental unit group of Society, and as a moral institution possessing inalienable and imprescriptible rights, antecedent and superior to all positive law.
>
> ii The State, therefore, guarantees to protect the Family in its constitution and authority, as the necessary basis of social order and as indispensable to the welfare of the Nation and the State.

In *The Land Of Spices* the institution of the family is of enormous importance, not because of its stability and positive role in society, but because of its destructive potential for its individual members. The family may very well be indispensable to the welfare of the Nation and the State, but in this novel the Nation and the State are not important. What is important is individuality, and this can only be achieved when the rights of each individual member are ranked above those of 'the natural primary and fundamental unit', the family.

In O'Brien's earlier novels, *Without My Cloak* and *The-Ante-Room*, attention is focused on the family; its position as the safe and loving guardian of the individual is not directly challenged. There are subtle suggestions that perhaps family life may threaten the freedom, even the sanity, of its individual members. Anthony Considine's possessive love for his son is in some ways a foreshadowing of Henry Archer's monopolisation of his daughter Helen's affections. But this potential problem is resolved in *Without My Cloak*: Anthony's son remains within the family.[45] *The Ante-Room* also takes the family as its nucleus: life revolves around the family home and dependent interpersonal relationships.[46] Individual sacrifices are made in order to maintain and sustain the structure. Agnes Mulqueen gives up her own hopes of happiness in order to protect her sister Marie-Rose. The sisters' relationship is further protected by the rather melodramatic suicide of the object of Agnes's love: Marie-Rose's husband Vincent. The family is protected by the denial of the desires of its individual members and the elimination of those who threaten its stability.

In *The Land of Spices* the setting is no longer the family home; there are, however, family homes in the novel and materially, they are attractive, even beautiful. Rue Saint Isidore No. 4 in Brussels, where Helen Archer spends her childhood, has beauty of 'a particularly good, unassuming form';[47] Castle Troy, Anna Murphy's family home, is 'a solid stone farm-house of good design'.[48] But both of these homes are a source of grief, not comfort, to the children who grow up in them. Helen Archer and Anna reject their homes and seek and find refuge in a convent community. Helen finds in convent life a place of comfort and security. Anna too turns to the impersonal life in Sainte Famille when her family home, Castle Troy, becomes a source of pain and disorder. Life in the convent of Sainte Famille is ordered and regulated and would seem to promote conformity, but the novel suggests it is also a place where individuality can survive and even thrive. This runs contrary to much received thinking on the type of education provided by convents like Sainte Famille.

In this novel the primary threat to the individual's autonomy are close familial relationships which weaken by nurturing over-dependency. To achieve the autonomy celebrated by O'Brien the two central protagonists must sever their ties with their families, no matter how torturous this proves to be. The growth to maturity is painful and lonely, and in Helen Archer's case lasts for many years. In *The Land of Spices* the family is presented as destructive. It disempowers its individual members, maiming and retarding them emotionally, due to an over-emphasis on the family unit as the most important structure in the individual's life.

O'Brien, in her essay *George Eliot: A Moralizing Fabulist*, praises Eliot because 'her young ladies did emphatically go out to confront their destinies'; this is exactly what she sends her own two central characters in *The Land of Spices* out to do.[49] Helen Archer, having radically broken the crippling ties that bind her to her father, gradually gathers strength and confidence and becomes a very successful and influential nun. Indeed, she becomes an independent, clear-sighted and useful individual member of a community, whose attachments are real, but helpful rather than disabling. She skilfully guides her young pupils and the nuns in her charge. With minimal interference she governs this large disparate group with intelligence, and even with guile.

In many ways she resembles that great sixteenth-century mystic Teresa of Avila whom O'Brien admired so much.[50] O'Brien sees Teresa as a genius, not just because of her writings but because of the way she lived her life. Helen Archer, too, achieves this status, given this definition of genius. She rises to the highest position in her chosen profession, a position of enormous power and influence, despite its limitations. She confronts her own destiny, comes to terms with her past, acknowledges her ability, and at the end of the novel, after a long and difficult apprenticeship, prepares to leave Ireland, her most challenging assignment, to confidently assume leadership of a community with over 1,800 nuns and schools spread out over the world. She is happy to 'return to work in so good a place, and to grow old striving with duties she believed in'.[51]

The most important element in Reverend Mother's growth to autonomy and fulfilment is her developing love for Anna Murphy. But this love is radically different from the love she experienced as a child. She learns slowly and painfully: 'To stand still and eventually understand was, she saw, an elementary duty of love.'[52] In the novel the kind of love that leads to growth is not the suffocating attachment Helen has to her father, nor the exclusive absorption Anna has in Charlie. Reverend Mother watches Anna grow and loves and protects her from a distance. She never approaches Anna, even when she is in despair after her brother Charlie's death; she allows Anna to come to her and then delicately and with total lack of sentimentality advises and guides her. The help she gives is mostly practical, ensuring that she sleeps and eats and is allowed space to recover. Anna is not aware of this love and care, so it does not bind her, or create dependency. When the time comes Reverend Mother fights ruthlessly for Anna's right to freedom, the freedom to study at university, not for any specific profession, but simply for its own sake.

The novel prefaces detachment of spirit and the freedom of the individual. This freedom, which depends on detachment of spirit, comes in two stages. The novel records a developmental process; Reverend Mother achieves freedom, but it is one that is contained within the narrow confines of convent life. She has no help in this long and at times bitter struggle. Reverend Mother's achievement is crucial in Anna's struggle. The future that begins 'in emptiness, on a wide horizon' for Anna cannot be attained without the assistance of Reverend Mother. Her self-confidence and belief in individuality ensure that the forces which struggle to keep Anna in a conventional and patriarchally defined position are overwhelmed.

Discussing Eliot's *Romola* O'Brien remarks: 'What a refreshment it is to be concerned in a fiction with a young woman who is more cerebrally than sensually conscious.'[53] *The Land of Spices* is refreshing for the same reason. Helen Archer's consciousness is 'active and unblinking'. The novel explores her consciousness with uncompromising thoroughness so that by the end of the novel we have an intimate knowledge of her thought-processes; what is presented is a mature woman, honest with herself, successful and even content.

Anna Murphy is, throughout the novel, more cerebrally than sensually conscious. As an adolescent she is accused of being an innocent, and laughed at for her lack of interest in and knowledge of sexual matters. At Chaplin's concert, when the whole senior school falls in love with the boring but beautiful young Jesuit priest, Anna remains aloof and uninterested. She is dismayed that the hilarity induced by this adolescent infatuation disrupts the performance of Schiller's *Wallenstein Tod*. 'Anna liked serious things to be serious', as indeed, the narrator tells us, does Reverend Mother.[54] Anna is never troubled by the *Schwarmerei* that is an accepted part of life in the convent. Her sudden realisation of Pilar's beauty could be read as a sensual awakening: 'She saw Pilar in a new way. She became aware of her . . . on a plane of perception which was strange to her.'[55] Anna's 'plane of perception' may indeed be sensual, but this is encompassed in the more dominant artistic perception. Anna experiences Pilar as 'a symbol', a 'challenge to creativeness', as 'a motive in art', and as the 'translation of the ordinary'. The echoes of Joyce's *A Portrait of the Artist as a Young Man* are very evident here, as they are throughout the novel.[56]

Anna's narrative is similar in many ways to that of Stephen Dedalus. They each witness the growth from childhood to maturity, the gradual awakening of aesthetic perception and the development of a sensitive artistic consciousness. Both reject much of what surrounds them in order to achieve some prospect of autonomy. Stephen must 'fly by those nets' of religion, family and race. In his flight he also rejects the feminine. Anna rejects family, but not religion, and she embraces femininity, finding in it, in the figure of Pilar, 'a motive in art', 'a passage of beauty as revelatory and true as any verse of the great elegy'.[57]

Anna recognises the hostile environment in which she lives and its potential power of entrapment. She knows that her growth must be 'in darkness and secrecy'. The one weapon that Anna has at her disposal is silence. This negative form of defence is exactly what Helen Archer uses when she is threatened. In spite of hidden resources of courage and stoicism and a valuable self-awareness, Anna, unlike Stephen, does not escape her family without outside assistance. Reverend Mother, who has remained discreetly in the background throughout Anna's twelve years in

Sainte Famille, comes into the open and grimly fights the agents who seek to control Anna's future. Reverend Mother, content that 'All was done that age could do for childhood', envisions Anna's future in terms that are very close to Anna's own. 'She had been set free to be herself. Her wings were grown and she was for the world. In poverty, in struggle, in indecisiveness.'[58]

Despite the differences in age and the distant nature of the relationship that exists between Anna and Reverend Mother, their thoughts, their reactions to different situations, their allegiances, their interest in literature and their aloofness from other people make them startlingly alike. Anna can be seen as the re-creation, in a different time and place, of Helen Archer. Brought in adolescence to a crippling crisis, Helen Archer makes a decision which excludes her from life. The life, in the world, which has been denied her, is to be lived by her double Anna. This doubling occurs elsewhere in the novel, and is a very useful and illuminating narrative technique. The autonomy achieved by Reverend Mother is restricted and confined. It is only with Reverend Mother's help that Anna gains the agency that will enable her to lead an independent life in the world outside the convent.

This reading of the novel arrives at the following conclusions. *The Land of Spices* can be read as a radical, if veiled, attack on everything that the Constitution of Ireland considered 'natural' and 'special' — the State, the family, the position of women in the home and marriage. The novel questions and throws open for debate many of the assumptions made by the authors of the Constitution. It also offers alternatives to each of these: an outward-looking European perspective is presented as an alternative to Irish Nationalism, the family is replaced by a successful community of women and women in the novel seek autonomy and agency outside the home and marriage.

But the alternatives themselves do present problems. The convent of Sainte Famille, so positively presented in the novel, in many ways simply reproduces the organisational structures of patriarchy, and has internalised many of patriarchy's most disabling methods. This is masked by the smell of good French coffee and Reverend Mother's liberal attitudes. The convent as an alternative way of life is only a temporary one for the many girls who go there. It is an autonomous community within its own walls, but has little or no power outside them. In *The Land of Spices* women who leave behind their families to find autonomy must abandon or deny any close attachments. They may set themselves free from the bonds of love but in doing so, they isolate themselves from emotion. Therefore, in *The Land of Spices* O'Brien remakes the trauma of homosexual desire into an enabling device, where 'the embrace of love', for the woman, can be transcended, allowing for the achievement of individual, if solitary, independence and self-realisation.

## Notes and references

1 Kate O'Brien, *The Land of Spices,* London, Virago, 1988.
2 ibid., p. 157.
3 ibid., p. 159.
4 ibid., p. 18.
5 ibid., p. 21.
6 ibid., p. 157.
7 ibid., p. 157.
8 Austin Clarke, 'The Land Of Spices: A review', J. Liddy (ed.), *The Stony Thursday Book*, no. 7, p. 33.
9 O'Brien, *The Land of Spices*, p. 155.
10 ibid., p. 275.
11 Kate O'Brien, *Imaginative prose by the Irish*, J. Ronsley (ed.), *Myth and Reality in Irish Literature*, Waterloo, Ont., Wilfrid Laurier University Press, 1977, p. 314.
12 O'Brien, *The Land of Spices*, p. 37.
13 Eavan Boland, J. Liddy (ed.), *The Stony Thursday Book*, no. 7, p. 46.
14 O'Brien, *The Land of Spices*, p. 141.
15 For a discussion of the problem of domination see Jessica Benjamin, *The Bonds of Love*, London, Virago, 1990.
16 Emily Dickinson, *The Complete Poems,* ed. T.H. Johnson, New York, Little, Brown & Co., 1960, p. 303.
17 O'Brien, *The Land of Spices*, p. 80.
18 ibid., p. 82.
19 ibid., p. 162.
20 ibid., p. 138.
21 ibid., p. 48.
22 ibid., p. 142.
23 ibid., p. 201.
24 ibid., pp. 48-9.

25  Simone de Beauvoir, *Le Deuxième sexe,* Paris, Gallimard, 1949, trans. H.M. Parshley as *The Second Sex,* Harmondsworth, Penguin, 1972.

26  O'Brien, *The Land of Spices,* p. 137.

27  ibid., pp. 154.

28  ibid., p. 21.

29  ibid., p. 164.

30  ibid., p. 236.

31  Adrienne Rich, *On Lies, Secrets and Silence: Selected Prose 1966-1978,* London, Virago, 1980.

32  Julia Kristeva, *Women's Time,* trans. Alice Jardien and Harry Blake, (1981) *Signs,* 7.

33  For a detailed discussion of Boland's positon on women writers in the Irish literary tradition see Eavan Boland, *A Kind of Scar,* LIP Pamphlet, Dublin, Attic Press, 1991.

34  O'Brien, *The Land of Spices,* p. 251.

35  *Bunreacht na hEireann/Constitution of Ireland,* Dublin, Brunswick Press, 1937, p. 4.

36  O'Brien, *The Land of Spices,* p. 7.

37  ibid., p. 92.

38  ibid., p. 15.

39  ibid., p. 16.

40  ibid., p. 54.

41  ibid., p. 75.

42  ibid., p. 211.

43  Adèle Dalsimer, *Kate O'Brien: A Critical Study,* Dublin, Gill & Macmillan, 1990.

44  O'Brien, *The Land of Spices,* p. 168.

45  Kate O'Brien, *Without My Cloak,* London, Heinemann, 1947.

46  Kate O'Brien, *The Ante-Room,* London, Virago, 1989.

47  O'Brien, *The Land of Spices,* p. 152.

48  ibid., p. 120.

49  Kate O'Brien, 'George Eliot: A Moralizing Fabulist', ed. J. Ronsley, *Transactions of The Royal Society of Literature,* Waterloo, Ont., Wilfrid Laurier University Press, 1977.

50  Kate O'Brien, *Teresa of Avila,* London, Max Parrish, 1951.

51  O'Brien, *The Land of Spices,* p. 279.

52  ibid., p. 20.

53  O'Brien, *George Eliot.*

54  O'Brien, *The Land of Spices,* p. 181.

55  ibid., p. 271.

56  James Joyce, *A Portrait of the Artist as a Young Man.*

57  O'Brien, *The Land of Spices,* p. 272.

58  ibid., p. 281.

# Select Bibliography

## Works by Kate O'Brien

### Novels, Plays, Diaries

*Distinguished Villa,* London, Ernest Benn Ltd, 1926.
*Without My Cloak,* London, Heinemann, 1931 (London, Virago, 1986).
*The Ante-Room,* London, Heinemann, 1934 (Dublin, Arlen House, 1980).
*Mary Lavelle,* London, Heinemann, 1936 (London, Virago, 1984).
*Farewell Spain,* London, Heinemann, 1937.
*Pray for the Wanderer,* London, Heinemann, 1938.
*The Land Of Spices,* London, Heinemann, 1941 (London, Virago, 1988).
*The Last of Summer,* London, Heinemann, 1943 (Dublin, Arlen House, 1982).
*English Diaries and Journals,* London, Collins, 1943.
*That Lady,* London, Heinemann, 1946 (London, Virago, 1985).
*Teresa of Avila,* London, Parrish, 1951.
*The Flower of May,* London, Heinemann, 1953.
*As Music and Splendour,* London, Heinemann, 1958.
*My Ireland,* London, Batsford, 1962.
*Presentation Parlour,* London, Heinemann, 1963.
*Constancy,* (unfinished and unpublished final novel).

### Shorter Fiction

'A Fit of Laughing', *The Bell,* Vol. 18, No. 4, 1952, pp. 220–71.
'A Bus From Tivoli', *Threshold,* Vol. 1, No. 2, Summer 1957.
'A View From Toledo', *Argosy.*
'Overheard', *Time and Tide,* 2 March 1935.
'Memories of a Catholic Childhood', *The Tablet,* 4 December 1976.
'Work in Progress', Kevin Casey (ed.), *Winter's Tales from Ireland,* Dublin, Gill & MacMillan, 1972.

## Critical Writings

*The Spectator,* fiction reviews, 1937–1956.
*The Irish Times,* 'Long Distance', 1967–1971.
'Avantgardisme', *The Irish Times,* 21 October 1965.
'Return in Winter', Sylvia Norman (ed.), *Contemporary Essays,* London, 1933, pp. 19–31.
'De Gaulle: And He Was And Remains Incorruptible', *Creation,* June 1969.
'Writers of Letters', *Essays and Studies,* Vol. 9, 1956, pp. 7–20.
'Irish Writers and Europe', *Hibernia,* March 1965.
'Imaginative prose of the Irish 1830–1970', J. Ronsley (ed.), *Myth and Reality in Irish Literature,* Waterloo, Ont., Wilfrid Laurier University Press, 1977.
'George Eliot: a moralizing fabulist', G. Rostrevor Hamilton (ed.), *Transactions of the Royal Society of Literature,* London, Oxford University Press, 1955.
'Why the Rage For French Films?', *The Star,* February 1938.
'Voice of the Children', *Irish Digest,* Vol. 43, March 1952.
'Why Don't They Emigrate To Our Smaller Cities?', *Irish Digest.*
*Preface to Impressions of Literature,* Collins, London, 1944.
'As To University Life', *University Review,* Vol. 1, No. 6, 1955.
'Ivan Turgenev', *University Review,* Vol. 1, No. 2, 1957.
'Lennox Robinson', *University Review,* Vol. 1, No. 5, 1959.
'Lady Gregory', *Kilkenny Magazine,* No. 2, 1960.
'U.C.D. As I Forget It', *University Review,* Vol. 3, No. 2, 1962.
'Aunt Mary In The Parlour', *University Review,* Vol. 3, No. 3, 1963.
'The Art of Writing', *University Review,* Vol. 3, No. 4, 1963.
'John McGahern', *University Review,* 1963.

## Radio and Television

'Self-Portrait', RTE Television, 28 March 1962.
'My Home Town', RTE Television, 1963.
'Thought for the Day', RTE Radio, 22–28 November 1969.
'Older and Wiser', RTE Radio, September 1973.
'My Kind of Poetry', RTE Radio, 7 October 1971.
'Moments from a Life', RTE Radio, 20 June 1991.
'Personal Choice', RTE Radio, 5 March 1966.
'Hometown', RTE Radio, 5 May 1969.
'At Feili Luimni', RTE Radio, 9 March 1958.

## Critical Works on Kate O'Brien

## Full-Length Works

Dalsimer, A., *Kate O'Brien: A Critical Study,* Dublin, Gill & Macmillan, 1990.
Jordan, John, J. Liddy (ed.), *The Stony Thursday Book,* No. 7.

Reynolds, Lorna, *Kate O'Brien: a Literary Portrait*, Gerrards Cross, Bucks, Colin Smythe, 1987.

## Essays

*The Irish Times*, obituary, 14 August 1974.

Boland, Eavan, 'That Lady: A profile of Kate O'Brien', *The Critic*, Vol. 34, February 1974.

Boland, Eavan, 'Kate O'Brien', *The Irish Times*, 24 August 1973.

Donoghue, Emma, 'Noises from the Woodshed', S. Raitt (ed.), *Volcanoes and Pearl Divers*, London, Onlywomen Press, 1993.

Hildebidle, John, *Five Irish Writers: the Errand of Keeping Alive*, Cambridge, MA, Harvard University Press, 1989.

Jordan, John, 'Kate O'Brien, A Note On Her Themes', *The Bell*, Vol. 19, No. 2, 1954.

Jordan, John, 'A Passionate Talent', *Hibernia*, 30 August 1974.

Jordan, John, 'Kate O'Brien: First Lady of Irish Letters', *Hibernia*, 11 May 1973.

O'Cinneide, Seamus, 'Kate O'Brien's pride in Limerick achievements', *Limerick Leader*, 24 August 1974.

Quiello, Rose, 'Disturbed desires: The Hysteric in Mary Lavelle', *Eire Ireland*, No. 5, 1990.

Ryan, Joan, 'Class and Creed in The Novels of Kate O'Brien', M. Harman (ed.), *The Irish Writer and the City*, Gerrards Cross, Bucks, Colin Smythe, 1984.

Ryan, Joan, 'Women in the Novels of Kate O'Brien', H. Kosok (ed.), *Studies in Anglo-Irish Literature*, Bonn, Bouvier Verlag, 1982.

Zack, W. and Kosok, H., 'The Image of Spain in the Novels of Kate O'Brien', *National Images and Stereotypes*, Tübingen, Gunter Narr, 1988.

Walsh, Caroline, 'In search of Kate O'Brien', *The Irish Times*, 14 August 1981.

Walshe, Eibhear, 'How Soon Is Now', *Graph*, No. 4, 1988.

Weekes Owens, Ann, 'Kate O'Brien', in *Irish Women Writers*, Lexington, KY, University Press of Kentucky, 1990.

## Reviews

*Without My Cloak*

'The Book Society News', December 1931.
'The Irish Book Lover', November–December 1931.
'Dublin Magazine', April–June 1932.

*The Ante-Room*

'Irish Book Lover', September–October 1934.
'Dublin Magazine', October–December 1934.

*Farewell Spain*
'Ireland Today', September 1937.

*Pray for the Wanderer*
'Irish Book Review', November–December 1938.

*The Land of Spices*
'The Bell', April 1941.

*That Lady*
'Dublin Magazine', September 1946.
'The Bell', August 1946.
'Irish Bookman', January 1947.

*Teresa of Avila*
'Irish Writing', March 1952.

*The Flower of May*
'Irish Writing', December 1953.

# Index